When Homelessness Was Too Much

Douglas Schnapp

Copyright © 2025 Douglas Schnapp

All rights reserved

No part of this book may be reproduced, or stored in a retrieval system, or transmitted in any form or by any means, electronic, mechanical, photocopying, recording, or otherwise, without express written permission of the publisher.

ISBN: 979-8-9891218-9-2

Cover design by Douglas Schnapp

Where We Left Off

The drive west, across eastern Colorado, was a mix of various levels of reality. The scenery was foreign, but I knew the view from my dreams. I saw miles to the horizon in all directions. The air was hazy; it lent a mystical quality to my golden world. As I experienced the drive in an extremely chemically altered consciousness, anticipation grew with each mile.

My eyes strained to focus to the horizon in front of me, knowing I was guaranteed to see the Colorado Rocky Mountains for the first time. I didn't know how much longer I had until shocking contrast on the horizon ahead would bestow a view of snowcapped peaks, thousands of feet above the golden land. The thought excited me as I pushed forward. I was happy.

The interstate highway meandered towards the Rockies, I knew that as fact. As I curved around with the road, I thought I saw something through the haze in the distance. The highway then curved back the other way. Were the drugs mixing with my anticipation and causing me to hallucinate? I wasn't sure. I kept driving. I kept looking ahead to the distance. Suddenly, I was sure. There, a group of mountains ahead of me; they reached into the sky above the horizon. The gray rock faces were topped with white snow.

I turned again with the road, and the mountains were gone. Off to the side of my focus, another section of the Rockies appeared through the otherworldly mist of the sky. Then, more appeared in front of me. I could see the wall of ridges, suddenly filling up the full expanse of the horizon in all directions west of my current location. I was heading towards a vast range of mountains, one which stretched as far north and south as I could see. While driving across the entire country, the ground had been flat during those weeks I had been on the road. Everything changed; a new experience with a completely different feel. I loved everything in that moment.

I reached Denver in late afternoon. I kept driving west. I meandered, with the road, up into the mountains. It was rush hour, and the mountain highway was congested with vehicles. I stopped at various spots amongst the mountains as I recorded videos. I made a decision as I was stopped at a scenic overlook above the city. I will come back to Denver another day. I wanted to check off another state from my travel list by day's end. I knew I could make it to Wyoming if I got back on the road.

...

The next morning, I jolted awake in my car. I gathered my bearings about me as I put on my glasses. The yelling, which woke me up, continued. Though the screaming and shouting was close enough to make out the words, the words made no sense. I pulled out my tray and torch. I did a hotrail. I then removed the shades from my car windows.

It was sunny outside. My eyes took a second to adjust. I stepped from my car. I was then standing in the parking lot of a rest stop between the Colorado border and Cheyanne, Wyoming. I had reached my goal; I made it to Wyoming in the middle of the night. I felt rested after a couple of hours of car sleep. I looked around to where I heard the screaming. I saw where it was coming from…and from whom.

I made eye contact with a vagrant, standing between the parking lot and the road. He was about a hundred yards from me; at the base of the sign for the travel center. I turned away to walk through the parking lot; into the rest stop to use the bathroom. The vagrant picked up ranting, right where he had left off.

"...and AMERICA! No, they won't go! NO! God blessed this land..."

When I walked back out to my car, a police officer was trying to reason with the guy's nonsense. It wasn't working. Eventually, as I prepared to leave the rest stop, the officer must have reached his limit in patience. He didn't arrest the vagrant. Instead, he stepped back into his patrol car and drove away. I thought to myself; I would have done the exact same thing in the officer's situation. I started my car and followed the officer out of the rest stop on my way back to the highway.

I reached Cheyanne, Wyoming. I explored the city. I ate at a Mexican restaurant. I recorded videos and interacted with people online. I found a park in the middle of the city. I spent a few hours rewiring the two twelve-inch subwoofers in the trunk of my car. When I finished, I put my tools away and began work on another project.

Desolation

There was a girl I had known in passing since I was a child in elementary school. Though a grade ahead of me, she went to the same school through all of my school years. Though Shannon and I didn't associate during our time from elementary school through high school, we randomly crossed paths at parties and other events. Later on, we were connected via social media as we periodically interacted in the real world, at bars and social functions. By the end of 2016, when I was single for the first extended time period in my adult life, Shannon and I began consistently interacting with one another.

Our dynamic blossomed quickly and organically. I shared everything with Shannon. The more I shared, the deeper I felt the connection. The more something became an experience just for the two of us, the more the moment became exclusively ours, the more invested I became…the more I was aroused and into it.

Shannon gave me instructions to please her. She told me what to do in videos for her. When I sent her the videos, she gave me feedback. Our dynamic grew more intimate with each task and video I completed for her. Our relationship set the groundwork for my online interactions when I joined the website, over a year later.

Our dynamic remained a constant in my life as time passed. The dynamic grew as life became something entirely new to me. When I stepped from all familiarity and began my foray into a strange and foreign existence, Shannon's presence in my life remained one of the very few dependable focuses I was able to maintain.

I smiled as I read the text message. I had spent the afternoon working hard on my car audio system. I was glad to be relaxing in my driver's seat at the rest stop; after leaving Cheyanne, Wyoming. The text message was the same two words Shannon had sent an hour prior, when I was finishing the car audio work in Cheyanne. Shannon gave me a reprieve for an hour while I drove west. When I let her know that I had made it to a rest stop west of the city, Shannon texted me those same two words again.

"Do it."

I replied an affirmative as I retrieved my equipment from a bag in the back of my car. I had previously modified one of my tattoo machines. I had wired the cord from the foot pedal to a trigger switch on the handle of the machine. I also replaced the plug to the power unit with a USB attachment. I was fully able to hook the machine to my car or battery pack and operate the machine while I was seated in my driver's seat. I received another two-word text message from Shannon.

"Video it."

I sent videos as I followed Shannon's directions. A half hour later, I sent the final video update. I put some thought into the cinematography of that final recording. The sun was setting. It was beautiful; looking out over the rest stop parking lot to the colorful sky as the light began to fade in the valley below. I began the recording with a steady framing of the sun as it set over the mountains in the distance to the West. I panned the camera to show a panoramic view of the sky's colors above the Wyoming valley. At the end of the scenic recording, the camera view reached the side of the passenger window on the inside of my car. I then panned immediately down to my lap. There, the camera focused on the green lightning bolt, complete with a black outline, on my right ball.

I put antibiotic ointment on the new tattoo, and I zipped up my pants. The video was well-received. Not just by Shannon, but by the select few others with whom I chose to share that moment. I sat at the rest stop and thought for a few minutes on something else. I then acted on my thoughts.

I went online and searched to find reviews of the best rotary tattoo machine available for purchase. I read multiple reviews. I found the proper website to make the purchase. I threw myself a curveball as I purchased the tattoo machine.

Though I was currently in Wyoming; heading west, I chose to have the expensive tattoo machine shipped to a locker at a grocery store in the center of Santa Fe, New Mexico. I was doing all I could to check off all the states on my travel list. New Mexico was out of my way the other direction. I created a reason to travel to New Mexico.

I set the delivery date for a week and a half later. I had time to visit Yellowstone. I had time to stop and see people as I traveled south through Colorado on my return from Wyoming. When I ordered the tattoo machine, I created a plan. I was going to check New Mexico off of my travel list for sure. I had created a new quest; I had a mission and a timeline to fulfill the mission.

...

I pushed westward through the evening and into the darkness of night. Wyoming was vast and barren with windswept hills and lonely clusters of mountains. Drugs ran their course, and I felt an urge to sleep.

There was an exit from the highway. It curved around steeply, up into a mountain pass. There was a small service station on the right side of the road up in the mountains. Everything was black in all other directions.

I pulled into the gas station parking lot. I sat in my car for a moment as I took stock of my immediate surroundings. There were a couple of other cars in parking spaces up closer to the store's entrance. Someone seated in one of the cars stared at me while I surveyed the area. Someone else inside the store walked to the front and stared at me through the glass store window. A small alarm bell went off in the back of my mind. I felt an urgent need to immediately leave the parking lot.

I hopped back on the road and headed further away from the highway. I checked my mirrors; nobody had pulled out to follow me. My music was off, and I heard a low rumbling from the dark section of road to my left, down a small slope. I looked over. I did a double take. I'd never seen anything like it.

Twenty years in the transportation and logistics industry, and I was still shocked. The sheer number: like nothing I'd ever seen outside of the largest distribution centers and most massive drop lots around the country. There were hundreds of semitrucks to my left. Some had their running lights marking their outlines, others were completely blacked out alongside them. It was too dark outside to see how far along the trucks continued. I could see truck lights in at least five rows of depth away from the highway.

Though apprehensive, I was intrigued. I was also tired. I pulled off the road to the left and down into the roadside corral of stationary tractor-trailers. I drove into the lines of massive idling machines. The noise of the countless idling engines vibrated my car in the absence of my music. I meandered back in the direction of where I left that service station. I weaved my way back as I cut deeper through the lines of trucks parked farther from the hill up to the road.

I parked in the fourth row deep, and I turned off all but my running lights. I didn't want to be conspicuous, but I also didn't want a truck to flatten me; pulling through my parking location to rest alongside the other semis. My small black sports car with blacked out windows wouldn't have stood a chance if a truck driver hadn't seen me until it was too late.

I sat for a minute amongst the sea of giant machines and their cargo. I again evaluated my current situation in that moment. I decided I was safe where I was. I put the shades up in my windows, I pulled out my drug supplies, I did drugs, and I stripped naked after I did drugs. I interacted on my phone with people from the internet.

I suddenly awoke to sunlight, filling my car with the morning. I was still naked. The shade which had been in my windshield had fallen from its place, and it was on the passenger-side floor. Maybe the trucks around me had vibrated it loose. I instantly put the shade back in place and dressed, as I embarrassingly woke up fully unclothed in that weird field of trucks.

Most of the trucks from the previous night were no longer parked there. I saw about twenty trucks still scattered around my immediate location. I kicked up dust as I hurried up and drove through the lot to an entranceway, back to the main road on the side of the hill. I wondered how many of the trucks had passed by the front of my car as they vacated the lot to return to driving to their destinations. Their views, looking down to my windshield as they passed me by, would have been fully unobstructed. They would have seen a heavily tattooed and fully naked sleeper in the midst of a midlife crisis adventure.

My car seemed to drive funny once I was back on the road. It pulled to the right. The drive was bumpier than normal. It felt better once I got up to highway speed. The outside air grew hotter that morning at a rapid rate. I could tell the temperature was already in the predicted high nineties. I drove for another hour. I did not have any water left in my car. I was also getting hungry. I had no food.

It happened in an instant. The sound, the smell, the feel. I knew exactly what had happened. The sound: a mix between a pop and a rip. The smell: smoke and burning chemicals. The feel: an instant pull on my steering wheel as my car vibrated like it was about to fall apart. My speed dropped from eighty-five to fifty very quickly. In my mirrors, I saw smoke trailing my car. I maintained control of the wheel as I let my car decelerate on its own. I didn't touch the brakes until I dropped below twenty miles an hour and found a good section of shoulder; one where I could pull off and have clearance from the right travel lane of the highway.

I stepped out of my car. The back passenger-side tire was shredded the entire way around the wheel hub. Smoke plumed from the wheel and dissipated into the air as my car sat directly on the rim. I had my spare tire with me, so I went to work locating the proper socket to remove the lug nuts and change the tire.

An hour passed in that awful heat, and I wasn't having any luck finding the socket. I had already sheltered twice in my car as random isolated storms ripped through the area. I had been driving through those random, single-cloud, mini-severe thunderstorms all morning. Though each storm only lasted a couple minutes, they proved to be an inconvenience while I was searching for the tools to begin repairs.

After that first hour, a dreadful thought crossed my mind. I remembered leaving a specific bag of tools back at my storage unit in Ohio. I knew I was going to be driving thousands of miles, so I wanted to lighten the weight of my car in every way possible. I remembered that the specific socket, the one which fit the lug nuts, was in that bag of tools back at my storage unit. My heart sank.

It had been two hours since I finished the last of the water in my car when I woke up in that field of trucks that morning. It was ninety-five degrees outside. Those wayward isolated superstorms did nothing to cool off the air. I hadn't seen a single car pass by me on the highway the entire time I had been looking for my tools. I was thirsty. I was worried. I was in the most desolate and isolated physical location I had ever been. The weather was extreme. My supplies were depleted…and my phone had absolutely zero reception.

The windswept landscape on both sides of the highway in all directions was dusty, rocky, and empty. I took my phone from the seat of my car and crossed over the picket fence on the north side of the highway. It took me about ten minutes to climb to the very top of the hill. I could see for miles in all directions from the top of the hill. All I saw looked the exact same. It was barren and dusty. Hills popped up across the landscape at random points. I saw no cars on the road, stretching to both sides of the horizon. My phone still had no reception.

From that vantage point at the top of the hill, I saw another storm in the distance. An isolated cloud formation was moving at me fast. I recorded video of the scene as I began to quickly descend the hill to reach my car and take shelter. I made it back just as the stormfront hit. Two minutes later, the storm had passed. My car, and the road, began to dry instantly in the heat.

I sat there, sweating in my car, for the next five hours. As storms rolled through, I had to keep all of my windows up. I may as well have just stood on the road in the rain. I was as soaked from sweat as I would have been had I been outside my car in the storms. Finally, as if a miracle, a car pulled up and parked behind me. I sat up in disbelief. Instantly, I jumped from my car. The police cruiser door opened, and an officer stepped out to meet me on the side of the road.

"Oh, my God! I'm so happy to see you. I've been here six hours without water. I can't believe another car finally came down this road."

The officer came upon me on a routine drive down the highway. He had water with him in his cruiser. He gave me six bottles to drink. I downed the first three in under a minute. The officer handed me a box of crackers. I ate half of them as we talked. The officer also had one more item which made him my hero; he had a tire iron. The officer changed my tire to the spare. He insisted I just sat back while he did the work. That officer, on that day, was genuinely my hero.

The officer looked up the closest places with tire shops from where I was stopped on the side of the road. I had the option to drive one hundred miles back in the opposite direction. I had another option as well; I could drive two hundred miles farther west, the direction I had been traveling...on the spare donut tire from my trunk.

I chose option number two. I decided to keep heading west. I thanked the officer sincerely for saving me that day. I then drove two hundred miles through Wyoming at eighty miles per hour on a donut. I made it to the tire store in that next city…and they didn't have a tire to fit my Lexus.

The tire store employee called ahead to another tire shop in Rock Springs, Wyoming. They had the proper sized tires to fit my car in Rock Springs. Rock Springs was yet another hundred miles west on the same highway; the road where I had already put two hundred miles on the donut. I didn't have a choice. I got back on the road, crossed my fingers, and I pushed down the gas pedal one more time.

I made it to Rock Springs. I found the tire store. They had one barely used tire that fit my car. They only charged me thirty-five dollars for the tire. I left the waiting room of the extremely large tire store within an hour. I had done my day's driving. I decided to post up in Rock Springs, cruise around and check out the city, and see who from the online world was close to me.

I tattooed myself as I sat parked at a rest stop overnight in Rock Springs. I interacted with online friends and did drugs. I stayed awake that whole night. Before the sun came up the next morning, I made a decision. I went into the travel center and bought a shower. I was excited as I gathered up my belongings after I showered. I walked back to my car. I put directions into my GPS for Yellowstone.

My excitement to explore new frontiers caused me to leave the rest stop in haste. I drove an hour north from Rock Springs and pulled my car into a gas station. The gas station was closed for another hour. I parked at the pump and waited. The sun came up as I waited to fuel. I didn't mind the wait. My anticipation had me feeling wonderful, and the drugs I did in my car helped me pass the time.

As with my first trip into Colorado earlier in the week, I looked for the mountains as I drove north towards Yellowstone.

The farther north I drove, the more mountains appeared on the horizon. I reached Jackson, Wyoming in early afternoon. I felt I had entered through the gates of an enchanted world of fantasy. I was no longer on flat ground. I could no longer see for miles to a horizon in all directions. I was in a special place; the majesty of nature surrounded me.

The natural beauty of Hawaii had mesmerized me years prior. I felt fortunate any time I took trips to the Caribbean on other occasions. I found beauty everywhere in the continental United States during my travels throughout my life, especially in my recent years of wanderlust. Nature had fostered and cultivated a wonderful part of my psyche since I was old enough to first make memories. It was that day when nature humbled me as I had never before been. That day for me, as I drove north from Jackson, Wyoming to Jackson Hole, was a game changer. That day...my mind was blown.

I sat in that field at the base of the Tetons for ten hours. I was thankful for everything in those ten meditative hours I spent at Teton Point Turnout. All of everything made sense. Those ten hours stretched with me on to eternity. I was nothing without all else, and nothing was everything...it all was, is, and would be ever after.

On that day, in that location, I felt something beyond what words could explain. I knew everything was ok...no matter what, in all situations, at all times, with all things...it was all ok. I had never feared death as an adult. At times, I sought it out or wished for it...but in that moment, in that location, on that day...I let go of my fear of living. I let go of everything, and as I did, I feared nothing at all.

That moment, as I bathed in the splendor of the Teton Mountains, in the field at the base of Grand Teton...I transcended. All which had happened to that point, all which had not...all over which I had control, all of which I did not...it all ended in the shadow of the Teton Mountains on that day in the summer of 2020. It all ceased to exist, and I stepped through. I stepped through to all beyond. As I stepped through, I felt it, and I knew it. It was electric. It was perfect. It was always there for me, and it would always remain. My perspective, on that day, shifted to that which lay in wait of my arrival.

As that so-important day came to a close, and as I continued my drive north from Jackson Hole, Wyoming…it all made sense. I knew I could have died in that moment, and all would have been right. I knew I could die at any point beyond, and all would be ok. I knew I could live, and anything at all could happen while alive, and all would be as it was meant to be. That moment split my life in two: all which came before, and all which would come after. In the shadow of those majestic mountains, as I sat there…I knew the moment had changed me forever.

…

I woke up in my car. I could see the morning sunlight through the cracks around the shades in my windows. I thought for a moment to try to sort out where I was waking up. I remembered driving through an open and large wooden gate at around three o'clock in the morning. I remembered, though the road had been black except for where my headlights had been shining, I was on the edge of a drop off. There was a guardrail to the right side of where I had parked. The small section of gravel between the road and the guardrail had been large enough to snuggly fit my car. I had parked under a metal sign which warned of the presence of bears in the area.

I could hear traffic zipping by my car to the left of me. I kept the shades on the windows of the driver's side and rear windshield. I removed the shades from the front windshield and the passenger side of my car. The sun instantly filled my car with light. The smoke from the hotrail was sparkling in the air. The sign, which warned of bears, was ahead of me, posted five feet above my car on a tree.

When I looked out the windows on the right side of my car, all I saw was sky. I leaned over to climb into the passenger seat. I still only saw sky…until I put my head up to the passenger window. I saw where I had parked and slept. I had parked on the very apex of an eight-hundred-foot sheer cliff drop-off. I had slept inches from a cliff; one which rivaled the proverbial cliff of my midlife crisis. I cracked the passenger door to look down.

There were four inches of pavement between my car and the drop. It was just enough room for the guard rail to be cemented there in place…and it was as far as I could open my car door before I hit it on the rail. I stepped out of my car on the driver's side. I waited by the guardrail until traffic passed and I didn't hear any more cars approaching. I then peed off the apex of an eight-hundred-foot sheer cliff drop-off. I was a homeless person doing homeless activities.

Prioritizing

Fast moving rivers cut through steep canyons. Abrupt shores, shrouded in pine trees, gave way to the calm of deep blue lakes. Waterfalls cascaded alongside challenging hiking terrain. Bison lounged lazily in the grass near the shoulder of the road. An unexpected collection of cars filled the expanse of the giant parking lot near Old Faithful. I waited on the observation deck, along with a hundred others, and I recorded the geyser's impressive eruption. I stopped alongside a meandering river to fulfill a video request from a woman online.

Once again fully clothed and driving, I crossed the Continental Divide. I stopped at an overlook high up in the mountains of Yellowstone. I could see miles out beyond me from that elevation. The Rocky Mountains in Yellowstone had lived up to all I had hoped. I stopped again after I drove down and out of the park. I recorded video of the sunset over the Tetons from the shore of Jackson Lake. In a day and a half, in that magical corner of northwest Wyoming, I saw and documented some of the most beautiful natural settings I had ever seen. My choice to drive north from Rock Springs had enhanced my life.

It was dark outside, and I was on my way back to Rock Springs. I knew I wasn't going to make the full drive back down the western side of Wyoming that night. I decided to drive as far as I could before I stopped for sleep.

I pulled into a gas station somewhere in the middle of the state. I paid for gas. I put the nozzle in my car's gas tank. I sat down in my car as it began to fuel. Two hours passed. I woke up to a police officer tapping on my window. The employee at the gas station, instead of attempting to wake me, had called the police.

I explained to the officer where I was going, and from where I had been driving. The officer told me of a nearby street with open parking. I found the location and pulled in between two other parked vehicles. I slept for three more hours. I left for Rock Springs as the sun came up the next morning.

...

My phone rang as I did laundry at a laundromat in Rock Springs, Wyoming. Though I had just hung up with her, Allison was calling me back. I stepped outside to the street to answer my phone.

"Hi, again…"

"I'll be back from the boat earlier today than I told you a minute ago. I want to see you. Can I see you?"

"Absolutely. my laundry is almost done. I'm about to go wash my car. Give me a call once you get back from the water. I'll let you know where I'm at later on."

"I'm excited to see you."

"I'm excited to see you, too."

"Bye, Doug."

"Bye, Allison."

I walked back in from the sunny outside weather to pull my clothes from the dryer in the laundromat. I smiled to myself. I had been interacting with Allison on the website since 2018, when I was still living in my house in Perrysburg. She was the only person I knew from the website who lived in Wyoming. Allison had recently moved from Cheyanne to Rock Springs.

I didn't know Allison was there until I made it to Rock Springs on the spare tire. Allison had been out of town on business when I was first in the city. She told me then that she would be happy to see me when she came back. I called her when I returned from Yellowstone.

That evening, I sat in my car amongst the campers and trucks parked in the back section of the Rock Springs Walmart parking lot. I had been working on a project to step up my travel game. I was framing a screen to fit in my passenger window so I could sleep in my car with a breeze at night and avoid mosquitos and other bugs.

Allison pulled up in her new silver extended-cab pickup truck. She parked next to me and stepped out of her truck. I stood up from my car and walked around the front to interact. We both smiled at each other.

Allison was ex-military. She was a couple of years younger than I. She was only five feet tall. Allison had long, straight black hair down to her mid-back. Her skin was bronzed and flawless. Her smile warmed my heart. She was as beautiful as I knew she would be.

The two of us talked for an hour at the edge of that Walmart parking lot. We watched the sun set from our elevated and unobstructed vantage point. We laughed and smiled. Our conversation was interesting. Suddenly, Allison seemed to have something else to say.

"Ok, come on. Follow me in your car. I want to take you somewhere. We'll drop your car off in my driveway. You'll see."

I had no reservations. I walked back around my car to my driver's seat. I was ready for whatever adventure Allison had in mind. Allison climbed into her truck. I pulled out through the parking lot behind her. Ten minutes later, I parked in her driveway. I hopped up into the passenger side. I buckled my seatbelt, ready for the ride.

Allison drove to the back of the newly built subdivision at the base of a mountain. She turned from her neighborhood onto the street running along the side of the mountain. She then turned off the road onto a dirt and gravel road, up the side of the mountain.

I recorded video during the off-road adventure. The truck wound its way up the side of the mountain. The truck's headlights were bright enough to show me something. At any moment, if Allison hadn't been sure with her driving, we could plunge off the side to our deaths. I tried to hold the camera steady as the bumps and rocks bounced the truck around while we climbed the steep mountain. I saw the lights of Rock Springs in the nighttime distance below us.

We reached the top of the mountain. The summit, along with all else in Wyoming, was windswept and barren. Allison pulled up to park on the dirt and rocks overlooking the valley below. The city below us was lit up in the nighttime. I could see across the valley to where the mountains on the other side of the city met with the starry sky above us. I could feel the pickup truck swaying in the wind.

Allison and I both saw the headlights behind us as a car pulled up. A moment later, two officers walked up to the sides of the truck. The location was a common spot for people to visit and smoke marijuana. Neither Allison nor I smoked pot. The officers ran our driver's licenses back at their cruiser. An officer returned a moment later to hand us back our licenses. The headlights remained behind us for another five minutes…then the police car pulled away to head back down the mountain.

It was hard to open the truck door against the high winds at the top of the barren mountain. I managed to hop out of the truck to survey the area. I recorded video of a strange and otherworldly weather station structure close to where we had parked. I hopped back up into the truck. Allison leaned over to me, and we began to kiss.

A first happened for me that night in the truck atop the

mountain with Allison. It wasn't a first I had ever wanted. As we undressed each other, Allison told me she wanted me inside her. Allison told me it wasn't possible for her to climax from oral sex. I told her I wished to try anyhow. I had heard that before, and I had proven other women wrong every single time. After half an hour with my mouth between her legs…I conceded to Allison. It was the first time I wasn't able to make good on my oral delivery.

Allison told me how good it had felt. She also told me how she was basically lacking a clitoris. She didn't need to mention that. I knew it within a few moments of when I began licking her. Though I had done drugs earlier that day, I had no issue getting up with her. After the attempt at oral, we consummated together in any positions we could manage in the extended cab of Allison's pickup truck. Fortunately, with intercourse, I managed to get Allison to the point she hadn't reached with oral.

The two of us spent the next few hours watching the stars over the valley. I thanked Allison for sharing such an amazing night with me. I thanked her for showing me such a wonderful location. I held on as I bounced around on the treacherous drive back down the mountain. Allison and I kissed for a few minutes when we arrived again at Allison's house.

Allison had relatives staying with her at the time, so I was unable to stay the night with her. I smiled at Allison. Allison told me to see her again. I told her the truth: it was the only time I had ever been to Wyoming after forty years of life…the probability of a return was rather low. She understood. We kissed again. It was bittersweet. I thought about Allison as I left Rock Springs that night.

I had a long drive ahead of me. My goal was to reach Cheyanne, on the other side of the state. I got gas in my car at the same rest stop from which I left to journey to Yellowstone a few days prior. I decided to fuel myself as I fueled up my car. I blasted down a series of huge hotrails. I blasted off from that rest stop fully fueled…and fully fueled.

I hit the nighttime highway with determination. The

travel lanes, except for the expected big rigs, were all but empty. I turned up the music and set up my phone to record the trip. I thought back to the speeds I hit on the drive west across Nebraska. I decided that the previous Nebraska drive had been practice for the drive east across Wyoming. With the music hitting, and the drugs hitting, I hit the gas.

Again, I peaked at one hundred and forty miles per hour. I kept the speed up for long lengths of time on my drive to Cheyanne. I ripped past semis as they meandered along at about eighty. I weaved through multiple vehicles on the rare instances I came up on any traffic at all. Like those days skirting the outsides of Detroit on the interstates, I lifted off the Earth. I was in space.

My mind raced; my reactions were on point. I was ever diligent, anticipating my roadway maneuvers before I put them into action. The red color of rear lights on cars shot towards me like I was in a video game. I changed lanes to accommodate. I had fractions of seconds to react and find clear ways forward. Headlights disappeared behind me into the black of night as fast as I could glance at my mirrors.

Time passed; I was too focused to measure how long. Miles passed; I kept a staggering pace. I knew it was the fastest I had ever covered the distance I covered that night. The speed (and the speed) kept my mind in an adrenaline-saturated state. I began seeing road signs for Cheyanne. I made it. As traffic picked up, approaching the city in the middle of the night, I governed my speed as I stayed on the cusp of the triple-digit mark.

When I reached the city proper, I came back to Earth and obeyed the speed limit. That drive through the desolate expanse of Wyoming in the darkness of night was a metaphor for a portal, one which returned me from an otherworldly and magical land, where nature was the focus. I was back to the daily life of cities, and people, and activity…and stresses, and worries, and concerns, and limits to the visions of what was out there beyond a manufactured world of clutter; where focus only extended to that which was immediately and currently visible.

I stuck around the city for a day. I went back to the park in Cheyanne the next morning to get some sunlight and work more on my car audio. I again ate at a Mexican restaurant. I drove around more and explored the city. The point came when I knew it was time to go. I knew I could lazily work my way down to New Mexico to pick up my tattoo gun when it arrived at the Whole Foods locker, but I had done my time in Wyoming.

I came upon Fort Collins, Colorado in the middle of the night. As always, I was busy sending and replying to messages on all of my social media platforms and apps. I had been in contact with a guy who lived in the city. The guy was looking to party. He invited me over.

Though I took steps to remove myself from the drug trade, I still used crystal all day, every day. The guy in Fort Collins mentioned he had his own crystal. That was fine with me. I still had an ounce from the last time I acquired crystal in the Midwest, and I planned to leave it in my car when I reached the guy's house...unless the quality of the guy's drugs was disgraceful, and I needed to go back out and retrieve my own to make the party happen.

...

By summer of 2020, I had been on the website for two and a half years. I was on all the popular dating apps for almost as long. Popularity online in an adult hookup world became strategic. As I traveled, I matched with people in close proximity via geolocation on the internet and apps. As I traveled through cities, I would begin interacting with many of my matches. I had many conversations going on at once with those close to where I traveled.

My conversations revealed which matches wanted me to stop to see them as I was passing through the area. Messages were received letting me know availability and locations. Often, when matches weren't available at the moment...whether they were at work or somehow otherwise occupied, they let me know when they were next available and wished to see me.

My travel throughout the country had me crisscrossing locations many times over. Along the way, new matches popped up anytime I was back through any area where I had already been. The new conversations with the new matches began as I was still connected to previous matches in the area.

Sometimes, I adjusted my travel to line up with certain matches and their availability. As I drove, I sent messages to my connections, whichever upcoming city I was approaching. Some people were available. I stopped to see them and hang out. Others weren't free at the time, so we made plans to try again on my next pass.

My interactions weren't based only on intimate experiences. Though some of my matches were only seeking no-strings-attached hookups, I was happy to just see people and go with the flow, whatever ways our time together was spent. The length of time spent was as varied as our activities together.

It was always exciting to create those dynamics with people all around the country. Some instances ended up being one-time things. With other people, sustained dynamics always gave me something I could look forward to when I was passing through a certain location in the country.

Meaningful friendships and long-term intimate dynamics popped up and lasted as I traveled. Unique situations created interesting memories in the times when those one-time meetings didn't blossom into the future. Very rarely, meet-ups went far off the rails. Usually, the worst-case scenario ended with my knowledge that the connection hadn't lined up, and I wouldn't be making a point to see that person again.

I had more and more connected people and places as I kept up on my travels. No matter where I was, in almost any location in any state in the country, I knew I had places I could go and people I could see. I felt alive as I traveled. I felt alive creating and sustaining dynamics with people everywhere. I felt secure; knowing I had places close by where I could visit, no matter where I was in the country.

I had friends with whom I could go out to dinner or just go get ice cream. I'd stop and meet people to hike in a park. I'd stop for sleepovers. I knew who wished to party, and I could stop and get high with someone and talk for an afternoon before I continued on down the road. When I was tired, I'd be invited to come take naps with people and rest. People would show me around their cities, the best locations for stunning nature photography and videos. Others wished to create videos and memories of an adult nature.

By summer of 2020, due to all the interactions and connections I had cultivated, I felt comfortable and familiar almost everywhere in the United States. I collected so many wonderful and meaningful memories…shared with people who became important to me on so many levels, in so many different ways. I was appreciative of the love and concern I felt from everywhere.

My dream had come true; I felt alive…but I hadn't fixed myself. I was happy, but I wasn't. I knew I had created a life of note. I knew I was living each day, not just going through the motions. My time felt full and immediate, and I lived in most moments. I was doing what I wanted, and I felt free…but something was still off.

The One that Counts

I thought back to the dawn of 2018, familiarizing with online interactions. I remembered receiving new invitations to homes all around the country. I remembered feeling the world had opened up in front of me. I remembered that first spark of an idea to travel and experience life.

I pulled into Dean's driveway in Aurora, Colorado. It was two and a half years after I was first invited to see Dean. I thought back to how foreign the invitation had felt as I sat in my living room in Ohio and interacted with Dean. I thought how so much had happened between that night Dean had invited me to see him and that current evening in mid-2020, as I stepped from my car to walk up Dean's driveway.

I stayed the night at Dean's house, but I left after breakfast early in the morning. I planned to see Dean again on my return from New Mexico. The pink and red sky of the sunrise over Aurora, Colorado that morning was beautiful. I recorded video after I filled up my car's gas tank. I then headed south, away from the Denver metro area.

The mountains outside of my passenger side windows were constant as I drove south on I-25. I was driving parallel to the eastern edge of the Rocky Mountains. The snow-peaked caps of the tallest mountains loomed high above. The wall of natural beauty extended as far north and south as the eye could see. Some of those largest mountains were fourteeners. Colorado has more peaks above fourteen thousand feet than any other state.

As I approached Colorado Springs, the wall of mountains to the west crept ever closer to the highway. As I passed through the city, mountains on the eastern ridge of the Rockies popped up on both sides of the road. Colorado Springs was split by the highway. I exited I-25 on the west side of the road. I followed the exit up and around the curves, onto the elevated surface streets of Colorado Springs.

My view from the eastern side of the city consumed my thoughts. I sought a vantage point to overlook the highway below, out to the wall of mountains beyond. A parking lot outside a strip of shops was the right location. I pulled in, and I parked facing out over the highway below.

It was a great spot with a spectacular western-facing view of the Rocky Mountains. It was the perfect spot to spend a couple hours doing drugs, enjoying the scenery, and interacting online. After an hour of hotrails, I reached a point in a conversation where I knew my perfect location wasn't perfect for what was about to transpire. I knew I needed to find somewhere slightly further up the mountain, a more secluded area.

I packed up my drug paraphernalia and pulled out of the parking lot. I took the winding road higher up onto the mountain, away from the traffic and people in the busier and more populus section of Colorado Springs. I found another parking lot which suited my needs.

I picked up my phone after I put on a shirt. I wanted to check the map. When the map came up, I saw something interesting. I'd heard of Pike's Peak, despite having never been in close proximity. I wasn't even sure why I knew things about the mountain. I learned something else as I looked at the map while I sat in my car on a mountainside in Colorado Springs; I learned I was within a half-hour's drive to the base of Pike's Peak.

There were storm clouds around some random spots in the mountains in both directions to the horizon. From what I could see, most of the peaks were sunny. I tried to figure out which peak was Pike's Peak. My vantage point was particularly good. I managed to sort out the many mountains in my frame of vision from the opposite side of I-25. The mountain which I determined to be Pike's Peak, towering into the sky beyond shorter peaks, was clearly visible in the sunshine. A wave of excitement hit me with the breeze blowing through my car windows. I had my plans for the day.

I drove down from the mountainside on the eastern side of I-25. I drove through the commotion of mid-morning Colorado Springs to the west. Within five minutes, the world around me shifted completely. I had just been in the center of Colorado Springs, surrounded by buildings, pavement, people, and cars. I had just been waiting at stoplights while people walked and drove all around me. I had just been in a heavily populated and trafficked urban location, surrounded by businesses and residences. All it took was five minutes of driving for my entire world to become something else entirely.

When I reached the point where the city abruptly stopped, nature took over with an impressive and astounding switch of environment: pine trees and forests, giant red rocks and roadside drop-offs alluding to the base of a wild mountainous region. Flowing cascading water, cliffs as high up as I could see, sharp curves on steep inclines kept me at full attention. I was suddenly in the Rocky Mountain wilderness. The complete shift all around me came fast. My brain was still adjusting when I realized I was quickly ascending in elevation.

I had to give more gas to my car's engine. I was angled back as I climbed upward into the mountains. I didn't have a full tank of gas, but I figured I had enough to summit Pike's Peak. By the time I reached the entranceway gate of the mountain, I had already ascended well above the city. I could no longer see any reminder of civilization besides the road and the traffic also heading to the top of the mountain.

To the left, there was a parking area at the gate to the summit of Pike's Peak. Shuttle busses were loading up passengers and dropping others off in the parking lot. I passed the loading area. I paid money at the gate to drive myself to the top. I recorded video through my front windshield as the gate in front of me lifted to allow my car through. I read the signs on the side of the road, and I mentally prepared my drug-filled brain for the drive.

I passed a lake early on in the drive. Then I crossed a bridge. There was forest all around me. I kept climbing higher. As time passed, my shoulders began to ache from the constant motion of the steering wheel. My ankle began to cramp from the constant adjustment of the gas pedal. Periodically, especially around corners, the view above the surrounding world was mesmerizing. I kept climbing higher.

A while later, I saw a stop-point in the road ahead. It was a checkpoint. I pulled up to one of the workers standing on the side of the lane. For me to continue ascending the mountain, it was mandatory that they check my car's brakes. The worker explained what was coming up on the drive.

Though the distance remaining to reach the summit of Pike's Peak was only a small fraction of the distance I had just driven, I was warned it was going to take me a longer amount of time. The road was about to become much steeper, and I was about to encounter many more turns, turns which were much sharper and more dangerous. My brakes passed the test, and I left the checkpoint.

I drove straight forward from the checkpoint. The trees lining both sides of the road were thick. I couldn't see anything beyond them. The road curved again. Up and around…and suddenly I was above the tree line. I could see to the ends of the world. I could see the deeper blue in the atmosphere above the curvature of the horizon. Beyond the endless sea of mountains, I saw above everything. I saw where Heaven came down and met with Earth. I smiled. My choice to summit Pike's Peak was the correct choice.

Once I crossed over to that strange world above the tree line, it felt like I was in an alien environment. The ground towards the top of the mountain was otherworldly, tan rocks of all sizes. It was the entire environment up above the trees and clouds. The top section of Pike's Peak was barren and uniform… and it was amazing.

The road, as I was warned, became immediately and

drastically more treacherous. My car struggled at the angle of incline. The curves bent back completely towards the opposite directions from which I approached them. I could see the winding road crisscrossing directly above me. I drove straight for a stretch, then I curved up and around. I was then driving another straight stretch, but in the opposite direction.

The curves had to be taken blind around some of the rock structures on the side of the mountain. Some locations, where possible, had small sections of guard rails. Mostly though, the road wasn't wide enough for guard rails; the ascending lane and descending lane were in a space just big enough for only the two lanes. The sheer drop-offs where the pavement of the lane ended were open air to thousands of feet below. I loved it, my Lexus did not.

Earlier on the drive, I passed through a layer of clouds. The sky was clear when I reached the final curve to the parking location at the summit of Pike's Peak. A parking attendant directed the line of cars to different open spaces in the parking rows. I was amazed at how many cars were parked in the rocks and gravel at the top of the mountain. I found a spot, four rows into the lot, and I parked.

My car had been smoking from under the hood since I reached the parking attendant. I turned off my car and popped the hood. When I opened the hood, it created a plume of smoke, the only cloud at the summit of Pike's Peak. The coolant in the tank was boiling. I knew the engine was far too hot to attempt to find the problem.

I closed the hood and got back in my car. It was cold at the top of the mountain, and it was windy. I pulled out a jacket from one of my bags. I opened another bag. I set up the tray and poured a line of crystal onto it.

I heated the end of a glass stem with my propane torch. I put the cool end of the pipe into my nostril. I plugged my other nostril with my fingers against the side of my nose. In a sweeping motion, my head went down across the tray. The hot end of the pipe, barely above the line of crystal, vaporized the crystal as I sucked it up into my nose. I then blew out the largest cloud at the summit of the mountain...except the cloud which was still escaping from under my hood.

The drugs hit fast. The feeling overshadowed my worry about my mechanical issues. I decided, as I zipped up my drug equipment and placed the bag under my seat, I wasn't going to let my car problems dampen an experience I knew was about to be amazing. I got out of my car and put on my jacket. I knew I was about to create memories.

I left my car to cool off, and I began to hike up the rock incline to reach the peak of the mountain. The air was thin, and I was out of breath constantly. Every few steps, I had to stop to catch my breath. I was breathing heavily as I walked up towards the summit. I made it up and around the final rock formation, and suddenly I was standing on the summit of Pike's Peak... trying to catch my breath.

People were wandering around up on the rocks. Some were standing still, taking in the amazing three-hundred-and-sixty-degree view of infinity. Others were taking pictures and recording video. I began taking pictures and recording video as well. It was amazing to be able to stand at the top of the world and look out over all of creation. I appreciated every minute I spent up there. I knew the drive down the mountain would be beautiful, and treacherous, and hard on my brakes...if my car even started again when I went to leave. I didn't care. I was, again, in a timeless moment. It all made sense.

...

I was almost to New Mexico. The sky was clear as dawn broke. The sunrise over Trinidad, Colorado was exceptionally beautiful as the light in the sky illuminated the squared-off peak of Trinidad's landmark natural monolith. Perched high above the highway at a rest stop halfway up a mountain's side to the west of the interstate, I gazed to the east as the sun illuminated Simpson's Rest. I was twenty-one miles from the New Mexico border, but I was two days shy of my delivery arriving in Santa Fe.

I sat, deep in thought, and I surveyed across the valley to the rock formation on the other side of the interstate. My view that morning was breathtaking. Had I not been there to see it, I wondered if it all would have still been there; existing without me. The crystal had been working on my brain as I drove through Colorado that morning. I wondered, was that sunrise real...or was it all just an illusion? Could it have been that all I thought to be real was only real to me? When I took that long ride, would all else cease to exist?

I snapped out of it. I was tired, and my brain had been running on fumes through the night. From my vantage point, the city of Trinidad looked interesting. I decided to explore the area for the day...beginning with the top of Simpson's Rest. Down the mountain, across the interstate, through the city, and up the other mountain; I had my path. I started my car.

Two online interactions were significant to me while I spent the day in Trinidad. A guy named Justin in some small city in northern New Mexico convinced me to stop and see him on my way to Santa Fe. A woman named Stacey in Pueblo, Colorado invited me to stop and see her on my way north from New Mexico later in the week.

I walked around underneath a viaduct in downtown Trinidad and recorded video of a storm as it moved in to shroud Simpson's Rest in rain. I texted Justin to let him know I would see him around midday the next day. I waited until the thunderstorm swept through the area late that afternoon before I decided to get back in my car and drive south. As the sun went down that evening, I crossed into New Mexico on the interstate.

I again felt that twinge of excitement as I approached the border of a state I had never before been. It never failed...even if I had done so much crystal that I couldn't get any higher from drugs, the thrill of exploring the unknown still registered on my chemically fried brain. New Mexico was the forty-eighth state on my list. I felt satisfied with my plan to drive to Santa Fe to pick up my new tattoo machine.

The feeling wore off quickly. It was pitch black as I drove through the mountain pass at the border of Colorado and New Mexico. The sky cast an eerie vibe that night. There was something ominous about. I didn't know why I felt a foreboding uneasiness. The drugs, after being awake for many hours, were beyond the point of keeping me going.

I found a rest stop in the emptiness and black of night. I felt alone, beyond just actually being alone. I felt on edge. All the vehicles at the rest stop were semitrucks. I didn't see a single person outside or in the restrooms. After I got back to my car from the bathroom, I put the shades up in my windows. I took my handgun from my ankle holster and placed it on my lap. I then immediately passed out from sleep deprivation.

I woke up the next morning in the Wild West. Sleep, as it always had, cured my previously onsetting paranoia. The dread and fear of the prior night had dissipated with the darkness. It was bright and sunny outside. My sense of wonder filled me with the desire to stay the course. The hotrails which filled my lungs as I was parked there in the New Mexico scenery reinvigorated my well-rested mind. My resolve to reach Santa Fe filled me with excitement.

Justin had been sending text messages while I was asleep. I replied to him. Justin gave me an address, and he asked what time I was going to be over to his house to see him. After I put the address into my phone's map, I told Justin I would see him at two o'clock. By four o'clock, I was back on the road and headed south, away from Justin's house and closer to Santa Fe.

I booked a suite for three nights. The third-floor balcony of my hotel room overlooked a large courtyard. I walked inside and set down my bags in the first room of my suite. I walked through the kitchen and through another room. I then reached my bedroom. The view from that side of my suite overlooked a parking lot, out into the city of Santa Fe. I was happy with the lodging.

As I waited for my visitor that first evening, I showered. Drugs were laid out on one of the desks in the bedroom. Earlier that afternoon, I had picked up my packages from the locker at the grocery store a few miles away. My new tattoo machine was set up on another desk, over by the bedroom window.

I had three packages waiting for me in the locker: my new rotary tattoo machine, another amplifier for my car stereo, and spark plugs. The rotary tattoo machine was rated the best machine of 2020. The amplifier was going to be the fifth in the system I was perpetually building in my car; used exclusively to power two ten-inch subwoofers which I had previously installed to complement the two twelve-inch subwoofers in my trunk. The spark plugs, items in my car which I knew needed to be changed out, were going to be changed once I was back in Colorado later in the week.

My phone had multiple new text messages. I saw them once I finished showering. As I dried off, I responded to a beautiful twenty-year-old trans girl. We had begun texting when I arrived in Santa Fe. She was on her way to my hotel.

"I'll be to your hotel in a half hour."

"Sounds good. I'm out of the shower. I'll meet you in the front parking lot when you get here. This hotel is big and confusing. It'll be easier if I just come out to walk you in."

"Ok, I'll text when I arrive…I'm hungry."

"We'll order food when you get here. See you soon."

I walked the girl back out to her car later that night. I made my way back through the corridors and courtyards to my suite. I was excited to use my new tattoo machine for the first time. I had another assignment from Shannon. I had been directed to tattoo a blue lightning bolt on my left ball to compliment the green lightning bolt Shannon previously required I tattoo on my right ball.

As with the green lightning bolt, the blue bolt bled a decent amount. The new tattoo machine worked very well, but the particular location of the tattoo again proved to be a challenge. I did drugs through the night as I interacted with Shannon, updating her on progress as I continued to fill in the spots where blood kept the ink from remaining under my skin.

Overall, it took six separate applications during that stay in the suite in New Mexico to complete the tattoo. I spent the three days exploring Santa Fe, tattooing myself, and intimately interacting with Shannon as I progressed. One of the other interactions during that time was with Stacey, the woman in Pueblo, Colorado.

Stacey was a forty-year-old blonde woman from the website. Stacey and I shared exceptionally good conversation in those few days. We made plans. Once I left New Mexico, I planned a stop in Pueblo, Colorado on my return trip North. We planned to spend the weekend together, since Stacey's teenage children were at their dad's house that weekend. Stacey also had a place for me to work on my car; I could install the new amplifier and change the spark plugs.

Ninety Seconds to Midnight

The nature of the dream startled me awake. I looked over. Stacey was still asleep. I walked to the bathroom as I tried to shake off the remnants of the nightmare. I put my tray down on the bathroom counter and looked into the mirror to be sure my previous night's haircut was evenly lined up. I was satisfied. I broke up a line of crystal and heated my glass stem with a new torch Stacey had given me when I arrived the night before. Stacey smoked pot, but she had no need for the torch; she didn't do crystal. As I blew out a large plume of smoke, the last of my post-nightmare feelings dissipated into the air with the cloud.

The task at hand proved more difficult and time-consuming than I had anticipated. It was hot outside, high nineties. I was pouring sweat and exhausted by the time I managed to change my car's spark plugs. I had been out in the direct sunlight for a few hours. A couple of the spark plugs took extreme effort and odd ingenuity to break free from their position. I banged up my hands, and I was covered in grease from the engine. It was mid-afternoon when I finally finished and walked back into Stacey's house.

Two days before that, I had been driving around exploring the natural scenery in Santa Fe. As I drove up a winding mountain road in a national park outside the city, my car again overheated as it had during my summit of Pike's Peak. I ended up stranded on an overlook in the wilderness of the park. I spent three hours in the forest, on the side of a mountain, while I tried to sort out what was going on under the hood.

I plugged my code reader into the computer of my Lexus.

I scanned my car. The Bluetooth results appeared on my phone screen. My Lexus had forty-nine separate error codes on the code reader.

After adjustments to different components of the engine, and after waiting for my car to cool off, I was able to drive back down the mountain to civilization. That nagging feeling of the impending doom to my car was amplified and pushed to the forefront of my thoughts. Again, my car had stopped working upon ascension of a steep mountain. Again, the coolant reservoir held boiling coolant. Again, I drove away knowing it was only a matter of time until the problems wouldn't allow me to drive any farther.

After I left Stacey's house, I reached Denver with no discernable car trouble. The pressure in my mind eased back. I put my bags down on the second bed in my hotel room. I was close to the Denver airport. My new spark plugs held up on the recent drive north from Stacey's house in Pueblo.

I checked my phone. I read the most recent message and replied back to the woman from the website.

"I made it to Denver. I'm in my room."

"Ok, I'm leaving my brother's house now. I'll be over in forty-five minutes."

After two hours with the woman in my hotel room, she dressed and was ready to leave.

"Well, I'm satisfied for sure. Thanks for being my first White guy. Your mouth is amazing. I'm happy I came over to meet you."

"I enjoyed it as well. I'll walk you to your car."

When I got back from the parking lot, I covered the smoke

detector in my room with a plastic grocery bag. I set up my drug paraphernalia and my tattoo equipment. I picked up my phone and began scrolling the messages I had missed during the previous two hours.

Bobby met me close to the hotel at a favorite sandwich shop chain restaurant, one which I was happy to see existed out West. Bobby was dropped off as I was sitting in my car eating my sandwich. I offered him one of the quarters of the roast beef on sourdough. Bobby took a bite, and he told me he saw why I liked the restaurant so much. We sat and ate. Once finished, I drove us back to my hotel.

I began interacting with Bobby on an app after the woman from the website left that afternoon. Bobby was twenty-eight years old. He was a White guy, originally from Michigan. Through his military service, he had lived in Denver, Colorado for the better part of a decade. Trouble after his discharge kept Bobby out in Denver on probation after a short stint in prison.

Bobby and I meshed like lifelong friends. Bobby couldn't do crystal with me on account of random drug testing, but he had no issue with my indulgence. Bobby drank alcohol instead, of which I had no interest. The two days with Bobby familiarized me with the city of Denver.

Bobby and I went all over the place: friends' houses to party, hotels to meet others, restaurants, bars, and shopping centers. I saw all sides of Denver proper: downtown, suburbs, inner city, business districts; it was a lot of exploration in such a brief time. My car was still holding up, but I worried about it. I felt I was pushing my limits.

After those two days, Bobby and I parted ways. I dropped Bobby off at a duplex where two of his friends lived. Bobby invited me in to hang out for a bit before I took off to leave Colorado. I had a weird feeling in that moment, and I opted to decline. I didn't wish to meet Bobby's friends. I didn't wish to hang out in a house. I wished to get on the road and head away from Colorado.

As Bobby walked up to his friend's house, I pulled out of

the neighborhood. The southern area of Denver was extremely traffic congested. I managed to find a gas station five minutes down the road. I pulled in and parked. I was amazed how many cars filled the roads and parking lots. People were everywhere as well, walking all around me.

My paranoia got the best of me. While parked at that gas station, I stepped from my car and checked for any signs of tracking devices. I hopped back in my car, blew down some more hotrails, and pulled up map directions from the heart of Denver towards Wyoming.

I had one more state in the continental United States to check off from my list. Though I knew I wouldn't be able to check off Alaska, I could at least get that forty-ninth state checked off: Oregon. A woman from the website, one whom I had been involved with for the prior year, lived in Washington and wanted me to come be with her. I planned to travel a route which took me through Oregon to reach her in Tacoma, Washington.

I reached an interstate highway south of downtown Denver. I began driving north through the metro area. My car seemed like it was running rough. By the time I cleared downtown Denver, on my way to the northern outskirts of the city, the air in my car had become hazy.

The sun was going down for the night, and the air around the city also seemed hazy. I didn't think much of it, but my worry for the car began to build as the engine began to run rougher. On the highway north of Denver, my worry was confirmed when smoke began to fill the car from the air vents.

I knew instantly that I was in trouble. I tried to look for exit signs and places within range to drive. Traffic packed the interstate as I drove north in desperation to find an exit from the highway. Then, as I was driving in the middle of the interstate at seventy miles per hour, in the midst of heavy traffic, my car shut off. The engine, the lights, the music, the power steering instantly gone. I was surrounded by vehicles on an interstate highway, all traveling at high rates of speed. That last bit of sunlight disappeared in the sky as my car filled with smoke…

and I was suddenly overwhelmed with dread.

It was dark outside. It was also hot. I was pouring sweat. When trucks blew by me, I felt the vibrations from the close proximity of their passing. The haze around me made it even harder to see in the night sky. I sprayed myself with bug repellant, but some mosquitos were not deterred.

The fire was out as of three hours prior. I made no progress attempting to diagnose the issue, let alone fix it. My hands were cut and bleeding. My arms, covered in grease and oil. I sat back down as traffic zipped by me at seventy miles an hour, barely more than a foot to my left. All I could do at that point was wait.

My car, after leaving Lansing, truly was my home. I had broken free from a way I chose to no longer live. I left the drug market behind, and opted to only possess a large supply of crystal for personal use as I experienced an unfamiliar life. I turned my back on seemingly endless money for peace of mind and reduced stress. None of that mattered in that moment on the side of the highway just north of Denver, Colorado. I had immediate problems consuming my mind, my sole focus.

My friend Lex, the friend who had helped me buy the Lexus in the first place, bought me a membership to AAA as I sat there on the shoulder of that busy interstate. It had been three hours since I somehow managed to maneuver my completely non-functioning car across two lanes of traffic to stop on the narrow shoulder of the highway.

That time, in my Lexus on the northbound shoulder of Interstate 25, I knew it wasn't that simple. I wasn't renting a room at my friend Jane's house anymore. I was on the other side of the country, in unfamiliar territory. That time, in my Lexus (my home) I knew I was in trouble.

Whether I liked it or not...I unexpectedly became a resident of Colorado. I managed a couple of hours of sleep in the bed in my hotel room. I walked out, unclothed, onto the balcony of my hotel room. I gazed across the parking lot. My Lexus was in a parking space in the back row of the parking lot. It was towed there the night before. As I had done during previous car incidents, I rode with the tow truck driver in the cab of his truck. I walked back into my room from the balcony and set up my hotrail supplies.

...

I woke up. I was on a big purple couch in a big basement of a big house. There were paintings on the walls and sculptures on pedestals. My belongings, all of my travel bags, were on the floor next to the big purple couch. I took a deep breath, and I stood up.

I stepped upstairs and walked into the kitchen. I squinted from the bright sunlight in the house, shining in from the many large windows. A place was set for me at the kitchen table. The food smelled wonderful. I took a glass of orange juice and sat down. I smiled at the other two people, already seated at the table. I greeted them, and I began to eat.

"Doug, would you like seconds?"

"No thank you. I have a lot of work to do. I need to get started."

As I walked back down the stairs, I noted the ornate and intricate woodwork of the railing. I sat down on the big purple basement couch, on one of the sections which wrapped around at an angle from the main section. I pulled out my phone and began watching instructional videos.

It was the third day I had slept there. It was the day when scheduled packages were set to begin arriving at the house. I had a good idea of what I was going to do from studying videos on my phone. As I watched more videos, Unique sent me a text message.

...

I spent most of the previous night out with Unique. The two of us first met on an app three days prior, while I was in the hotel room. Unique was a pretty Black girl. She was twenty-six years old. She lived in Denver.

A day after I left the hotel, I met Unique in person. I was wandering the streets of Aurora, feeling lost and defeated. After a couple of miles of walking in the night, I needed a break. As I sat with my backpack and a travel bag outside of a busy gas station in inner city Aurora, Unique pulled into the parking lot and picked me up.

It was midnight as we rode through the busy streets of Aurora. Suddenly, out of nowhere, Unique yelled something. She whipped the steering wheel around and made a sharp U-turn across four lanes of traffic.

"That guy's on flakka!"

As the tires screeched from the quick change of direction, I started to ask Unique what she was doing. I stopped mid-sentence. The words clicked in my head when I saw what had captured Unique's attention. My mouth dropped open slightly as I tried to comprehend what I was seeing. Unique pulled into another gas station and parked her car. We sat in the car and watched the guy from across the parking lot. I couldn't help myself; I began to record video.

The guy, a White guy, was in his early twenties. He was dressed like a college student. He was decently groomed with a normal haircut, khaki shorts, tennis shoes, button-up shirt, and no unusual physical features. Had the guy been standing still, he would have blended into the normal menagerie of people out in Aurora that night. His actions, however, were those of people I had seen in videos online. In fact, I felt as if I was watching one of those "dangers of drugs" videos taking place directly in front of me.

We watched as the flakka guy talked to himself; fully

animated hand gestures and head movements accompanied his words. Suddenly he would freeze, no talking or movement, and he stared into nothing. Then, he'd bolt across the parking lot to another side. At one point, flakka guy did a decent imitation of "the robot" dance move, rigidly moving his arms and neck in fast stiff motions.

"I told you! Flakka!"

"This dude needs help…"

"Welcome to Colorado."

"I don't want this guy to get hit by a car, but I also don't want him to wake up in a jail cell. I have no idea how to help him."

Flakka guy suddenly froze, and then he sprinted to the entrance of the gas station. There was a display of gallon containers of windshield washing fluid for sale outside the entrance to the gas station. The flakka guy took a full three minutes to dramatically explain something to the washer fluid display. He then began walking, in slow-motion, towards a guy pumping gas.

"I don't want to get involved, but if he starts fighting that guy at the gas pump, I'm going to have to try to break it up."

Flakka guy, as soon as he reached the guy at the gas pump, turned around and ran off across the road, into the night.

"That was super weird…"

"Alright, I'm pulling out of here."

Unique pulled out from the gas station, back to the road.

We came to a stop behind a line of cars at a red light. The light turned green. Suddenly, flakka guy came out of nowhere and zipped in front of the four lanes of moving traffic. He managed to dodge all the cars, and he again ran off into the night.

...

I read Unique's text message as I sat on the big purple couch. Unique told me she would be over in an hour. I told her I would see her then. Out of respect for my current situation, I held off on doing any crystal on the big purple couch in the basement. I chose to wait until I was with Unique as we ran errands, tasks I needed to accomplish to forward my progress. Unique smoked crystal. She had made a water pipe which she used to smoke crystal. The quality of Unique's crystal was, surprisingly, on par with the quality of my crystal.

Two packages delivered before Unique arrived to pick me up: a sensor and a water pump. Two more showed up while I was out with Unique getting high and buying other needed items: a PCV valve and another sensor. I was still waiting on a particular gauged socket. The socket was scheduled to arrive the following day. The remainder of the needed parts were picked up from local retailers around the Denver area.

Crystal Clear

My new car club membership provided a limited number of service calls annually. I called Dean, and I asked Dean for a favor. I used another membership service call to have my car towed again. That second tow was from the hotel to the street alongside Dean's house in Aurora, Colorado.

Dean lived with his semi-elderly mother in an immaculate house in one of the more upscale neighborhoods in Aurora. The six-thousand square foot home was a work of art. The previous homeowner had been a master Russian woodworker. Every detail of every part of the home's interior was beautifully crafted: the railing, the floors, the walls, and the furniture. The paintings and sculptures accented the living space. Even the front and backyard were decorated with sculptures and artwork.

Dean owned a hair salon. In 2020, he was out of work due to the coronavirus pandemic. Dean was concerned for his mother's health at the time, but he permitted me to stay in his basement for those first two weeks while I rebuilt my car's engine.

The engine parts had been delivered, I had been watching instructional videos, and the socket I needed to remove the belts from the engine had arrived. I began taking apart my car's engine on the street in Dean's neighborhood. It was a beautiful and sunny Colorado summer morning.

That evening, I finalized plans with a blonde trans girl, one whom I first met when I arrived in Denver earlier in the month, before I went down to New Mexico. Bethany was twenty-five years old. She lived in Denver with roommates, but she rented a penthouse suite in a luxury hotel that evening. I ordered a car from a ride service, and I told Bethany I would be at her hotel in half an hour.

Bethany was beautiful; her vibe was sultry and erotic. Bethany earned her income as an escort. She took the night off work to spend the evening with me. Our time together was off the clock. Bethany told me she felt something between us during our online interactions. Bethany didn't want money to have any bearing on our experience together. If money had been a factor, I wouldn't have made plans to meet her.

Bethany didn't like crystal, so I did hotrails by myself on a table in the dining area of the hotel suite. Bethany preferred another drug. She smoked black tar heroin. I hadn't done heroin since that Thanksgiving night in 2018, when my friend Makayla babysat me to be sure my accidental overdose didn't become a fatality.

The Denver skyline was visible from the top-floor hotel balcony. I did crystal all through the night. Bethany and I smoked heroin. Bethany had an interesting heroin pipe. It was a hybrid glass marijuana bowl attached to a water chamber. Bethany, same as I, enjoyed crafting her own smoking devices.

As I lay on the bed against the headboard, Bethany straddled me while topless. With only a thong on Bethany, and me in my boxer shorts, we shotgunned hits of heroin back and forth to one another. I would hit the pipe, put my mouth to hers, and blow smoke into Bethany's mouth as we kissed passionately. Then Bethany would hit the pipe and do the same to me. I felt my eyelids becoming heavy from the heroin. The hotrails kept me awake as I smoked heroin throughout the night.

As the sun came up, the car service dropped me off on the street by my Lexus. I unlocked my car and sat down in the driver's seat. Before I could gather up tools to work on the engine, the heroin put me to sleep. Two hours later, I was awake again. Two hotrails after that, and I popped the hood to continue the disassembly of my car's engine.

Dean's mom brought me a cup of coffee. She let me know that breakfast would be served at the table on the back patio in five minutes. I thanked her and went inside to wash up in a bathroom. I walked through the house and out the door to the patio. Dean and his mother were seated at the table.

I sat down in front of my plate. I set my coffee cup next to my orange juice. On my plate, there were eggs, bacon, and toast. The eggs were sunny side up. I shook some salt and pepper onto the eggs. I passed the pepper to Dean. I then watched Dean do something which changed the way I ate eggs forever going forth.

"Oh, my God…"

"My aunt showed me this when I was a kid. Trust me, I've done this my whole life."

"Really?"

"Yes, try it."

"Alright, I'll give it a shot."

Dean handed the pepper back to me. Dean looked at me and raised his eyebrows. I smiled. I took the shaker and completely covered my eggs with a black layer of pepper. When I took a bite, I tasted what had been missing from breakfast every morning. It was as if I had discovered a new food. In that moment, I was converted.

For the next week, my focus remained on disassembling my car's engine, replacing parts, and rebuilding it. I took breaks in the daytime to go do things with Unique. Dean and I took time to go to the store, go out to eat, or to get ice cream. At times, I walked through the neighborhoods to the auto parts store or the grocery store. I continued to interact with many people online, but I only met up with others in the evenings, once it was dark outside, when the lack of light inhibited my ability to work on my car.

I spent two thousand dollars on the engine parts. I worked hard in the sweltering summer sun. I walked half a mile back from the auto parts store one day with a bag full of supplies, dragging a new floor jack. I tired myself out. I shed blood and sweat, and I finally finished the repairs...and my car didn't start.

One day, in Dean's basement, I bumped into a pedestal, one which had some pottery artwork on it. The sculpture fell and broke. When Dean arrived home, I told him what happened. I apologized, and I gave Dean a hundred dollars to make amends.

I wished I could have given more money to Dean, but my car issues had been depleting my funds at a fast rate. Since I had stepped away from the crystal market, I no longer had a source of incoming income. I was still stranded, and I wasn't sure how I was going to get back on track.

Dean and I had a talk one afternoon. Multiple issues: the broken vase, Dean's fear for his mother's health during the pandemic, all of my bags and belongings filling up the floorspace in the basement...the two weeks I spent in Dean's basement reached the end. I appreciated the hospitality.

My friend Lex often traveled for work. She built up reward points at hotels, many rewards points. Again, through her help, I had a partial solution to my predicament. I still had other concerns beyond immediate lodging. I had a basement full of belongings at Dean's house, I had a broken car, my personal supply of crystal was dwindling down low, and my money had also diminished, leaving me borderline broke.

One problem at a time. With lodging situated, my next immediate concern was my luggage in Dean's basement. All the bags and items were my most important items; the items I always took when I traveled. My storage unit back in Ohio was completely filled from floor to high ceiling, wall to wall. Over the couple of years of travel, items were picked from storage to accompany me on trips. Other items were taken out from my car and packed into storage. I fine-tuned my travel items to what was needed, what was valuable, what was important to me, and what was useful as I traveled the country.

Though my Lexus trunk and back seats had been packed completely full of my travel items while I traveled, I knew it wasn't smart to reload my belongings from Dean's basement into a broken-down car on the side of the road. It wasn't just my concern for theft while my car sat unoccupied on a street and away from my current physical location. A big concern was the possibility I would come back to my car one day to find it had been towed, all of my belongings gone with the car.

Storage Space Available. First month; only one dollar. Reserve online now. Move in immediately.

With fees and taxes, it became: "first month; fifty-seven dollars." I was desperate, though. I made it happen. I had to pull the trigger in a timely fashion. I confirmed the rental as I sat on a chair outside of the restaurant in my hotel's parking lot. It was sunny and hot outside. I was four miles from Dean's house. I had three of my bags with me: a backpack, a travel bag with a shoulder strap, and a roller suitcase. Since I reserved a storage unit, I decided to walk the four miles, through Aurora, back to the basement where the rest of my belongings were waiting for me.

I had walked much of the Aurora area in the nighttime. That four-mile daytime walk back to Dean's house was challenging. It was midday, the sun was bright, and the temperature was in the high nineties. My backpack and shoulder bag weighed me down. My suitcase caught issue with any bump or curb on the ground.

I stopped in the back of a parking lot to rest. A car pulled into a parking space along the side of the building where I was sitting. Besides that car, the section in the back of the parking lot was void of people; or so I thought. The two thug-looking guys in the car noticed me seated on the pavement with my luggage. They stared in my direction. I nodded to them.

To my surprise, a third guy walked out from around the corner of the building a few feet away from me. He walked right past me, toward the parked car. The guy's gun was sticking out of the back of his waistband. My gun was in plain view in the holster on my ankle. That third guy glanced in my direction before stepping into the back seat of the parked car.

I casually averted my gaze and scanned the rest of the parking lot. I remained seated on the cement when the third guy stepped back out of the car and put something in his pocket. As the car with the two guys backed out of the parking space and pulled away, the third guy walked by me, back behind the building from which he had emerged five minutes earlier. I decided my break was over. I gathered my bags, and I continued on towards Dean's house. It was no longer an option to remain seated on that curb.

Dean pull his FJ Cruiser up to the front of the lot. I punched the code into the keypad by the main doors of the structure. I came back out to Dean's car, wheeling a large cart. I thanked Dean for his help as we finished loading all my luggage onto the cart. I let Dean know I would take it from there. I pushed the cart into the elevator, and I ascended three floors up the warehouse to my five-by-five-foot storage unit.

After unloading all my items in a manner which allowed easiest access to the items I would need the most access, I was left with a small floor space in front of the door. I closed the door and shut myself inside the cramped space. Through the thin metal walls of the structure, I heard other people loading and unloading items into their units all around me. I heard conversations clearly, in close proximity.

I made sure the door was securely shut on the inside by wedging a screwdriver along the door's track. I unpacked my bag of drug supplies in the semi-darkness. When I determined there wasn't another person in the immediate vicinity of my storage locker, when the closest voices I heard came from a separate hallway, I fired up the torch and blew down a hotrail. I blew the smoke into a balled-up sweatshirt. Most of the smoke was absorbed, but some dissipated into the air in the tight quarters.

I placed the sweatshirt on one side of the open floor space. Six hours later, one of my extra loud snores woke me up.

The Golden Ratio

Some nights, I stayed in hotels. Other nights, I had a reclining lawn chair, with blankets and pillows, set up on Dean's back patio. On those nights, I slept under the stars. I had electricity from the house to keep my phones and battery packs charged. Dean's mom brought me coffee each morning. We ate breakfast outside at the table on the patio. I used the downstairs bathroom to shower when needed. I tattooed myself in the backyard under the sun.

Eventually, the sleeping situation at Dean's house evolved. Dean ran an extension cord from a power outlet on his house to my car on the street. There were nights when I wasn't in a hotel, where I chose to sleep in my car instead of sleeping in the open air of Dean's back patio. Some nights, the weather wasn't conducive to sleeping outside. On those nights, the extension cord from Dean's house plugged into a power strip inside my car to charge my phone and power my tattoo equipment. The cord also powered a small nightlight and my small desk fan.

My arms were heavily tattooed during my time in Colorado. I had again been using crystal intravenously, at a more consistent rate, while I was out West. I tattooed myself strategically to camouflage my needle use. In the crease of my left arm, the vein I used most for injections, I tattooed a large blue and black design. I filled it in completely. From that point on, nobody could tell that I had been shooting drugs.

For the first time since I first began using crystal in the spring of 2017, my supply was almost diminished. When I decided to leave the game and head west, I thought I had enough drugs to last. I hadn't anticipated becoming stranded in

Colorado.

I needed to sort out my situation. I reached out to Unique. She made something happen to help me out. At four in the afternoon one day, while I sat in my broken-down car, an SUV pulled up behind me on the street. I stepped from my driver's seat and walked back to the trunk. A blonde, White, younger guy stepped from the SUV. He walked to meet me on the street at the back of my car. I extended my hand in greeting. We shook hands. The blonde guy asked me a question.

"How do you want to do this?"

"The amount she told me is right there in the trunk next to the speaker box. Drop it there when you pick up the money."

The whole exchange took thirty seconds. The guy got back in his car and drove away. I stayed back at my trunk for another couple minutes and worked on the speakers in case any nosey neighbors happened to be minding my business. I then took the brown rolled-up lunch bag and put it in my pocket. I walked back to my driver's seat and quickly used my phone to secure a ride service to somewhere else.

The car from the ride service dropped me off at an apartment complex in inner-city Denver. I had been interacting with a Mexican trans girl. We had been communicating using a translation app. I spoke no Spanish, and she didn't speak a word of English. We knew we wouldn't be doing any talking upon my arrival. As I walked up to the appropriate apartment, I wondered how the intimacy was going to go down without any verbal communication. I was high, and I looked forward to the challenge.

It proved to be no challenge at all. The girl took my hand after she opened the door. She led me through her apartment to her bedroom. She motioned me to her bed, and we both removed our clothes. After we finished, we kissed, and I walked back outside to wait for the next car to pick me up. It was nighttime when I walked out to the road from the apartment. Two minutes after I reached the curb, a car pulled up and stopped in front of me. I got in, and the car pulled away from the complex.

...

Unique put me in touch with her uncle. He was a mechanic in Denver. He offered me help. He planned to meet me at my Lexus to see if he could figure out why my car wouldn't start. Unique's uncle told me that if he wasn't able to get my car to run, he would be able to find me a reasonably priced car to buy. I happily accepted his help, and we set up a day and time to look at my car.

"Do you feel that? That's not good at all."

I felt and heard the knocking in the engine. I had blown the head gasket.

"You need a new engine. You're better off finding another car. I'll look for something for you. I'll let you know when I find something."

Dean came out of his house to talk to me as Unique's uncle was leaving. I told him my bad news.

"Well, looks like my car is done. Man, I don't know what to do."

"A good friend of mine is a mechanic. I'll give him a call for a second opinion."

Two days later, Dean's friend came over. Dean's mechanic friend, like the trans girl from the week before, didn't speak a word of English. Dean functioned as translator. After an hour of inspection, adjustments, and translated conversation, the second opinion was the same as what Unique's uncle had told me two days before. Again, my heart sank. My car was dead, and it was stuck there on the side of the road…and I lost any hope that I could fix it and continue on my westward journey through the country.

...

I rode with Unique in the middle of the night. We parked on the street next to Unique's house, facing into the neighborhood from the outskirts. Suddenly, an hour after we first parked to talk, we both stopped talking. Unique and I shared a glance at each other in that moment of silence. I had a bad feeling. I could tell Unique had a bad feeling, as well. We both listened carefully in the night. The car windows were down. Until that moment, the two of us heard nothing in the silence but our own conversation. We didn't speak. We both heard it. It was coming closer. We whispered to each other.

"What is it?"

"I don't know, but it's coming."

"Get as low as you can in your seat…"

I slid down as low as I could get while still being able to see over the dashboard. It was coming fast. It sounded like it was coming from a side street. As the screeching of the tires and roar of the engine broke through, the car slid out into the road, two streets up from where Unique had parked her car. The car skidded around the corner to face us and accelerate in our direction.

From where I was, I saw two silhouettes in the front seats of the dark sedan. Under the streetlight, I clearly saw the third person; he was out of the window of the back door, seated in the space of the rolled-down window. On his face, a wild-eyed stare. In his hand, a gun. I watched as the car completed the turn two blocks up from them.

"Is that a gun?"

"Yes, get down."

The engine roared as the driver accelerated. The car sped up and drove directly at the car parked a block in front of Unique and me. At the last second, the car pulled back to the center of the road. It flew past the parked car. Again, the driver accelerated directly toward the next parked car on the next block. Unique's car, where Unique and I were both watching while slumped down in the front seats.

Again…at the last second, the driver swerved and avoided hitting Unique's car directly head-on. The car cut back into the middle of the road to rip past us. Unique and I were both frozen. It all happened so fast; we couldn't react. I hadn't even been able to fully duck down in the seat. I just watched as the car with the guy hanging out of the side window flew by us and kept driving. A second later, the tires screeched again as the car turned out of the neighborhood behind us. I heard the engine fade off into the night as the car sped off.

In my mind, I kept that image of the guy with the gun. His eyes, wide and crazy, seemed to focus on nothing as he stared ahead into the night. His body swayed each time the car swerved toward and away from the parked cars on the street. The gun in his hand, the noises coming from the car's tires and engine, the sheer instant chaos which broke through that silent night in that empty neighborhood…Unique and I snapped out of it. We both knew that we urgently needed to get away from there.

…

I had a hotel room situated between Aurora and Denver.

Damian knocked on the door while I was in the middle of tattooing myself. I put the tattoo equipment away and began heavy drug use with my new friend. We made some videos that first night. The next day, we walked through the city to another hotel. The two of us stayed two nights in the second hotel, and then I decided that I needed to make a change.

I thought back to the day before; when I used a ride service to travel from the hotel in Aurora to Unique's uncle's auto shop in Denver, then back to Aurora. The trip cost fifty dollars each way. If I rented a car, the car would cost that much per day. The rental made sense.

Damian's sister picked Damian and me up from the hotel and brought us back to her apartment. I made some phone calls. A car service took Damian and me to the Denver airport. After I filled out the proper paperwork, the two of us loaded into the rental car and left for the city. I rented the car for the following week. I was mobile again.

Damian and I were on the highway loop one afternoon in Denver rush hour traffic. The roads in Denver were beyond congested during peak hours. All lanes of traffic were packed on the highways. All exit ramps were backed up. Many stoplights required waiting through multiple cycles of light changes before passing through the intersections.

My GPS map wasn't displaying a correct route to get through the city. After a half hour of frustrating driving, I ended up looping around and stopping at the same red light were we had stopped a half hour earlier. My patience was wearing thin. Damian noticed, and he took the opportunity to try to make me angry. Anytime I said anything, Damian replied abrasively; seeking a rise out of me.

"Oh man…we were just at this light a half an hour ago."

"You don't know how to read the map."

"Yes, I do. I showed you how it looped us back around."

"Nope. It's you. You don't know what you are doing."

"Seriously? I don't have the patience for this…"

"It's you. You can't read the map."

"Dude…I'm serious. I'll drop you off on the side of this highway…"

The stop-and-go traffic was unrelenting. The negative replies to everything I said were as frustrating as the traffic. Our words escalated and became more heated. Damian was trying to get under my skin. It worked. Five minutes later, I pulled to the shoulder at the top of a busy overpass. As I slammed on the breaks, Damian flung open his car door and jumped out to the road. I drove forward in the slow traffic. I saw Damian in my mirror. Damian walked down the side of the overpass to the road below. I shook my head while I drove away.

Once I pulled into my storage unit a half hour later, I checked my phone. I called Damian, and Damian picked up. I apologized for my role in the escalation of our conversation, and I offered to swing back into the city and pick him up. Damian apologized as well. He told me he wanted to see how mad he was able to make me. I told him I could be back that way in thirty minutes. Damian politely declined.

The Exception

    I again felt freedom as I drove south from Colorado Springs. I visited Stacey again in Pueblo. I spent another day in Trinidad after stopping for the night in southern Colorado. I recorded the sunset from a field at the foot of the Rocky Mountains. I continued ignoring texts from Justin as I passed into northern New Mexico. I was again out on the roads, enjoying the sense of freedom I felt behind the wheel of the rental car.

    I did drugs in parking lots, and at scenic overlooks. I met new people from my phone. Some plans materialized; others fell through. I showered at truck stops. I updated friends with status reports. I took time in the car, and in the shower rooms of truck stops, to video-interact with intimate online partners. At random intervals, I tattooed myself along the way. I explored new locations. I did my best to leave all of my immediate concerns on the side of the road back in Aurora. I knew, in those rental car moments, I needed to live…and I needed to appreciate that fleeting feeling in life, that which comes from magical experiences.

    I was living it up on borrowed (rented) time. When that first week with the car ended, I extended the rental for a second week. Unique's uncle hadn't finished his work on the SUV, so I opted for more time with the rental car. I was approaching the end of that second week, and I knew time was becoming a concern. Having the freedom to travel as I wished, I didn't want it to end.

    Unique's uncle told me that he found a pinhole leak in the transmission housing of the SUV. He gave me some options; I could take it as-is; risking a breakdown, or I could hold off until he found the time to attempt a repair. Unique's uncle wasn't sure when he was going to be able to work on the car, and my car rental fees were adding up quickly.

...

A woman from the website had been in contact with me since well before I began traveling out West. Her name was Gina. According to her profile name, the info in her profile, and her messages; she was a lesbian seeking only women. She had been the one to reach out first. She had been the one initially pursuing a dynamic. She had been the one, once she learned of my plans to head across the country in her direction, who insisted I make a stop to see her.

"You're interested in me? According to your profile, you specifically seek women."

"Yes, but you're the exception. There's just something about you…"

The exception: I always seemed to be the exception. I didn't particularly enjoy being the exception. It gave me an odd feeling; one which made me wonder if the novelty would wear off when what was sought wasn't who I was. Age, race, gender, body type, even tattoo coverage…I was always someone's exception to their previously stated desires and turn-on/turn-offs. Was I a trophy? Was I an experiment? Was I a placeholder to fill time until they found what they were actually seeking? It left me with a sense of loneliness.

Gina lived in Littleton, Colorado. She was in the process of moving to a new apartment during the weekend I agreed to meet her. That Friday evening, I pulled into the parking lot near the soccer fields of Columbine High School. I left from a friend's house a few miles away.

I stepped from my car to walk down to the lake adjacent from Columbine. In the late afternoon, the sun began to set. The reflection of the pink and purple clouds on the clear mirror lake surface was as beautiful as the sky itself. The pristine calm of the water was only disturbed by random families of ducks swimming in the water. It was a wonderful place for me to collect my thoughts and record video of an amazing natural scene. I was at peace during that brief moment in my life.

When I got up to leave, after spending the weekend with Gina, I checked my phone. I had a reminder text from the airport car rental company. It was Sunday. My car was due back on Monday. I made up my mind in that moment. I wasn't going to return the car on Monday. I still needed to drive the rental car until Unique's uncle was ready with the SUV.

Two things happened on the Tuesday of that following week: the rental car company billed me an additional nine hundred dollars, and the deal with Unique's uncle fell through. I called the rental car company. I told them I was going to keep the car for another full week since they billed me an additional week's price. I wasn't worried about another bill from them. They had already taken the last of the money in my bank account. I was worried about the SUV no longer being an option. My time in Colorado reached a new level of desperation.

I was basically out of money. While I had the rental car, I had to jump back in the game to make cash to survive. I let go of insignificant amounts of crystal here and there, but it wasn't enough to cover living expenses. I decided I would turn the car back in at the airport the following Sunday when the rental company was closed. Unique agreed to follow me to drop the car off and give me a ride back from the airport. We planned to drop the car off in the middle of the night. I still had a couple more days to drive.

I went down to Pueblo that first night to see Stacey one more time. I returned to Dean's house the next morning. I put in as many miles as I could. It was past the middle of September, and I was still in Colorado. I thought I would have checked Oregon off from my travel list by then. Instead, I realized I wasn't going to be checking Oregon off the list at all.

I spent the afternoon setting up a donation page on social media. I posted about it on other social media outlets. I set up the page to receive enough donations to buy a car and head away from Colorado. I decided I needed to consolidate my two storage units. I needed a car which was big enough to fit everything from my Colorado storage unit as well as all the parts I could strip from my Lexus before I left it on the street. I planned to drive everything back to my storage unit in Ohio. From there, I would have some breathing room to sort out my next moves.

Around midnight that night, I met someone from a social media app. In the middle of the night, I picked up the Mexican trans girl from a neighborhood close to downtown Denver. It was late. It was dark outside. Nowhere was open, and we couldn't hang out at her place. Her family was all home.

Taylor told me that she had an idea. She told me to drive, and she would direct me to where we were going to go. I headed west towards the outskirts of Denver; to the side of the city where the eastern slopes of the Rocky Mountains began. The two of us headed up into the mountains west of Denver. As dawn broke, Taylor and I ascended Lookout Mountain. We stopped at an overlook to watch the sun rise over the Denver metro area. Taylor told me she was going to take me to one more location before we found a hotel. I drove us through Golden, Colorado and further into the mountain towns west of Denver. We reached Morrison, Colorado. The sun was bright in the morning sky.

I stopped in the middle of the road to let three deer casually cross in front of the car. We were at Red Rocks Amphitheatre. I was in awe. I thanked Taylor for her guidance. I let her know how happy I was to share that once in a lifetime experience with her that morning. The two of us came down out of the mountains, and I used my phone to find a hotel once we were back in Golden.

Though Taylor and I shared intimacy in the hotel room that day, I was a disappointment. The drugs didn't allow me to fully perform in the way I had hoped. I felt bad about it. We slept for a few hours. When the two of us walked outside to get back in the car, snow covered the ground. We were shocked. It wasn't even the end of September.

All Good Things

Again, my friend Lex saved me. The social media donation page was a success. I made enough money in three days. A large chunk of that money came from Lex. The urgency of my situation cooled down. Though desperation diminished to a level which no longer consumed me, the unseasonable early snowfall reminded me that winter was soon approaching Colorado. I had some money again. I could eat and survive. I still had drugs. I just needed to find a car.

On that last night in the overdue rental car, I drove to the city of Boulder. I parked in a busy parking lot to shoot drugs and interact with Shannon on my phone. The evening progressed, and the sun set beyond the mountains. The parking lot, no longer full of people shopping and visiting restaurants, began to take on an eerie vibe.

Cars still littered the large parking lot, but I didn't see a single person once the sun went down. For two hours, I sat alone in my car that evening. I shot crystal one more time and said goodnight to Shannon. I began to think about how I should spend those last few hours with the rental car before Unique followed me to the airport to drop it off.

...

Days after returning the rental car, I was in my own world. I was closed off in my broken-down car on the side of the road. Something startled me as I was sitting there in my car cocoon. I instantly felt a threat to my isolation bubble. As I sprang from my seat, I flung open my car door. I was almost instantly standing in the street outside my car. I caught the last hurried step as the woman stepped back on the sidewalk and hurried away from my car.

The woman was walking a dog on a leash. She stared straight ahead, away from me as she moved hurriedly down the street. She didn't fool me at all. I knew exactly what she had done and what she was up to. I called her out on it. I was mad. I knew I had surprised her. I had caught her in the act.

"Hey!"

The woman glanced back and picked up her pace.

"HEY!"

She stopped when I yelled toward her again.

"I know what you're doing. You're out here every night. I saw it the other day, and I know, for a fact, you just checked the door handle on my car. Keep your hands off my car."

"I'm out walking my dog in my neighborhood…"

"And you didn't expect me to be in my car while you're out checking door handles."

The woman began to walk away faster. I remained next to my car.

"I better not catch you doing that again."

There was no response. I texted Dean to come out to my car for a minute.

"Hey man, make sure your cars are always locked. Some lady walking her dog was just checking door handles. She just checked mine while I was sitting here."

From then on, the woman stayed on the other side of the street when she walked her dog at night.

...

I was wandering amongst the sculptures and flowers in Dean's backyard one morning while on a break from tattooing myself. My phone in my hand was vibrating at a steady pace as I interacted with people online. A message on an app caught my attention.

"I want to cuddle in bed in underwear for the rest of the day with you."

I was receptive instantly. I let Skye know that I needed to be picked up. Skye pulled up in front of my Lexus. I grabbed my backpack, and I hopped in the car. It was a twenty-minute drive to Skye's apartment complex on the other side of Aurora. The sun was shining, the sky was blue, and I had that tingly feeling of anticipation. I was looking forward to cuddling. I failed to mention to Skye that I wasn't wearing underwear.

For the following week, Skye and I played house together. We went grocery shopping and cooked food together in the apartment. We ran errands and stayed in bed together. I tattooed both of us. Skye gave me a nice Carhart winter coat. The coat was much needed. Though the days were still hot, the nights were getting cold in Colorado.

It was dark on our drive back from Saint Mary's Glacier. Skye wanted to take me to the Idaho Springs area of Colorado to see the glacier. By the time we parked the car and began to hike, it had already become dark. Before we reached the glacier, the two of us turned back. Some other hikers had crossed our path. The hikers told us that we still had another half an hour to hike to reach the glacier. Skye and I figured we would cut our losses and not risk hiking in the dark and cold night.

Skye drove me to my car. We sat there for a few more minutes as we finished our conversation. We kissed, and I stepped from Skye's car. I needed to find a car of my own, and Skye was set to begin a new job at a veterinary clinic the next morning. I was wearing the Carhart coat…I was prepared for the cold night of sitting in my Lexus on the side of the road in Aurora.

As I sat there in my car, I received a message from Laura. Laura had been following me on the website since early 2018. She lived in Phoenix, Arizona. Laura told me she made arrangements to take a week's vacation the following week. She invited me to stay with her in a hotel in Aurora for her vacation. I accepted the offer.

The next morning, Unique knocked on my car door to wake me up. She waited as I gathered up the items I carried with me; mostly drug paraphernalia and small items of value I didn't wish to leave in my car while I was away. I stepped from my car and hopped into the passenger seat of Unique's Volvo.

"What's the plan?"

"You're going to ride with me to Denver. I need to stop at some stores and then go to the DMV. I have an appointment. I need new tags for my car, since it's almost…MY BIRTHDAY!"

"Well, happy early birthday. Let's roll."

Unique passed me her water pipe. I took a large hit of crystal. As I breathed out a large cloud of smoke, I instantly woke up. The day was ahead of us. I felt good. I pulled out my phone, and I began to search for potential cars on the online market.

After stopping at a few stores, we drove deeper into Denver. Eventually, we pulled into a crowded parking lot. Unique left me in the car with her water pipe while she went to handle her business. I watched her walk up to the back of a line of people outside the buildings. I then scanned the area where Unique was standing.

I saw the situation at the DMV that day; the situation directly resulting from that year's coronavirus pandemic. Disappointment and bad thoughts filled my head as smoke from the crystal filled Unique's car. The line of people, spaced out at standard increments on the pavement and sidewalk, extended the length of the buildings on the side of the parking lot. The line then turned, and it extended the length of another building. My thoughts began to race.

Unique told me she had waited two weeks to get the appointment. I saw the line barely moving. I began to think of the complications I was going to face once I actually found a car. I sat in the car for two more hours with the sun beating down through the car's windows. Unique was a resident of Denver. Unique already had a car. All Unique needed to do was renew her registration. By the time she finally made it back to her car, I had fully exhausted my brain with negative thoughts of the roadblocks I would face when I did manage to procure transportation to leave Colorado.

…

A car service picked me up from my car on a Friday afternoon. I placed some of my luggage in the trunk. I climbed into the car and sat down next to Laura. Laura hugged me, and we kissed. Though we had interacted online for a couple of years, it was the first time Laura and I had met in person. As we rode through the city to the other side of Aurora, the two of us discussed plans for the upcoming week. We both wished to remain in the hotel room and order food the whole time.

When we reached the hotel, I helped the driver stack Laura's luggage onto a cart outside the hotel lobby. The air in the city was hazy, not just the air around the hotel. I noticed it the entire drive through the city. The driver left, and I went inside the hotel with Laura.

As the sun set, the haze in the evening air continued its progression. Laura and I saw three distinct forest fires in the distance. The smoke above the mountains was prominent in the sky. The sunset was beautiful as a result. I had never seen anything like it. From the smoke to the clouds, the sky, and the sun itself…it was breathtaking. I recorded that first sunset as I did the following sunsets each day from that vantage point high up in our hotel room. The scene was magical and otherworldly. The colors and the sky, the light through the smoke, my mind was blown.

At the end of that week together, Laura gave me an open invitation to come live with her in Phoenix. The offer was appealing, but my two storage units required my immediate attention. I had to decline Laura's offer. I was sad to part ways with Laura, but the timing hadn't lined up. She went back to Arizona, and I went back to my Lexus on the side of the road in Aurora, Colorado. The air was still hazy, and the fires were still blazing.

I needed a vehicle which had enough space to accommodate the items in my storage unit as well as all the parts I stripped from my Lexus. I found a Subaru Outback on an online car market website which fit that description and was in my price range. I set up a time to meet with the owner for a test drive.

The stars lined up for me that day. The car ran well. The owner and I made a deal. We drove to an ATM so I could take out the remainder of the cash I needed to buy the car. Back at the owner's house, I loaded up four additional tires into the hatchback Subaru. I then had eight tires. I only needed four tires on the car. I took the extra tires anyhow. We went inside, and the owner filled out a bill of sale. He gave me the bill and the title. At that point, I was the owner of the Subaru, title, and all.

For the next few days, I alternated between removing components from my Lexus and painting my Subaru. I parked the Subaru directly in front of the Lexus on the street next to Dean's house. I ate meals with Dean and his mother, and I showered at the house. As always, I recorded video to document my activities. As always, I continued my online interactions and dynamics, high on crystal.

As I finished the final coat of black paint on the Subaru, the sun was almost completely set below the horizon. The neighbor from across the street walked over to talk to me. I extended my hand. We smiled as we shook hands.

"Hi there. I've seen you working hard out here."

The neighbor told me how he caught two teenage kids breaking into his car in his driveway. He had them on security camera. The kids had been caught on other security cameras as well, not just in Dean's neighborhood, but in three adjacent neighborhoods. Someone who lived in a neighborhood across the street had also caught the teens in the act. Once police were involved, the teens gave up a lot of information.

It turned out, the lady walking her dog each night was out checking for unlocked car doors. Once it was dark each night, the teens returned to any of the cars which were known to be unlocked. They then stole items from those unlocked cars. The lady walking her dog was the mother of one of those teens.

I shook my head in disbelief as I heard that story. I told the neighbor of my encounter with the lady walking her dog. When our conversation ended, I instantly went into Dean's house to update him. Though I knew my encounter with that lady wasn't related to drug paranoia, I was still amazed to hear the way that situation worked out.

I decided I needed one more ounce before I was ready to leave Colorado. As I sat in the car the following morning, I reached out to Unique. I wasn't able to get in contact with her. I then texted Bethany. Though she didn't use crystal, I figured anyone with a black tar heroin connection would most likely be able to score some methamphetamine. Bethany texted me back a moment later. As suspected, she knew a guy. Bethany named a price for an ounce. It wasn't cheap, but it was still within reason. She told me it would be available at eight o'clock that night. I thanked her, and I told her I would be in touch.

A twenty-five-year-old Puerto Rican girl and I arranged a date at a popular sports bar in Denver that afternoon. I drove to Denver to meet up with her. Traffic was terrible. She made it to the bar before I did. There was a festival taking place on the streets outside the sports bar, so I had to park blocks down the street. I was out of breath when I reached the bar.

The girl met me outside. The bar was completely packed; the outside and inside were full of bargoers. The two of us walked together through the lower floor of the bar, out to a back patio. We ordered food. The girl ordered a couple drinks. She found it odd that I didn't drink. Our entire interaction from that point was confusing.

The girl was exceptionally beautiful. She told me how attracted to me she was. The vibe was off for me, though. I couldn't figure it out. She seemed half interested in me, but she said random things during our conversation which almost seemed to be insults. When I made jokes, the girl stared blankly at me. She said things which didn't seem to be jokes, and she asked me why I didn't think she was funny.

When the bill came, I reached for it. The girl took offense.

"I'm paying for it. I invited you."

When I tried to retort, the girl genuinely became angry with me. She gave me a ride back to where my car was parked. After she explained how she didn't like my new Subaru, she drove away.

Unique texted me while I was eating my meal at that sports bar. I happened to be on the side of Denver where Unique lived. She told me to stop over. When I got there, Unique introduced me to her brother. The two of them lived together.

Unique then motioned me to follow her to the deck in the backyard. As we talked, Unique gave me a price for an ounce. I instantly accepted. I handed her the money from my pocket. She told me she would have the crystal first thing in the morning.

Bethany was unhappy with me when I cancelled my order with her. I told her I couldn't do the price she wanted. Out of courtesy, I told Bethany that if she could match the price that I was getting for it from someone else, then I would still follow through with the deal. Bethany told me she couldn't do it. I told her I was going with my other option. Bethany was mad, and she hung up on me. I never meant for her to take it personal. It was business.

The morning later, I was finishing loading my Subaru with Lexus parts. The four extra Subaru tires were jammed into the open space in the empty Lexus. I knew I needed the room in the Subaru for the items in my storage unit. I filled the inside of the Subaru with car stereo equipment, personal belongings, and Lexus parts. Before that though, I blacked out all the back windows with spray paint left over from painting the car. I didn't want my belongings to be seen through the glass.

I visited the lady working in the office at my storage unit. I closed out my account. I emptied my items from the unit onto a large pushcart. I pushed the cart down the hallways, into the service elevator, and out the front doors to my Subaru. I loaded up my car, and I returned the cart to the lobby of the storage unit. The Subaru was packed as full as my Lexus and BMW had always been as I traveled the country previously, before my plans were put on hold when I broke down in Colorado.

I set a new timeline. I planned to wrap up my affairs and be on the road east within the following five days. With my car loaded completely to the top, I left the storage facility to meet Unique in the parking lot of a strip mall in Denver. Unique had an ounce for me. I needed that crystal to fuel my remaining activities in Aurora and to then drive across the country once again.

I called the DMV about an appointment to get license plates for my car. Two weeks. The waiting period for an appointment was two weeks. I knew, from the time I rode with Unique for her appointment, that I wasn't going to be able to get plates for the Subaru. I made up my mind to drive across the country with no license plates on my car. My time in Colorado had expired.

I worked on the Subaru in the warm sun. My Subaru, on the street in Dean's neighborhood, was parked in front of the Lexus. I looked back at my Lexus. I felt a sadness, knowing I was about to leave my car in Colorado. Though I had only owned it since the previous November, I traveled thousands of miles in the Lexus, across most of the country.

While in thought as I stood there, I saw a glint in the sunlight inside the Lexus, below the rearview mirror. I walked over to the Lexus and opened the door. I pulled a knife from my pocket and cut the fishing line from around the mirror. That little metal ninja star was the last item I recovered from my Lexus. It had been hanging from the mirror, as it had in all of my previous cars. I bought the little ninja star from a store in a mall in Toledo, Ohio. I was a teenager when I bought it. It had been with me through my travels. I would have forgotten my ninja star had the sun not shown me the light.

I returned to adjusting the wiring between the Subaru's alternator and battery. I made sure everything was secured and ready to travel. When I was satisfied, I quickly stood up. I forgot that the car's hood was only halfway open. The corner of the hood caught me directly on the top of my head.

I was instantly dazed. I jammed my neck; the hood stopped me from fully standing up. Blood began to stream down my face and the sides of my head. I felt almost drunk from the head injury. I tried to think, but thoughts weren't coming to me clearly. As blood trailed behind me on the sidewalk, I staggered my way towards Dean's front door. I managed to knock on the front door before I collapsed into a chair on Dean's porch.

Dean's mom opened the door. Through blurred vision, I saw her reaction to my injury. I heard Dean's mom yell for Dean. One of them brought me a bag of ice, and the other brought out paper towels to wrap my head. I wasn't sure who brought what. The bleeding eventually stopped, and I was left with a gash across a swollen knot in the middle of my head. Once I recovered in the chair, I helped Dean wash the blood from the porch. I thanked Dean for the medical treatment.

I then thanked Dean for the hospitality during the entire time I was stranded in Colorado. I let Dean know that I would always be genuinely grateful for his help. Dean was a devoted friend to me in a time when I needed one. I knew it was my last twenty-four hours in Colorado.

The next morning, I took a look around for the last time. I checked throughout the Lexus. I had everything I needed and wanted to bring with me. I started the Subaru, and I pulled from Dean's neighborhood. My mind was heavy with thoughts…and saturated with drugs. I felt free, I felt excited, and I felt empty inside.

When I reached the eastern outskirts of the Denver metro area, a weird feeling came over me. I was leaving. I stopped at a gas station. I sent a few text messages while I was inside the store. After I paid for gas, I walked outside and filled up the tank. I looked around one last time. I got in my car, and I left Colorado.

Isochrone Curve

I decided to pass over the border to Kansas before I stopped for sleep that first night of the trip. The Subaru held up well. At a rest stop in Kansas, I shut my eyes. Colorado was behind me. I was sad to leave, but I was excited for the next chapter. I had drugs, and I hopefully had enough money for gasoline and food during the rest of the trip.

I woke up with the rising sun. The heat and bright light were unbearable; directly on me, the sunlight shone through my car's closed windows. I realized, in that uncomfortable moment, that I needed to prioritize acquiring and fitting new window shades for the Subaru.

The cross-country drive back to the Midwest was mostly uneventful. I didn't have license plates, so I inevitably encountered law enforcement. The first incident occurred at a gas station in Topeka, Kansas. The officer walked up to my car as I sat in a parking space, eating a slice of pizza. I explained my story, why I didn't have plates on the car. I told the officer about finally leaving Colorado after months of being stranded on the road in Aurora. I told him about the wait for an appointment at the DMV. I told him about my storage unit in Ohio.

The crystal had me talking more than the officer cared to listen. The officer let me go, but I asked one question as the officer turned to walk away. The question was answered in detail. I appreciated his response, and I let the officer get back to his business. Thanks to the officer's answer, I had directions to the best fried chicken in the Topeka area.

Days later, I reached Illinois. I saw the police cruisers positioned in the median of the highway to catch speeders.

Traffic was the heaviest I had seen during the pandemic times. I drove past the cruisers with cars in the lanes beside me. I drove past the cruisers with cars in front of me and behind me. Three minutes later, I saw the blue and red lights behind me.

    I pulled over to the side of the road, and the officer approached my car. Again, the crystal had me talking. As soon as I rolled down my window, I jumped right into my story. The officer looked at me wide-eyed as he took in sentence after sentence of dialogue. I told the officer about months spent in Aurora, the wait for an appointment at the DMV, and my storage unit back in Perrysburg. I told him about my last interaction with the police and the fried chicken.

    When the officer finally managed to speak a sentence of his own, he told me to hang on for a minute while he walked back to his car. I looked around to make sure all of my drugs were put away. My car was packed with my belongings. The only available open space was where I sat in the driver's seat. My drugs and paraphernalia were stashed amongst the clutter. I wasn't sure exactly where all of my illegal items were, but nothing was in plain sight.

    Five minutes later, the officer was back at my window. My license had come back clean. The officer handed me a paper. He told me to keep it in case I was pulled over again on my drive. He told me it would save time. It was a note which explained that I was going to get plates once I was back in Ohio. The officer quickly bid me a safe trip and sent me on my way before I could again bombard him with incessant talking.

...

    I reached Ohio early that Halloween morning. I stood in the darkness and knocked on Adrian's door. A moment later, Adrian greeted me, and I walked inside. I put my bags down next to the couch, and I fell fast asleep moments after lying down on that couch. I managed a few hours of non-car sleep for the first time in a while.

I did some hotrails with Adrian and his boyfriend when I woke up later that morning. After we ate breakfast, I gathered up my belongings. I let Adrian know that I would be back in the evening. I had a full day's worth of work to do at my storage unit. I had items to unload from my Subaru, I had a completely full storage unit to sort through, and I had to select the new priority items to load back into my car for travel.

I needed to pick out which items from my car and from storage I was going to try to sell. My y-pipe exhaust system, which Dan had never managed to replace on my Lexus, was going to be an item I tried to sell. My custom Lexus bumper, which I put on my Lexus just prior to leaving to head west, was also going to go up for sale. I had removed it from the Lexus in Colorado. It barely fit in my Subaru. Those two items were extremely space consuming, so I prioritized selling them first. I already had a party interested in the bumper.

Methamphetamine got the best of me while at my storage unit. Hours were spent rummaging, sorting, and moving items all over the unit and the pavement outside it. I came across a can of gold spray paint, left over from painting the emblem of the Lexus bumper months before. The crystal put an idea in my head. An hour later, my Subaru, formerly white and then all black, had gold tiger stripes all over it.

Ideas inspired by crystal meth were seldom thought through to logical conclusions. The y-pipe Lexus exhaust system was easily seven feet long from end to end. On one side, there was a single metal tube resembling a bazooka. On the other side, the two pipes with catalytic converters curved outward from the center of the assembly.

I had another crystal idea, and I put it into crystal action. I strapped the y-pipe to the roof rack of the Subaru. The front bazooka end extended forward above the middle of my car's windshield. The two rear metal tubes sat above either side of the roof rack extending to the back of the Subaru's roof. It literally looked like a military weapon on the top of the car...especially once the crystal convinced me it was a good idea to spray paint the y-pipe gold to match the tiger stripes all over the car. I had created a rolling, driving eyesore.

The modifications to the tiger striped doom bringer were set. I unloaded much of my haul from the other side of the country. I picked up new items from my storage unit to aid in my future travels. I made a stop at a rest stop on my meandering route from Perrysburg back to Adrian's house in Findlay. The crystal in my brain managed to send me about an hour out of the way west from Adrian's house. Crystal seemed to lead me to seek out rest stops anywhere I went. If there were no rest stops on my immediate route, crystal encouraged me to divert until I came across one...even when my destination was closer than the rest stop.

I parked the doom bringer, and I walked to the restroom in the main building at the rest stop. When I got back to my car, I realized I had locked my keys inside my ridiculous looking vehicle. It was sunset, and the air was cold. I shook my head, and I got to work. So many times, my cars had been unlocked by prying open and wedging the corner of a window. I needed some sticks and a rock.

I looked around until I found what I thought would work. It didn't work. For six hours, it didn't work. My phone was locked in my car. I had nobody to call. It grew dark outside. I walked a substantial distance to the opposite side of the rest stop where there was semi parking. I figured I could find someone with tools to help. The first truck, I knocked with no answer. The second truck's driver was sitting in the front seat. As I approached, before I even spoke, the truck driver yelled, "No!" and rolled up his window.

When I got back to my car, I abandoned the effort on my driver's side window. Crystal told me the passenger side had a better chance of success. Another hour went by. It was windy and snowing. A car of four people in their early twenties pulled into a parking space a couple of spaces down from me. Three of them went into the building with the restrooms. The fourth walked over to me.

"What do you have going on over here?"

The guy tried to help me while his friends were inside the building. The other three tried to join in the effort once they returned to the parking lot. Nothing worked. I thanked them, and I told them I would manage somehow. They left and got back onto the highway. Two minutes later, I almost had the window pried open enough to reach in with a stick and unlock the door...and then the entire passenger side window shattered.

Glass exploded into the car and all over the parking space next to the Subaru. I pulled a battery powered vacuum cleaner from the back of the car and sucked up all the glass from the front seat and the pavement. I unloaded the new window shades I had made. I duct-taped the layers of shades to the inside and outside of the broken window.

I dreaded the drive back to Adrian's house on that cold pre-winter night. I knew I needed to get to a hardware store the next day for caulk and a thick sheet of Plexi glass. The tiger striped doom machine was downgraded another notch that night at the rest stop. My modifications to my Subaru were a physical manifestation of the modifications which crystal was doing to my brain.

Game On

It was cold outside, but Adrian had the heat turned up high in his house. I sat on the couch in boxer shorts. Suddenly, I was hungry. I had my long black trench coat with me. I decided it was easier to throw that on and go get food from a gas station without getting dressed.

At first glance, I looked like a stereotypical flasher. My chest and legs were bare. I looked unclothed underneath the trench coat. It was late, and I didn't care. I assumed I wouldn't see anyone but the gas station clerk that late in Findlay, Ohio. That small farm town was empty at peak hours, and it was one o'clock in the morning.

When I reached the gas station five minutes up the road, I saw three guys in their twenties standing outside the entrance. I parked at a gas pump since I needed gas anyhow. The three guys stared at me from across the parking lot. They saw me step from a ridiculous car wearing what looked to be only a trench coat. They quickly seemed to lose interest. One of the guys ran around the side of the building while the other two walked into the store ahead of me.

As I grabbed a drink and a carton of eggs from the refrigerator at the back of the store, I heard the two guys talking loudly with the cashier. I walked across the store and over to the counter to pay for my items and prepay for gasoline. The two guys were in front of me in line. One continued to converse with the cashier, but the other turned to me and stared. I nodded to him. The guy then began to speak.

"Uh, what are you doing?"

"I'm buying eggs and a Yoo-Hoo."

"Uh, why?"

"Because I want eggs and a Yoo-Hoo."

The guy continued to stare at me, indignant. I stared back. The guy finally broke his gaze when the cashier, whom I assumed was one of his friends, told the two guys to step aside so he could ring me up. The two guys walked out of the store, and I paid for my items. I asked the cashier a question.

"What was that about?"

"Don't mind them. They're idiots."

I stepped out into the night with my eggs and Yoo-Hoo and began to cross the parking lot to go pump gas. Suddenly, I saw movement to my right side, on the other side of the lot. From over the hill, between the gas station and the business next door, the two guys reappeared. With them was the guy seen earlier running behind the building when I pulled up. There was also a fourth guy I hadn't seen before. They were in a hurry, heading directly for me. I was halfway between the store and my car, alone in the night.

I waited to be sure they were intent on me. They were. The guy who spoke to me in the store had a huge smile on his face. I let them get closer. I stopped in the open parking lot between the store entrance and the gas pumps. I stared at them. They looked like they were closing in on their prey. Their prey, on that night, was me.

I let them reach the edge of the row of gas pumps. I calmly reached my hand into the right-side pocket of my trench coat. Surprise. I pulled out my nine-millimeter handgun. All four sets of eyes instantly widened. I kept the gun pointed down, but I reached over with my left hand and racked the slide.

All four surprised guys instantly scattered. The guy who previously ran behind the building again ran behind the building. The other three, no longer frozen in their tracks, turned tail and booked it back up and over the hill to the building next door. I stood there for another thirty seconds. I unracked my gun and casually walked to my car and pumped thirty dollars of prepaid gas.

...

I originally left Michigan in spring of 2020 to start over. I left the Midwest to get out of the game. The game pulled me back in. I didn't know what else to do. I chose the route which had been good to me. Despite the stress and the complications, I knew I was able to get ahead again with the business model I followed for the past few years. In my mind, my chemically compromised mind, it was an easy choice to make.

Back at Adrian's house, I started making phone calls. The first call I made was to set up a junkyard in Colorado to come pick up my Lexus from the side of the road. Out of courtesy, I told Dean I would have my Lexus removed from the street beside Dean's house. The junkyard offered me three hundred and fifty dollars for scrapping my car. They insisted I didn't need to be there for them to tow it and pay me. They told me a tow truck would be there in three days to pick it up.

I got in contact with a guy interested in buying my Lexus bumper. The two of us set up a plan: I would drop the bumper off at a shipping company, and the guy would then send me half of the money upon the shipping receipt. Once the bumper arrived in Texas, he would send me the other half of the agreed price. The guy would pay the shipping costs.

My next phone calls became a sort of grassroots fundraiser for illicit substances. I wanted to take a ride. I wanted to pick up supplies. I wanted to jump right back in the game, right where I left off before leaving the Midwest. I was trustworthy, and my friends and associates knew it. Close to a thousand dollars was sent to me to jumpstart my efforts.

I made a phone call to someone I hadn't spoken with since spring of that year. I told my plug that I wanted an amount beyond what I could cover at the moment. I knew more people were in the process of freeing up funds to front me. I told my plug that I would see him in a few hours. I had to drive to him, and I was planning to drop off the bumper along the way.

I did just that. I dropped off the bumper at a courier service along the way. The guy in Texas sent me the first half of that money and the shipping cost. I switched gears as I left the courier. I texted my plug, and I added to my order.

I stopped at a rest stop a bit later. Two other friends sent me money. I sent them messages confirming I would see them once I made it back from the spot. I texted my plug again and added to the order another time. Trust goes a long way in life. Money came in because my friends in the game knew I was good on my word. I reached my destination, having added on to the order yet one more time along the way. Just like that, I was back in the game.

Those next couple days were spent driving here and there, dropping off items and recouping the funds I lost during my time across the country. I also received money from the man in Texas when he confirmed the arrival of the Lexus bumper.

I heard back from the junkyard in Colorado. The tow truck driver called me as he was on the street next to Dean's house. Though I was told I didn't need to be present for them to tow my car, the driver told me that I had been misinformed. There was nothing I could do about that. I was not going back to Colorado. I accepted that I was not going to get paid to scrap my Lexus.

Dean told me the city came out and towed the Lexus a week later. I let go of that situation once I confirmed my car was no longer sitting on the street by Dean's house. That officially closed the chapter of my life with my Lexus. I was happy the car was handled so Dean didn't have to think about it or see it anymore.

It was early November of 2020. I thought I could make a clean break from the lifestyle I had been living up until spring of that year. I managed to leave Lansing, Michigan in the past, but I was right back doing what I had been doing to make money. It was game on.

I was online interacting the same as I had been. I was receiving payments from the website. I was meeting old and new people from the internet for intimate connections. I was doing drugs at the exact same high rate daily, and I was traveling all over the place. Without Lansing as my home base, I was more homeless than ever.

I left Adrian's house. I headed to Chicago. I planned to meet up with someone I had met on the internet. We were going to spend a weekend together, and then I was going to head to a spot outside Ann Arbor, Michigan. I had found somewhere to stay in Michigan while I put a plan of action together.

I texted Karen as I left Chicago. I let her know I was on my way. I then typed in her address in Ann Arbor, Michigan and settled in for the drug-fueled hours of driving ahead of me. Karen was a former scientist with a PhD. She was highly intelligent. She finished school early after skipping a few grades when she was young. I first met Karen on the website in 2019. She was a year older than me, and she lived alone in a quiet neighborhood outside Ann Arbor.

Though Karen was married, her husband lived in North Carolina, working his job as an environmental engineer. The couple had been separated since before I first met Karen the prior year. Karen no longer worked as a scientist. She remained at home most of the time to focus on her mental health. Though I had never met Karen's husband, Karen assured me that I was good to come stay with her in his absence.

I hadn't slept for days. I hadn't slept since mid-week before I went to Chicago. I did drugs to try to keep my eyes open as I drove. I knew I was pushing my limit and needed to sleep. I was determined to reach Karen's house without pulling over somewhere to sleep. Hours later, I made it to Ann Arbor, Michigan. I was on the home stretch, and I felt relieved when I pulled my ridiculous car into Karen's driveway.

Burnin' Down the House

I was happy to see Karen. My mind was compromised from the lack of sleep. I set up the hotrail tray and blew down some lines with Karen. I was so tired. I was exhausted mentally and physically. Shortly after I sat down on the big black leather reclining couch in the living room, I fell out. I didn't just fall asleep; I almost instantly went into a comatose level of unconsciousness as my mind and body gave out on me completely.

I remembered waking up just one time during the many hours I was unconscious. I didn't know where I was. I didn't recognize anything. I seemed to be in a house, but I didn't know whose house. In a trance-like state, I remembered stumbling down a hallway to look for a bathroom.

As I made my way back to the living room, I stumbled past a woman I didn't recognize. I remembered the look on her face. She looked angry. Neither of us said a word as we passed by each other. I heard a door in the hallway close behind me. I fell asleep as I slumped down to the floor in the living room. I didn't even make it back to a couch.

I could tell much more time had passed when I again regained semi-consciousness. I was awake, but I remained lying there on the floor in the same position with my eyes closed. I heard talking. It was a woman's voice. I listened for who else was involved in the conversation. There was only one voice. The conversation was one woman speaking to herself.

I was still tired and had no desire to open my eyes. I rolled over at one point and opened my eyes for a second. I focused on a couch in my line of sight. Personal belongings were stacked around Karen, where she sat talking to herself. She hadn't seen that I was awake, and I closed my eyes again. A moment later, as a result of what I heard Karen say, my eyes instantly opened wide. I jumped up from the floor.

"Karen, hi. I'm sorry I slept for so long. I hadn't slept in days."

Karen stared at me. She had a concerning look on her face as she mumbled to herself.

"Karen! Snap out of it."

Karen instantly looked shocked. She stared at me in disbelief. Then, she spoke to me.

"You can see me? You can see me here in front of you?"

"Of course I can see you. I'm sorry I slept so long. I needed the sleep. Don't do it. I see you. You exist, I promise you."

A moment prior, I had suddenly jumped up from the floor in response to Karen's conversation with herself. Karen was convinced she was a ghost. She was going to burn the house down with us in it to prove she no longer existed. I jumped up to reply to her just in time. All the items stacked on the couch around Karen were items from her life which were important to her. Until I jumped up from the floor, she was convinced she had to start the fire.

Karen told me that while she was awake and tweaking by herself, she had spent hours shaking me and yelling to me, trying to wake me up. Her mind concluded I was dead. Since I hadn't recognized or acknowledged her earlier when I walked in a haze to find a bathroom, Karen took it as I was unable to see her...because she had become a ghost. I was relieved that I woke up when I had. I was relieved I had paid attention to her conversation with herself as I was lying on the floor. I was relieved that I managed to convince her she was a real person, and we both, for sure, were very much alive.

I was no longer tired. I set up my hotrail tray, and I began my day in typical fashion; by blowing down a few large lines of crystal.

I told Karen my plan for my time at her house: I was going to order parts and audio equipment online, and along with multiple trips to local stores for supplies, I was going to turn my Subaru into a camper/stereo on wheels. I was going to stay in the game for the immediate future. I was also going to cash in on the website. After that, I was going to get my registration and plates for the car. It was also the year I needed to renew my driver's license. When all of that was done, I planned to head down to Florida, away from the cold of winter…and closer to Shannon.

I was working towards being able to head to Florida, but I encountered a snag. I received notification from the website that my payment was delayed. I had to let Karen know I was going to be there a bit longer until the payment came through. I needed the money. I made money during that time, but I wanted that payment from the website for funding to travel across the country again. Karen understood, and it wasn't an issue.

I didn't pry into Karen's business, so I didn't know her situation with her separated husband. One afternoon, there was a knock on the door. I looked through the peep hole. I instantly walked back to Karen's bedroom and knocked on her door. It was law enforcement. I stood in the living room as Karen answered the door. It was a welfare check. Karen's husband had called the police when he couldn't reach Karen on the phone that day. The officer left soon after arriving, but Karen mentioned that it happened frequently.

I met my friend Meg on the website during a week when Karen was out of town. Meg also used crystal, and she had her own supply. She came over to Karen's house one night to hang out. I tattooed her side by her stomach. We kissed, but we didn't have sex. I instantly liked Meg. We got along well. We began to hang out on a regular basis.

I finished the structural work on my Subaru. I finished the wiring and the audio system. I painted the outside once more, light green with black accents and a white roof. It looked ridiculous again, but my crystal-soaked brain was happy...for the moment. Suddenly, I decided I needed to paint my car again. I went out and bought more spray paint. I then painted my Subaru one more time. I painted it completely black, same as it was before.

I finally received the check from the website. I finalized my plans to leave the Midwest once again. By the beginning of the next week, I planned to be back on the road. One more week in the cold Michigan weather. I was then going to head down to warm Florida and better times. I was again excited to escape the Midwest. I had tried earlier in the year, and after being stranded in Colorado, I was back in Michigan. It was time for redemption.

Karen had been busy behind the closed door of her bedroom. She had procured an online, long-distance boyfriend. Her boyfriend coincidentally lived in North Carolina, the same state as her husband. Though Karen's new boyfriend, Tom, was on parole for something in North Carolina, he showed up at the house in Michigan, invited by Karen. Tom was a decent enough guy, and I had one more client before I left for Florida.

I mostly stayed in my camper-car in the garage. Karen and Tom stayed on the opposite side of the house in Karen's bedroom. I walked from the garage into the house one morning after I returned with Karen's car from a trip to reup. Karen and Tom had been waiting on me.

I took off my long sleeve shirt and hung it over the back of a chair in the dining room. I sat down at the head of the dining room table and unzipped my backpack. I took out a couple of handfuls of bags from inside the backpack. I repeated the process a couple times. A moment later, I had lined up the sixteen bags on the table, each containing an ounce of large, high-grade crystals. I pulled out a digital scale, and I began to weigh out eightballs from one of the bags. Karen paid me prior to taking the trip, so I tossed an eightball to Karen and another eightball to Tom.

As the two of them pocketed the bags, I continued to weigh out the contents from the bag I had used to supply them. There was a knock on the door. I froze. Before Karen even made it to the front door, I heard a key unlock the door. A police officer stepped into the house and Karen's husband barged in past him.

Karen's husband found out previously that Karen had a boyfriend. He learned from Karen's family that her boyfriend skipped out on his parole and was visiting Karen in Michigan. Karen's husband came back to his Michigan house from North Carolina when he heard the news, and he brought the police with him to arrest Tom.

At the moment I froze, Tom ran through the kitchen into the garage to hide. I stood up in front of the dining room table. As the officer, Karen's husband, and another officer entered the front room of the house, I thought of options as fast as I could. I had a pound of crystal laid out on the dining room table. Before any of the visitors looked in my direction, I quickly took my shirt from the back of the chair and threw it over the top of the dining room table. I then walked to the living room to keep any attention away from the dining room table.

Karen's husband yelled at Karen the entire time he was in the house. The officers attempted to calm him down multiple times. Karen's husband looked at me. I wasn't who he was looking for. He turned to Karen.

"Where is he?!"

Tom came back inside from the garage. Karen's husband saw Tom as he walked into the living room to stand next to Karen. Karen's husband ran up to Tom and got directly in his face.

"That's him! It's him right here! Arrest him!"

One of the officers told the husband he needed to step outside with him to calm down. The other officer remained in the living room, close to the front door. I slunk my way back to the dining room table. I was in direct view of the officer, but the officer was occupied speaking with Karen and Tom. Karen's husband was outside, yelling incessantly. I saw through the window that at least one more officer had joined the commotion outside.

In the moments when the officer inside was distracted and focused away from me, I began to scoop up my shirt on the table with the bags of drugs underneath. The moment came when I was sure I could scoop up all from underneath the shirt into my arms with the shirt. I casually picked up my belongings and walked from the dining room as nonchalantly as I could.

I walked through the kitchen, still in view of the others. Once I made it to the hallway leading to the garage, I balled up my shirt in my hands to be sure I didn't drop anything. In the garage, I stashed my shirt and its contents under the bed in my camper-car. My hands were shaking from adrenaline. I stayed in the garage, but I locked my car and worked on a project on the other side of the garage.

Eventually, I heard the door shut. Everyone had left the house except for Karen and Tom. I walked back into the living room. The three of us were in shock. The police hadn't been in contact with authorities in North Carolina, so they had no cause to take Tom with them. All they had was the word of Karen's irate husband. Tom dodged a bullet that day…I dodged a nuclear bomb.

I texted Meg. Meg lived an hour west of Ann Arbor. After that incident, I felt I needed to be at least that far away from Ann Arbor. I packed up all my belongings. I already had almost everything loaded in my car in preparation to head to Florida. Within an hour, I left in my camper-car to spend the night at Meg's house.

The next morning at Meg's house, I realized I had a couple more items still at Karen's house which I wanted to take with me to Florida. I let Karen know I would be by the house in the afternoon. I went to leave Meg's house and walked out to the Subaru. I got in, and I pulled out from the apartment parking lot. I only made it about fifty yards from the apartments and I pulled over alongside the curb.

I had a flat tire on the back passenger side. My spare tire was situated beneath the bed I had made, a bunch of modifications, and all my luggage underneath everything in the hatchback. It took two hours in the cold to finally manage to free up the spare. A half hour after that, having changed the tire, squeezed the flat tire into the back of the car, and loaded my belongings into the back around it, I was finally ready to drive. I checked my phone. I had a message from Karen an hour prior.

"You probably don't want to show up here now. The police are back."

I called Karen. Officers had returned, and they found Tom hiding in a crawlspace. Karen's husband had set it up, but the officers needed visual confirmation that Tom was indeed the correct person wanted by North Carolina law enforcement. They arrested Tom on the spot, and they gave Karen a court summons to appear and answer for harboring a fugitive.

Had I not had a flat tire, I would have arrived at Karen's house at the same time that incident happened. I drove to a fast-food restaurant. I sat in my car and talked to Karen for an hour. I decided I wasn't going to stop back at her house for my belongings. They were nothing important anyhow. I tried my best to console Karen on the phone. I told her I would stay in touch as I was traveling. I hung up the phone and headed to Ohio.

I reached an auto supply store across the border in Ohio that evening. I bought a new high-performance car battery to support my camper-car's audio system. I installed it while in the parking lot. I then drove another hour down to Adrian's house in Findlay. I planned to stay there overnight, since the DMV was closed for the day. I decided I was going to drive back up to Perrysburg the next day to renew my driver's license, register my car, and get license plates.

Alone in the Night

"Where are you?"

A valid question. People asked me that question more often than any other. I ignored it. I had other things on my mind. I spoke into my phone as if in my own world.

"You know something? I'll do crystal for the rest of my life."

I was thinking aloud. Previous addictions always ended. I couldn't find a single reason to stop using methamphetamine. Over the past few years, the benefits of constant crystal consumption easily outweighed the downsides of around-the-clock indulgence in my chemically altered mind.

On crystal, I had no desire to use any other substances. I had more energy; sleeping three hours every two days also gave me much more time. I stayed busy; my creativity was expressed through work on various projects at any given moment. I connected sexually; intimacy was prolonged and more meaningful. I was outgoing; fear and anxiety were easily overcome. I felt alive; I sought out others to share my world...if only for isolated fleeting moments.

The drugs allowed me to maintain all those interactions and meetings; drugs moved me through the world of adult social media popularity at an accelerated pace. I took more risks which led to more new and unique experiences. I saw the benefits of methamphetamine in all aspects of my life. The drugs gave me perspective through crystal-colored glasses. An endless supply of the highest grade; I never worried about running out of drugs. The money from crystal kept me going in times of need.

Though I was content with remaining an indefinite user of methamphetamine, I was again working towards freeing myself from the game. I was homeless, but the entire country was my home. It was a trade-off I happily accepted. I relished the effects of continuous indulgence. The drugs sheltered my mind from any negative side effects of those same drugs.

Much had been seen from the media regarding the stigma of drug addiction. All other drugs had been those detriments; the familiar problems stated in news reports and studies. Crystal was different. I had seen lives ruined by methamphetamine, in the media and in person. I didn't respond to crystal in all those negative ways like the others. I knew I had a golden ticket. I had a pass. I didn't want for the drug; I didn't struggle without it. While high, I looked past the fact that my life had been turned completely upside down.

I had privilege, one which kept me from ever knowing a day of wishing to get high without the means to do so. That part of the crystal meth scene didn't exist in my world. My view was skewed. My world, from my viewpoint, was full steam ahead... but it wasn't steam; it was smoke. There was so much smoke that I couldn't see past the cloud in front of me. It was the dawn of 2021, and I jumped into the year, full of excitement and wonder.

I hung up the phone. As I drove, I thought about my stop that morning in Arlington, Ohio. That look on my dad's face when I walked in; was it disappointment? Yes...it was disappointment for sure. Something else was there as well. I smiled when I first stepped into the gunsmithing shop on my dad's property. When my father looked up at me, he didn't smile back. I saw the recognition register, and that next look caused my heart to sink. After six years without contact, the look on my dad's face made me rethink my decision to stop by and see him. I pushed past it. I greeted my father...

I shook the memory of that morning from my head. In that moment, I had other concerns. It was dark outside. I approached the bottom of Ohio on southbound I-75. Late evening traffic, north of Cincinnati, had been growing more dense by the minute. The Subaru camper/car had begun to experience electrical issues on the drive. I had already stopped outside of Dayton to try to sort out the issues with the car's wiring. With the wiring in check, the signs pointed to the alternator.

Then, as with previous cars on previous cross-country trips, the Subaru simply shut off. No engine, no headlights, no power steering, no anything. I was on the busy freeway, and I was careening through traffic at seventy miles an hour in a rolling camper/car with no power. Unlike previous car failures, I had an out. There was an exit ramp up on the right. I saw the ramp, and I also noticed that the exit instantly became a slope downward from the elevated freeway.

The exit was reachable, even considering current catastrophic camper/car conditions. Though I needed to cut across three lanes to the right, there was a gap in the traffic around me. I pulled the wheel hard, using muscle in place of the inoperable power steering. I reached the ramp. As I coasted down the hill, I continued at highway speed. There was one car far ahead of me at the bottom of the ramp. I hoped the car would make it to the intersection before the green light changed to red at the bottom of the hill. The light changed to yellow. The car ahead of me could have easily made the light…

"Keep going! Keep going! Keep going! No!"

I stomped my foot down on the brake pedal. My Subaru camper/car slowed down to stop behind the other car at the very bottom of the hill. Just after the three cars in cross-traffic began to fill the intersection in front of me, the light quickly turned green again. The car in front of me took off into the night. I stepped from my car and began to push. There was no longer momentum from descending the hill. I had to start from scratch. The road was flat. With much effort, I pushed my car through the intersection and down the street on the other side.

As I struggled, a car pulled up next to me. The driver offered his help. I climbed back into my driver's seat, and the other car lined up behind my Subaru. The other car pushed me half a mile down the road to the first and only available parking lot.

"Thank you for your help. You're a lifesaver."

"Yeah, man; no problem. Be careful out here tonight. This isn't a good part of town."

I watched; that other car disappeared down the road and into the night. I took a deep breath, and I evaluated my situation. I was in a bank parking lot. There was nothing else around. I was alone in the Cincinnati darkness. I could hear the cars passing a few hundred yards away on the interstate above me. The surface streets were empty. Random streetlights illuminated the dark Cincinnati sky.

I shook my head. My cross-country trip from Michigan to Florida; already a multitude of difficulties and complications were testing me. Still north of Ohio's border with Kentucky, I had a long way to go. Had I been driving in a functional car on the highway, I would have been ten minutes from crossing over the Ohio River. A functional car was no longer part of my reality. In the flash of a headlight, my reality had become an ordeal.

...

It was one o'clock in the morning. I listened to the reply; the tow truck driver was confident in his answer. I ignored the confidence and asked again.

"Are you sure? Well, I'll be here. I have no other option."

"Yes, I'll reach the shop in Kentucky at five thirty. I'll be up to you in Ohio just after six. Hang tight and try to stay warm. Be careful. I know that part of town. It definitely isn't where you want to be stranded."

That was the second warning about safety in that location. I just shook my head as I hung up the phone. Since sleep in the wintry night wasn't going to be possible, drugs were on the schedule for the duration. Drugs would have been on the schedule regardless, but it was time to go above and beyond. With the shades up in the windows, the torch ignited, and the lines dumped out on the silver serving tray, it was time to get to work. How much crystal would it take to override the stress of the night? It was time to find out.

There was too much smoke. After a half hour, I had to open the doors and step from the car for some fresh air. The clouds flowed from the car doors and dissipated into the brisk night air. The winter wind instantly chilled the sweat covering my body. There was a sound in the distance. It was music: bass. The distant thumps slowly grew louder as I let the last of the drug smoke out of the car. I had to make a decision. Where was I going to be when the car with the loud bass reached me? I thought on it for a split second. I was going to be inside my car with the shades covering all the windows.

The volume increased as the car blatantly headed in my direction. I sat back and peered through a crack alongside the shade in one of my car's windows. The car, blacked out with dark window tint, stopped moving; it idled on a street across from the parking lot where I was camping. The music cut off. As the car inched forward, the driver adjusted position to directly face my Subaru. Headlights illuminated my vehicle in the dark Cincinnati night. Five minutes passed, and I adjusted my grip on my handgun.

The car began to drive; not in the direction it had been heading, but it turned to pull into the parking lot. My Subaru was parked directly in the middle of the lot. The other car, still without music, slowly circled the lot around me like a shark circling its prey in the ocean. I sat still inside my vehicle. The other car circled three times. I watched through the cracks on the sides of the window shades. Out of nowhere, the other car suddenly left the lot and disappeared down a street, into the night.

I kept my gun in my hand. I made sure all of my drug paraphernalia was secured out of sight. The loud bass thumped again as the other car drove away. I listened as the beats faded off. Time passed. It was hard to stay warm. The side effects of crystal on my circulatory system caused my fingers and toes to ache in the cold. I continued to keep a vigilant ear to listen for approaching people and vehicles. The night was silent. It was eerie.

Two hours passed. I froze. Was it the same car as before? I again stashed my drugs. I continued to listen intently as the faint sound of bass notes floated to me in the darkness. Again, the music slowly grew louder. Whether it was the same car or a different car, it was for sure getting closer. It was again decision time. I decided to act. I strapped my gun around my upper arm, and I pulled the lever to pop the hood. With my gun blatantly visible around my left arm, I grabbed a screwdriver and began to work on the wiring to the alternator of the Subaru.

I heard the car as it reached the same cross street where that earlier car had previously stopped. The hood of the Subaru blocked vision between me and the emergent vehicle. I stood up from the front of the engine compartment and walked around towards the back of the Subaru to get a look at who was approaching. It was the same car as before, windows completely blacked out.

I held a steady gaze towards the windshield of the car a hundred yards in front of me. As it had earlier, the car's music cut off. As casually as possible, I opened the back door to the Subaru. I tossed the screwdriver into the back, and I pulled out a metric socket wrench. As I turned to walk back to the engine compartment to tighten the bolts on my car's alternator, the car with the tinted windows peeled out and turned down a side street. I heard the music kicking back on as the car's engine roared. Both the engine and the music again faded out into the night. That was the last time that I saw the car with the blacked-out windows.

At five fifteen, the phone rang. The tow truck driver was running ahead of schedule. He was leaving the shop in Kentucky. At five forty-five, I watched the tow truck pull into the parking lot. After securing my drugs in my backpack, I stepped out of my car to meet the driver. The two of us hooked the Subaru to the cables, and I steered my car as it was pulled up onto the bed of the truck by the tow winch.

It was still dark, and the interstate through Cincinnati was void of almost all traffic. Soon, we were across the Ohio River and in Kentucky. I used my phone to find a location of an auto supply store in Kentucky. After another half hour, the Subaru was safely unloaded into a parking space in front of the store. When the tow truck was out of sight, I took the drugs out of my backpack and did a couple hotrails.

Get in the Zone

My physiology was in tune with my drug regimen. My body and mind were conditioned and fully accustomed to methamphetamine. Though crystal generally reduced appetite, I was at a homeostasis. I ate food on a regular schedule. I was also able to do substantial amounts of drugs and fall asleep, especially when I had been awake a while. As the sky lightened from black to a dark purple that morning, I put away my drug equipment and went to sleep in the bed in my Subaru camper/car. The sun was about to rise, and I wanted to sleep a few hours before the auto supply store opened.

It was mid-morning when I woke up. Other cars were parked in various spaces in the store's parking lot. I went into the store and asked about the alternator I needed to buy for my car. There wasn't the needed alternator in stock at the store. The clerk made a phone call. A store on the other side of the city had one in stock. Luckily for me, one of the store employees was about to make a trip to pick up parts from the other store. With the alternator added to the list, I went back out to my car to do drugs and wait.

I sat in the driver's seat of the Subaru. For some reason, paranoia was bad that morning. I kept thinking that random customers were aware of my drug use. A lady walked into the store. Through the glass storefront windows, I saw her walk up to the register and begin speaking to a clerk. I immediately packed up my drug equipment and decided to sit on the curb in plain view for the rest of my waiting time. The drugs were locked in the car, and I felt some relief from the paranoia.

Halfway through changing out my alternator with the

new one later that morning, a police cruiser pulled up and parked two spaces over from me. The paranoia came back in a wave which washed over me. I remained on task, but I watched the officer walk into the store and stand by the door to speak with the clerk. The officer stayed at the store for the remainder of the time I spent changing alternators. With shaky hands, I finally finished the job. I walked back into the store to thank the clerk for his help. I bid the clerk and the officer a good day, and I immediately drove from the auto supply store's parking lot.

I kept my eyes on my mirrors, but the police car never pulled out behind me. The paranoia, still with me, had me hurriedly driving away. I didn't take any extra time to look up directions back to the interstate; I just sped down roads in the directions I assumed would lead me to the highway. After stressfully careening through the surface streets, my paranoia was finally left behind when I found an onramp to the interstate. There were no police behind me, and I was back on track to Florida.

Back on track...for one hour. One hour of driving on the interstate; that was all I managed. On an overpass in dense afternoon traffic, my fuel pump went out. I couldn't believe it; broken down again, and I was still only in northern Kentucky. Cars honked as they ripped past the Subaru while I was stopped on the narrow right shoulder atop an overpass. With each honk, my frustration grew. Horn honks were met with middle fingers; all in vain. More time passed. The next tow truck finally arrived.

It was dark outside again when my Subaru was dropped down into a parking space in the back row of a truck stop parking lot. I made sure my car was set down into a parking space as much out of the way as possible. I knew I was going to be there for some time. The truck stop/travel center was large. There were many spaces in the parking lot. The truck stop/travel center was busy. Many of the spaces were occupied with vehicles.

Coming from a background in transportation and logistics, I had an advantage. Having traveled the country many times over on my perpetual road trip, I felt comfortable in the setting where I had been placed. I was parked amongst a row of personal vehicles belonging to long-haul truck drivers. The cars were there to remain as the truck drivers were out on the road working. I knew the cars would sit for up to a couple of weeks at a time while the drivers hauled freight around the country. Though I was stranded, I was content with my car's position, secure in the parking space at the rest stop.

My first order of business that evening at the Kentucky truck stop: add on to the already ridiculous hotrail stem I used for drugs. Hotrail stems were straight glass tubes. Once they were heated too many times with a torch, the stems cracked and broke off at the ends when overheated. I had been taking the broken stems and connecting them together into one huge pipe back when I was still in the garage in Michigan; my temporary home where I worked to make my Subaru into a camper at the end of 2020. My thoughts: the bigger the stem, the more crystal I could scrape from the inside of the glass. Scraping crystal was oddly satisfying. The hotrails of crystal residue got me just as high as first-pass crystal.

The pipe was made from broken pieces, added together when glass stems broke from heating them. The pipe approached two feet in length. Epoxy, colored electrical wiring, and hot glue held the pieces together. Since only the end of the pipe was heated to do hotrails, the other substances beyond the glass ends weren't subjected to the torch. I made sure the stem on the end of the pipe was still long enough to be cool where the binding items held the pipe together at the start of the next stem. I painted a colorful spiral design around the outside of the pipe using my tattoo ink. Clear epoxy resin covered the length of the ink design, protecting it in a clear coating.

Crystal had that effect on me; I was always busy doing and creating anything that swirled into my head. I moved from task to task, creation to creation. As my mind swirled with thoughts, my work was never done. Car work, car audio work, tattooing, documenting, creating media, interacting online with people all over, sharing intimacy, random projects popped up all the time...

That Frankenpipe wasn't my first order of business that evening. I had been distracted when I pulled Frankenpipe from its secure hiding space within the dismantled dashboard of the Subaru. As I did drugs, the colorful spiral of the pipe mesmerized me. I had another broken pipe to add to my glass monstrosity. In that moment, I was consumed with pipe dreams.

A minute after blowing out the last cloud, I remembered what I actually needed to do before anything else. I put the giant pipe away, and my brain began to properly prioritize my task list. I needed to get online and order a new fuel pump. I found one and placed the order...to the parking lot of the random Kentucky truck stop. In the shipping notes, I described my car and parking space location. There was no next-day delivery. The fuel pump wasn't going to arrive over the upcoming weekend. Delivery was set, and the fuel pump was scheduled to arrive the Friday of the following week.

There was a Denny's restaurant connected to the travel center at the truck stop. I knew I was about to consume more southwest skillet breakfasts than I had in all the time in my life leading up to that point. There were showers at the truck stop. There were all the amenities needed for over a week's worth of parking lot camping. People were everywhere inside and outside the bustling service center. I settled in, and I got to work; extending my hotrail pipe another few inches.

...

Was that the phone ringing? I tried to shake off the fog from only an hour of sleep. I was dropped off at my car earlier that morning by a lady I met on the internet. The prior night was spent at the lady's house. That hour of sleep that morning was my first sleep in two days. The fog began to lift. It was, in fact, my phone ringing. I knew I needed to answer it. Projected delivery of the new fuel pump was that morning. I searched around me in my camper/car to locate my phone before the ringing stopped.

The phone went silent. I found it a moment later. It wasn't a call from the delivery, but there was a message I had missed. I fully woke up as I read the message, more bad news. The message was regarding the delivery of the fuel pump, and I hadn't been awake to reply in a timely manner. My trip to Florida was becoming more and more challenging, and I was only two states further than where I had started.

"We attempted to deliver your package, but we were unable to complete the delivery."

The remainder of the day was spent on the phone. I did drugs in my car in the parking lot at the rest stop in Kentucky while I tried to sort out the situation. The delivery driver, according to customer service, wasn't comfortable delivering to a car in a parking lot. According to customer service: without an address, the delivery would not be able to be completed.

Feeling dejected, I wondered what the future held for me. The year was off to a shaky start. Before the dark of night set in, I made sure that the top of my fuel tank was securely bolted back into place. I didn't want to accidentally blow myself up while doing hotrails in the camper/car. With nothing else to look forward to that day, I got a full night of much needed sleep.

After eating food from Denny's the following morning, a random thought entered my head. I dressed and headed into the service center. I walked up to a cash register and asked the clerk a question.

"Hi. My name's Doug. I was supposed to receive a delivery yesterday. It's a part for my car. Did you guys happen to get a package with my name on it?"

"I'm not sure. Let me get the manager and see if he knows anything."

My heart raced as I waited to speak with the manager. The service center, as it had been each day I was there, was extremely busy. Ten minutes passed as adrenaline mixed with the meth in my body. Though I was told the delivery couldn't be completed, I had a feeling of hope that morning. Sure enough, after showing my driver's license to the manager of the service center, I walked back out to my Subaru with a new fuel pump in my hands.

A week and a half of winter camping in a broken-down car at a rest stop in Kentucky, and I saw an end in sight. Having previously removed the old fuel pump, installing the new fuel pump was a fast process. The moment of truth was upon me. I bolted the cover back onto the fuel tank. I left my tools out in case the installation wasn't successful.

As I sat in the driver's seat of my car, my mind was all over the place. Before trying to start my car, I pulled out my two-foot long Frankenpipe and blew down a couple large hotrails of crystal. I was ready. Hope was with me. I was about to find out if luck was on my side. I stuck the key in the Subaru's ignition. I took a deep breath, and I turned the key.

"Yes!"

First try, the engine turned over and the car started. Relief washed through my drug-saturated brain. I removed the shades from the windows of my car, and I put my tools away. I was ready to get back on the road. I wondered if good fortune was finally on my side. Though I had a reprieve for the moment, good fortune was not on my side.

Two hours on the southbound interstate in Kentucky, and the alternator began to act up. I knew it was about to go out. It had happened to me before in a different car. I had learned of the faulty line of alternators coming from the particular auto parts chain store after changing out three alternators in a row back in 2018. I didn't have any other options when I was towed from

Ohio to Kentucky two weeks earlier.

Though the alternator was failing, my new fuel pump was working fine. After searching online for the closest particular auto store to exchange the alternator, I plugged the directions into my phone. I needed to make it another forty-five minutes south to reach the store. Having had the issue before, I didn't stress over the situation.

I took my alternator out, and I returned it to the store. To avoid a repeat of the issue, I walked across the street to a different auto supply chain store and purchased another alternator. I walked back to my car in the parking lot of the first store. I did a hotrail, and then I quickly installed the new alternator in my Subaru. I was back on the road in under an hour, crisis avoided.

Hours later, I was on the interstate in the dark of night, approaching southern Kentucky. Though the alternator was fine, an unforeseen problem arose due to the previous faulty alternator. As I reached a split at the top of an overpass where two interstate highways intersected, in the middle lane, in semi-heavy highway traffic, and still on a steep incline… the new battery died: damaged from the issues with the faulty alternator.

And like that; my real problems began. If only I could have been back at that comfortable rest stop in northern Kentucky where I spent the majority of the previous two weeks. That rest stop: where just that morning I had done everything in my power to vacate it and leave it behind. I had it good at that rest stop. Life was easy. I had taken it for granted.

My car came to a stop in the middle of the interstate split. I immediately put my car in park. I set the parking brake to prevent my Subaru from rolling backward, down the hill behind me, into oncoming highway traffic. There were three lanes of traffic splitting off to my passenger side and onto the overpass to my right. Two more lanes split to the left of me, beyond my driver's side, and onto the overpass of the other highway.

I was a few hundred feet from the apex of the split. Traffic zoomed by me on both sides; horns honking as cars passed. I had no power. I couldn't even use the four-way hazard lights in the dark night sky. Trucks, flying by me at seventy miles per hour, shook my car with their proximity. I was in immediate danger. I needed a plan, and I needed to move fast.

I thought for a moment as I did drugs in my car. I knew what I had to do. I set my phone in the holder hanging from my windshield, and I began recording video. I had to pick my moment carefully. The truck traffic was particularly heavy at the split. Any false move could easily result in death. I watched the groups of cars and trucks as they quickly approached the split and veered off to the two interstates on either side of me. I saw the gap in the distance behind me. I waited in anticipation; my moment came. Suddenly, it was time.

With a small gap in the traffic almost to me, I lowered the parking break and put my car in neutral. I adjusted the steering wheel. When the last car passed by my driver's side door, I jumped out onto the pavement beside my car. I gripped the steering wheel with one hand and pushed the door frame of my car with all my might. As the Subaru began to roll backwards down the hill, toward the next group of vehicles of oncoming traffic, I jumped back in my car.

I muscled the steering wheel the best I could as I sat in my seat; turned to face out the back windshield to watch where my car was rolling. The Subaru began to pick up speed as it rolled backward down the hill. The next group of oncoming traffic was approaching. The headlights in the distance grew brighter. I pulled hard on the wheel, and the Subaru cut across the three lanes of traffic to the shoulder on the right side of the overpass.

My Subaru reached the shoulder halfway down the hill. Just as all of my wheels cleared the line which marked the shoulder, the next group of oncoming traffic reached the overpass split. As I applied the brakes and my car rolled to a stop on the shoulder, the horn from a passing semi hurt my ears. My car vibrated from the closeness of the encounter. I had managed to roll my car backwards down a hill on an interstate into oncoming traffic without being smashed to bits.

I was safe on the shoulder of the highway as long as cars remained in their travel lanes as they drove by. The most immediate concern that night had been managed. It was then that I began to realize all of the other concerns I faced. I took another moment to do drugs while I watched the video which I recorded of pushing my car to safety. I then took a moment to evaluate all the latest problems in my world.

There was no phone service.
I was in the middle of nowhere, which meant I had nowhere to walk.
It was cold. It was nineteen degrees and dropping.
I had a couple bottles of water, but I had no food.
A dead battery was not something I could remedy.
As the night went on, nobody stopped to help.

The next morning, it was the cold which woke me from sleep. My legs were numb and sore from the winter freeze. The sun was bright when I took the shade from my windshield. I heard cars zipping past me. I reached for my phone…and I realized I had another problem to add to the list.

At first, I thought my phone was off. Then, I thought my phone had died. Finally, I figured my phone was too cold, and it would turn on once it was warmed up. I was wrong. My phone, at the worst possible time, had completely broken. I still had a backup phone, the phone which held a charge for a maximum of ten minutes. I found the phone and plugged it into a battery pack.

The stress was overwhelming. I made a conscious choice to spend the entire day hanging out and working on my car as if I were spending my leisure time there by choice. The stress of the trip, to that point, was enough to cause a reset in my brain. There, on the side of the road, in that situation, I took a mental vacation from everything. I was stranded, and my mind had checked out. I did drugs and worked on various projects for the remainder of the day.

By nightfall, my focus shifted to my attempt to remain warm for one more night. After wrapping my legs in blankets, I managed to get some sleep. The pain in my legs from the fifteen-degree night woke me up the next morning, the same as it had the day before. It was lightly snowing as I stepped from my car to walk around and get some circulation in my legs. I almost fell over when I first tried to stand up outside the car. My legs were in bad shape. I managed to get the blood flowing after five minutes of walking around on the shoulder of the highway.

I knew I had to do something that day. I had managed fine without food, but I was down to half a bottle of semi-frozen water. I emptied out my backpack. I grabbed a socket wrench and popped the hood of my car. After removing the battery, I put the wrench away. I scribbled a note on a piece of paper and left it on the dashboard of my car, visible from outside the front windshield. I didn't want my car to be towed in my absence.

"Stranded. Walked to find phone service. Back shortly."

With the extremely heavy car battery in my backpack and the receipt for it in my pocket, I grabbed my backup phone and began walking up the hill of the overpass. Once I reached the point where the overpass dropped off to the road below, I climbed over the guardrail and worked my way down the steep slope to the surface street. Exhausted from hiking with the battery on my back, I walked along the side of the road below the interstate overpass.

I turned on my backup phone. I sat down on the car battery to rest and catch my breath. I knew, once my phone booted up, that I would only have an extremely limited timeframe to find phone service and contact a ride service. I checked the bars on my phone; nothing. I held the phone up above my head. A single bar appeared. It wasn't enough reception to use the ride service app, but it gave me hope. I left my backpack and battery where I had been sitting, and I walked down the road. Eventually, my backup phone showed three bars of service.

"Your ride is fifteen minutes away."

"Your ride has been cancelled."

"Your ride is seventeen minutes away."

"Your ride has been cancelled…"

After time passed, my phone was dangerously low on power. I managed to reach a driver on the app. Just before my phone died, I sent the driver one final message.

"This location is where I am for sure. Please show up. My phone will die in the next minute or so. I will be here. Please help me. I'll see you in twenty minutes."

Twenty minutes passed. I was about to give up hope when I saw a car approaching from the curve up ahead. I waved my hands. The car pulled up and stopped. It was my driver. I promised the driver a huge tip for taking the time to help me. The driver had been planning to go off duty and go home for the day. Had it not been for that one driver, I wouldn't have had any other options. I charged my phone in the car. Forty-five minutes later, I was dropped off at my Subaru with a new battery. I made sure to tip the driver the maximum amount before my phone died again.

That night, after more than two weeks, I finally left Kentucky. I made it out. My car had no more issues on my drive south. After a couple more days, and a couple of nights of sleep at rest stops along the way, I reached Florida. It was past the middle of February in 2021. The weather was warm and sunny. The trip was behind me. I had made it.

Self-Sabotage

Florida: the Sunshine State. It was bright and sunny the next morning when I left a friend's house. I had things to do; a car to work on, laundry to wash, food to eat, drugs to consume. I drove through the Tampa Bay area. I reached out to Shannon. We picked a time to meet up at a gas station. I found a park close to the particular gas station. It was on the water. It was a good place for me to get some more work done on my car.

A couple of hours later, I packed up my tools. I was pouring sweat. The Florida heat was in full effect. I drove five minutes down the road to the gas station. Ten minutes later, Shannon pulled into a parking space next to my Subaru. I gladly stepped from my car to hers. My air conditioning in the Subaru camper/car didn't work. The air conditioning in Shannon's car was on, full blast, as the two of us got high and engaged in car intimacy.

After Shannon went on her way, I remained in the parking lot. I painted my car. I worked on the stereo system as the night sky grew dark. There was a twenty-four-hour laundromat in the strip mall on the far side of the parking lot. I began to do laundry in the middle of the night.

I heard something behind me as I sat on the sidewalk outside of the laundromat at three o'clock in the morning. I looked back. I was surprised to see a raccoon running towards me on its hind legs. I jumped to my feet to face the raccoon. I yelled at it.

"Get out of here! I'll kick you in the dick!"

The raccoon, startled by my voice, switched its trajectory.

It remained on its hind legs but took off to the left and around the corner of the building. I stayed on alert from that moment until my laundry finished as dawn broke the next morning. As time passed, no other wildlife tested me.

I loaded up my car with clean clothes as the then-bustling parking lot filled with an absurd number of early morning work commuters. I put my car in gear and joined the fray. The sun was up when I crossed over the Sunshine Skyway Bridge to reach the south side of the metro Tampa area. I found a rest stop on the side of the highway. That was where I posted up to do more work on my car.

I had been in contact with a trans girl from an app on my phone since the last time I was in Florida. Chloe lived in Orlando. I was a few hours away, but I agreed to visit Chloe when she invited me over to her house that day. I packed up my tools once more, and I put Chloe's address into my phone's GPS. I sent an ETA in a text message, and I pulled out from the rest stop.

Later that night, I pulled into the gas station parking lot back where I met Shannon the day before. I was tired from driving to Orlando to see Chloe and then returning to Tampa later that same evening. I had been looking forward to the soft-serve ice cream at that particular Tampa gas station since I left Orlando earlier that day. I turned off my car after I pulled into a parking space at the gas station.

Instantly, I lost my car keys. I hadn't even gotten up from the driver's seat of my car. I literally turned off my car, pulled the keys from the ignition, and suddenly my keys were gone. Crystal meth accounted for my actions for the next hour and a half. I moved around, I looked all over, multiple times I unloaded and reloaded all the items packed in my camper/car. I wanted ice cream, but I was stuck in my car looking for my keys.

After an hour and a half, my tweaked brain finally felt relief. I managed to find my keys. They had fallen into the crack between the driver's seat and the backrest to the seat. At eleven thirty that night, I finally locked up my car and walked inside to get ice cream from the gas station. I was pouring sweat from the crystal-fueled frantic key searching over the previous hour and a half. Absorbed in drug-induced paranoia, I thought everyone in the gas station knew I spent all that time looking for my keys.

During the next few weeks, I stayed busy. I tattooed myself at the beach below the bridge over Tampa Bay. I met up with Shannon and did car stuff with her on a regular basis. I continued to work on my car at different rest stops and parks in the Tampa area. I met random people from the website and on the apps. I met random people while I lived the car life in Florida.

I got a call from Shannon one morning. She had a new job, and her new company put her up in a hotel in Jacksonville so she could attend meetings and conferences. Shannon invited me to join her across the state in Jacksonville for those three days. I accepted the invitation. I agreed to meet Shannon at the hotel when she checked in.

My car drove without issue across the state to Jacksonville. Shannon and I recorded videos together in the hotel room. We did drugs together. While Shannon attended meetings, I remained at the hotel. I did drugs and created requested videos which I sent to Shannon. One particular evening, Shannon wanted to dye my hair. We went to the store and picked up hair dye. Shannon then dyed my hair in the hotel room.

When the time came to check out, Shannon went her separate way back to the Tampa area on the west side of Florida. I took a detour. I headed south from Jacksonville to visit Liam again in Titusville. I hadn't seen Liam since I previously stayed with him in Titusville after leaving my living situation with Zoe back in 2019.

My car began to drive funny on the trip to see Liam. During my time at Liam's house that next week, I attempted to diagnose and fix the Subaru. Liam and I did drugs around the clock. Liam's demeanor shifted from welcoming to paranoid. Liam was convinced that my presence in the retirement community would lead to neighbors reporting him for violating community guidelines. Not wishing to add stress to Liam's life, I left to head back to Tampa at eleven o'clock at night. It was a week after I had arrived from Jacksonville. My welcome had run its course.

Five minutes after leaving Liam's house, I was pulled over by the police before I could even clear Titusville. It was dark outside at eleven o'clock that night. The wiring in my Subaru was causing issues. I had no rear lights as I drove. I convinced the officer to allow me to drive back to Liam's for the night and then make the drive to Tampa the next morning in the daylight.

Liam wasn't happy when I showed up again shortly after leaving his house. He thought he was safe from neighbor complaints without any visitors. Liam once again had a visitor. He let me back inside, but he immediately went to bed. Liam had to work early the next morning. I stayed up and blew down hotrail after hotrail to try to improve my evening.

The next morning, Liam and I hugged. He apologized for his lack of hospitality, and he explained to me how he feared being kicked out of the community. I thanked Liam for the one more night of having me there. When Liam went to work, I drove back across the state to Tampa.

I watched sunrises and sunsets over the water from the beach on the Sunshine Skyway Bridge. I tattooed myself as I sat outside of my car in the sand. Cars were allowed to drive on the sand of that particular beach. I watched kite-boarders in the water. I was included in other people's cookouts on the beach. I ate hamburgers, hot dogs, and potato salad. I took soap with me into the bay to wash up amongst the saltwater waves.

When I left the beach, I worked on the air intake and hoses under the hood of the Subaru at various parking lots around the Tampa area. I met up with Shannon periodically. I tried out new restaurants in the area. I continued to interact with people on my phone. I continued to do drugs constantly. I still had a good amount of crystal with me. My money was running low. I made a one-time deal with someone I knew. I sold the last eightball

I could spare. The rest of my drugs were strictly my personal supply.

I took a drive down the west coast of the state to Fort Meyers. A lady from the website was housesitting at one of her friend's houses for a week. She invited me to spend time with her at the house. My car made the multi-hour drive. I navigated the surface streets of Fort Meyers. I was not impressed with the city as I drove through it. I eventually reached the house. Cher greeted me with a hug and kiss at the front door.

My first night at the house in Fort Meyers did not include sleep. Cher went to bed. I didn't. Cher didn't do crystal, and she wasn't thrilled to find out that I was always zooted on the stuff. I was paranoid all night. At one point, I opened a drawer in the kitchen to grab a fork. I instantly yelled and jumped back in reaction to a drawer completely full of cockroaches of all sizes.

The next night, Cher went to sleep again. I remained awake yet another night. At that point, I passed beyond the audio-hallucination period to full on hallucinating. In the dark of night, I peeked out of the blinds to the patio in the backyard. I saw four people outside of the sliding glass back door. I took cover behind the couch and pulled out my gun. I aimed and held steady for the next hour. Nothing happened, so I cautiously crept my way to the door. With my handgun aimed to the backyard, I quickly pulled the curtain back. Nobody was there. Later that night, the scenario repeated. Again, I pulled the curtain back and pointed my gun. Again, nobody was there.

Cher went to work the next day. I stayed at the house. I did drugs, I interacted on my phone, I worked out, and I managed a short nap. When I woke up, the hallucinations were gone. Cher arrived back at the house after her workday ended. Cher and I had a talk. Cher had ended a previous relationship due to meth consumption. Cher and I decided that I wasn't what she needed in her life at that point. I left Fort Meyers. Again, I headed back to the Tampa area.

It was evening as I drove across the multiple-mile bridge

over Tampa Bay. I was hot and sweaty. I was exhausted. I was in a bad mood. I was halfway across the bridge, out in the middle of the bay. My Subaru ran out of gas.

"I'm over it. I don't care anymore."

"Doug, where are you?"

"I'll send you a text with the mile marker and road. After that, I'm going to sleep."

I hung up the phone. I found a mile marker close to where my car had stopped. The expanse of roadway across Tampa Bay was a series of bridges and small islands of land supporting the pavement of the road. My car had come to a stop almost halfway across the bay, on one of the small islands in the middle of the water. There was enough room for my car to sit between the pavement and the guardrail where the water of the bay began. I was facing north, over two miles from reaching the top of the bay. There were two miles of water behind me on the south side of the bay. I was in the middle of Tampa Bay.

I texted my location to my lifelong friend, Andrea. I needed to sleep, and I turned off my phone. I had hardly slept during the previous week, so I knew I was about to crash hard. The heat was going to be a concern. I had to keep my windows up; mosquitos were a far more immediate issue that night.

I woke up the next morning as I cooked in the sun. I sat up, soaked in sweat. I saw a tow truck parked behind me. The driver was walking towards my Subaru with a can of gasoline. As the tow truck driver emptied the contents into my gas tank, he explained the situation to me.

"I work for AAA. We got a call that someone was stranded out here. The police have already been out here."

"Huh?" I was still in the process of waking up.

"They knocked on the windows, but you didn't wake up. Your friend called us again to check on you."

"What's that?"

"I only have one gallon of gas for you, but it will get you off of this bridge."

I was confused. I assumed it was Andrea who had helped me out, but I didn't understand the part about the police. How did the tow truck driver know the police had been out earlier in the morning? Why would they have just left when they got no response as they tried to wake me? Whatever. Once the tow truck driver drove away, I blew down a hotrail.

I drove across the rest of the bridge and to the first gas station I saw. I fueled up. I got ice cream. I changed out of my clothes, clothes which were completely soaked in sweat. I wrung out the shirt I had been wearing overnight. My sweat dripped down to the pavement of the gas station parking lot as I stood outside my car in the hot Florida sunlight.

Proprioception

There was a nice suburb city just outside Tampa where Shannon lived. I saw many similarities between Westchase and my home city of Perrysburg. The two cities were close in population and demographics. I spent time with Shannon in Westchase when she was available to see me. I spent the rest of my time exploring the Tampa area and working on my camper/car.

I still had a good reserve of crystal for personal use. Shannon got high with me when we spent time together. I would do a hotrail and blow the smoke into Shannon's mouth as we kissed. Though I knew I was good for a while on my supply of drugs, I had another worry building. Each day, little by little, my money was running out.

Per usual, I pulled into a small parking lot alongside a neighborhood in Westchase when Shannon told me she was done working for the day. I turned off my car and waited. Ten minutes later, Shannon pulled up alongside my Subaru in the parking lot. I grabbed my bag of drug supplies and a bag of adult novelty items, and I hopped into the passenger seat of Shannon's SUV.

Per usual, Shannon and I slowly rolled around the neighborhood until we found a good place to park; one which was away from any public traffic. Shannon had dark tinted windows in her car, but the two of us still tried to remain as inconspicuous as possible when we engaged in illicit activity. Once Shannon parked, I pulled out my bag of drug supplies and got to work lining up hotrails on my tray.

I blew down three large lines of crystal. Each time I did a hotrail, I kissed the smoke to Shannon. I had been using crystal all day, but Shannon hadn't. I could see the drugs take hold of Shannon as the two of us sat in the car on the street in the quiet neighborhood. I then opened my other bag. Right there in Shannon's car, the two of us acted out whatever fantasies Shannon wished to do. I was at peak arousal obeying Shannon's wishes. I loved the dynamic between us.

A brief time later, Shannon dropped me off at my Subaru. As Shannon pulled away, I decided I wanted to drive back to the rest stop on the Sunshine Skyway Bridge. I had spent many nights at that rest stop since I arrived in Florida. I put my key in the ignition of the Subaru and turned it...and nothing happened. I tried again; still nothing. I checked under the hood. I adjusted some things. I checked some items inside the car. I turned the key again...nothing.

Half an hour later, I received bad news from Shannon. Her new company had fired her after receiving a bill from the hotel she shared with me in Jacksonville. The bill was a damage and cleaning fee for the hotel room. According to the hotel, eight hundred dollars in damages were accrued; including fees for hair dye in the bathroom and on the towels, as well as ruined sheets and bedding. The company fired Shannon over the phone half an hour after I realized I was no longer mobile in my camper/car. I was stranded in a broken car and suddenly not on good terms with Shannon at the same time.

I sat in my car and stared straight ahead. I knew my life had flipped upside-down. I also knew I wasn't prepared for anything from that moment on. Without a working vehicle, all of my website connections were no longer in reach. Without transportation, my homelessness was suddenly confined to my immediate location.

Fear crept into my mind. I reclined my driver's seat. It moved back two inches. All of my belongings were packed into the camper/car all around me. I sprayed myself with bug spray...

and I went to sleep. Prior to slumbering, my last thought was comforting; one day I would go to sleep and not have to wake up.

Heat, as usual, was what woke me up the next morning. I found my bearings as I remembered that my car no longer worked. I took a deep breath and reached for my drug bag. A couple of hotrails later, and I decided I needed to do something to fix my situation. My car had no cover from the sun. It was morning, and the sun was already cooking the Subaru.

There was a small pond and some trees adjacent to where I was parked. As I relieved myself amongst the trees, I decided which direction I was going to push my car. I could see into the neighborhood. I decided to push my car down the street until I found a location with an overhanging tree to provide shade during the warmest portion of the day.

Within an hour, I was sitting in my car again. Sweat was pouring from me. I was exhausted, but I was in some shade deep into the neighborhood in Westchase. I was parked on the street beneath an overhanging tree. I was surrounded by houses and sidewalks in a normal neighborhood in suburbia. My broken-down, crazy painted, out of state camper/car; a car packed full of all my belongings, stuck out in the normalcy of the neighborhood. The fact that the camper/car was where I currently resided was even more conspicuous.

I knew I was in for a rough time. Life was complicated, and the urgency of the situation was overwhelming. My repeated car hardships continued to accumulate and wear on my psyche. Consistent and excessive drug use, lack of proper sleep, and legitimately being homeless had me slipping further off the edge than ever.

I did some more hotrails of crystal methamphetamine as I took it all in. Moments later, I stepped from my super-heated car into the sunlight of the hot Florida afternoon. Moments after that, I received my first dirty looks from the first of the neighbors who were out walking in the neighborhood.

...

The flowers alongside the walkway in Hassan's front yard were in full bloom. The smell was delightful. Hassan smiled as he stepped outside and basked in the sunlight of the spring afternoon. Mrs. Johnson waved to him as she walked her dog on the sidewalk across the street. Hassan returned her wave, nodding his head towards his neighbor. Birds chirped randomly from the trees. The sky, deep and blue, was free of clouds. Hassan saw neighborhood children riding their bikes in the street a few houses down.

Hassan took a deep breath and stretched his arms above his head. Since he worked from home, he made it a point to step outside for a few minutes every couple of hours for a break and some fresh air. As he stood there on his small cement front porch, he focused on the sight; familiar over the prior two days. His smile slipped, just slightly. As he began to walk into the lawn of his front yard, Hassan asked the same question he had already asked earlier that day.

"Nothing yet?"

The answer came back to him as it had before.

"No. Not yet."

Hassan stood there on his lawn between his house and the street. He scrunched his face into an expression of concern. He turned to walk back inside. He let go of one more sentence as he stepped into his house and shut the front door.

"Let me know if you need anything."

I watched the front door shut. I felt bad, almost a sense of shame, as I picked up my socket wrench and got back to work on my car. Since Hassan first introduced himself to me, he had provided me with food and drinks. He took me to the auto parts store twice to pick up parts which I thought would fix my car. Hassan offered to pay for the parts, but I covered the costs myself. Hassan had even offered to start a neighborhood fund to send me back North and have my car shipped to meet me there. I couldn't grasp the thought of traveling across the country separately from all of my most important and valuable belongings; an entire camper/car full of my life.

I felt anxiety from the hospitality. I felt the only way I could pay back the favors was to get my car running again and out of the street in front of Hassan's house. To that point, my attempts to make good were miserably failing. Though I appreciated the hospitality, I knew I was quickly wearing out my welcome.

I experienced a multitude of reactions while stranded in Westchase. Hassan had been on the far positive end of the spectrum of reactions to my sudden arrival in the quiet Florida neighborhood. Stress was building up in my compromised brain. Each new stressor added to my urgency as I was hit from every angle around me.

In the beginning, the dirty looks were balanced out with waves and greetings from random passers-by. Soon, I noticed odd behavior. It made me uncomfortable. Cars drove past me in my Subaru. As they approached, they slowed down. I saw the occupants of the cars recording videos as they passed. Sometimes I saw neighbors recording videos as they stood outside down the street. Paranoia skyrocketed. Why was I suddenly the focus of videos being recorded by people in the neighborhood? The answer came to me by way of an unusual messenger.

I had just put away my pipe and stepped from my car one afternoon when a man on a bike suddenly skidded to a stop at the front of my car. Startled by the bike rider, I flinched as the man hopped off the bike.

"You're famous around here right now. Two thousand views on the neighborhood group chat in the past two hours. What's your name? I'm Scott."

"Wha...what are you talking about?"

"Sit down and eat lunch with me. My name's Scott. What's your name?"

As Scott sat down on the curb, he handed me a happy meal from McDonald's. Scott had another happy meal for himself. Scott opened his happy meal and began to eat. I cautiously took the food I was offered.

"What, you aren't hungry? Sit. Eat. Your name's Doug, right? Let's get to know each other."

I slowly sat down next to Scott. I thanked him for the food. As I removed a cheeseburger from the colorful box, I cautiously confirmed my name to Scott. I then followed with two questions of my own.

"What are you talking about; I'm 'famous?' How'd you know my name?"

"You're a big deal this week. Here, look. You're the biggest news in the area."

My heart sank as I looked at the phone Scott held in front of me. There it was all up in my face: post after post on the neighborhood's social media page, different views and angles of me and my broken-down camper/car. Pictures and videos, all with hundreds (a couple with thousands) of comments and views. I felt awful. All I wanted was to fix my car and be on my way. I wanted as little attention as possible. I was suddenly and embarrassingly trending as a circus novelty.

As I slowly chewed my food, I read comments on the posts Scott showed me. Some commenters were sympathetic and compassionate. Some were angry and downright awful with their words. I wanted nothing but to disappear as I sat there on the curb in the Florida sunlight. My nightmare paranoia became real life as my tweaked brain tried to process the sudden exposure to so many people at one of the lowest points in my life. It was beyond embarrassing. I was at a loss. Scott saw the mortification on my face, and he quickly tried to find words to put me at ease.

"It's ok buddy. We just want to know what's going on, and we want to help you. Don't pay attention to those negative commenters. They don't know anything."

"Uh…"

"Hassan first posted to the neighborhood group. You told him your story, didn't you? He wanted to see if we could help you out. All us neighbors just want to see you get going again."

I was still frozen without words. Suddenly, I was overflowing with speech at a panicked rate. Words began to spill out in incomplete thoughts and sentences.

"I need to get out of…I need to explain myself…I don't want…I just want to fix my car…"

"It's ok buddy. Add me as a friend. Stay in touch. You'll be alright." Scott handed me the toy from his happy meal. "Here, take mine."

I managed a smile. Scott hopped back on his bike and rode away, waving as he told me that he would see me again soon. I looked at the happy meal toy in my hand, and I felt my eyes water up. I just wanted to leave, and I couldn't. I was stuck right there in the middle of a public humiliation, fully exposed at a low point in life…and some of those people were far from sympathetic.

Scott and I became friends on the social media platform, and Scott accepted my request to join the neighborhood group on the site. I posted on the group's home page. I introduced myself. I explained my travel and how I had broken down. I apologized for being a burden to anyone wishing I was gone. I explained that I meant no ill will…I just wanted to get my car running again so I could be on my way. I soon erased my post and exited the group. I just wished I could disappear. I didn't want the attention at all.

As days went by, people continued to drive by and record video. Some people came by with food and cases of bottled water. Sometimes people even asked for an order from local restaurants and came back from the restaurants to eat with me at my car. A local news reporter attempted to interview me. She then gave me a hundred dollars and picked me up three sub sandwiches from a local sub shop. I was grateful for the help, but it was thoroughly embarrassing.

The dirty looks continued as well. So did visits from police. At one point, two officers bought me lunch and ate with me as they questioned me about my plans to get running again. I was lost. I had no idea what I was going to do. It was an early morning visit from a police officer on day ten when I reached my breaking point. Though the officer was cordial, the message was clear that multiple residents of the neighborhood wanted me gone immediately. When the officer drove away, I went into autopilot. I didn't think, I just acted. I couldn't remain in that situation a single minute longer.

The Nash Equilibrium

There were no clouds in the sky. It was bright outside. It was hot. My car was all the way in the back of the Westchase neighborhood. I hopped into the driver's seat and put the key in the ignition. I switched gears to neutral, and I stepped back out onto the street. With one hand on the steering wheel and the other on the frame of the door, I began to push.

I pushed as I guided the steering wheel. I pushed my car all the way to the other end of the street. I took a break at the turn. I wiped sweat from my face, and I chugged down a bottle of water. Then I pushed some more.

I navigated turns and stopped at stop signs. I ignored the random people who chose to record video instead of help me. I pushed out and around a car which pulled up in front of me to keep me from stopping on a particular length of road. As I pushed my car by myself in the heat, the occupants of the car watched from their air-conditioned seats in their running vehicle. It took extra pushing and steering at the same time to maneuver my way around the car. An hour passed. I kept going. After three other streets of pushing, I reached the far-side entrance to the neighborhood.

The road outside the neighborhood was congested with traffic. It was two lanes in each direction, and the speed limit was forty-five miles an hour. I barely bothered to not get hit as I pushed my car out of the neighborhood and into the traffic. I kept pushing my car in the right travel lane. Cars slowed down and moved over into the other lane to avoid hitting me. My mind was elsewhere. Nobody stopped to help. I continued by myself in the heat for a full eight-tenths of a mile to the first stoplight intersection down the street.

It was then, at the red light of that intersection, that a lady in a car behind me offered her help. I hopped into my Subaru. When the light turned green, the lady pushed my car with her car through the intersection. Barely able to speak from the heat and the activity, I thanked the lady as I began pushing my car again. There was an entrance to a Costco parking lot another quarter mile ahead of me on the right. I didn't make it that far.

Completely exhausted, I only made it to the beginning of the turn lane for the Costco. My body gave out from the heat and exertion. I grabbed a folding chair from the back of my Subaru and managed to walk it over to the grass on the side of the road. I left my car there in the turn lane as I sat in the chair and battled against unconsciousness. I gave up. I didn't have any energy left to push my car the rest of the way. I closed my eyes as I sat in the folding chair in the grass of that field. The sunlight faded to black. The sounds of the traffic on the busy roads, and in the intersection behind me, faded away to silence.

The sound startled me awake. I was lost in a fog of reanimation. The air around me was warm and bright. I was seated in a chair. There was grass under my feet. A shopping complex came into focus in the distance. The noise around me was from traffic. I heard the sound again. That time, I knew what it was. It came from behind me. I stood up and turned around. The source of the sound, as expected, was there in the road behind my broken-down vehicle.

Two police cruisers, with lights flashing, were parked on the street. The officer, the one who used the siren to wake me, stepped from his cruiser to join the other two officers as they talked in the road. I folded up my chair and walked to meet the police as they stood between their cars and the Subaru camper/car. I readied myself to explain my situation again and attempt to garner sympathy and help.

Moments later, from the driver's seat, I guided my car into a parking space at the fast-food restaurant on the corner of the intersection. The police had pushed as I steered the rest of the way in the turn lane, onto the auxiliary road to Costco, and into the parking lot of the restaurant. I thanked the officers for their assistance. Before the police left the scene, one officer pulled out a digital camera and took multiple pictures of my camper/car.

In the moment, I didn't care. I was simply happy to be done pushing my car for the time being. Life was difficult, exhausting, and immediate. I blew down a hotrail of crystal as I sat in my car and rested. I was fully spent. The drugs barely had any effect on me physically, but they helped put my mind at ease. I had no idea what step to take next in my life. Suddenly, the idea came to me. I was going to walk into the restaurant and buy some chicken strips, chicken strips with ketchup and buffalo sauce.

In the middle of the night four nights later, I again sprayed myself with bug spray. The mosquitos were relentless. Though nobody at the fast-food restaurant said anything to me about being parked in their parking lot, the crystal made me as paranoid as ever. I felt exposed. The fast-food restaurant was situated on the corner of the intersection. Anyone who drove by on either of the roads had a clear view into the parking lot, empty except for the very noticeable camper/car. One more hotrail, and I decided I needed to make a change.

In my mind, I planned my route. I was going to push my car across the parking lot, taking a right onto the auxiliary road between the restaurant and the much larger Costco parking lot. Once on the auxiliary road, I would need to take a left about twenty feet farther, and then I could cross the open pavement to reach the parking spaces at the very back of the Costco lot.

I knew the task was about to be extremely challenging. There were three storm drains in the fast-food restaurant's parking lot. The pavement angled down sharply where it led to each drain. I would need enough momentum as I headed toward each dip in the parking lot to then be able to get my car up the opposite side of pavement beyond each storm drain. I would have to steer my car while I pushed it across the lot. Once to the other side, I would need to push the car up the pavement which led to the auxiliary road. While guiding the steering wheel, I would then need to make it over another incline as I turned into the Costco lot.

I set up my phone in the holder hanging down from the center of my windshield. I recorded four hours of attempts to make it across the three storm drains in the restaurant parking lot. Finally, after many attempts, I made it to the auxiliary road. I was pouring sweat. On the verge of passing out, I took a break to do drugs while my car sat between the two parking lots. Half an hour later, my camper/car was lined up in a parking space at the back of the Costco lot. I made it…and I fell asleep almost instantly.

A noise above me woke me up a couple short hours later. The first blues of sunrise began to lighten the sky from the black of night. I looked up through my windshield. I saw the source of the noise. A news helicopter was hovering high above my parked car. Was I hallucinating? Was it the helicopter of the Tampa news anchor who previously gave me a hundred dollars?

I recorded video as I stepped from my car in the early morning darkness. The video I recorded proved to my chemically saturated brain that there had actually been a news helicopter in the sky above me for almost ten minutes. My tactic of recording videos had set my mind at ease. It hadn't been the drugs. It had actually happened. Though my mind was eased by the video proof, my paranoia spiked due to a helicopter hovering above my car for almost ten minutes. Again, I wished for nothing more than to disappear.

A shiny black Cadillac pulled into the parking space next to my Subaru. I waved the smoke from in front of my face, and I stepped out of my car. A kindly older gentleman stepped from the Cadillac with something in his hand. The man handed me a hundred-dollar bill. I thanked the gentleman for his charity.

Three mornings later, I heard another car pull up close to

where I was parked. I peeked through the crack of my window shade and instantly grabbed my drug paraphernalia, stashing it out of sight. I waved the smoke from in front of me as I quickly stepped from my car. I walked to meet the police officer between my Subaru and his cruiser, parked two spaces over. I readied myself to tell my story once again.

My time, after my interaction with law enforcement, was then dedicated to pushing my car to another parking lot. The officer had explained that I needed to be somewhere else besides Costco. I complied. Later that day, I saw Shannon pull up next to me in the parking lot of the small grocery store adjacent to Costco. After I sat down next to Shannon in her car, I explained my situation, what I had been through since I previously lost contact with her. Shannon called a tow truck for me.

...

As summer began in Florida in 2021, I spent three full weeks in a Walmart parking lot. I met the other people who lived in their cars in that same parking lot. I worked on my car. I continued to do drugs and interact with people online. Sometimes, Shannon came to visit me. We shared intimacy in her car after we did drugs. Shannon went shopping for non-perishable groceries with me at the Walmart. Shannon and I were the only two English-speaking people inside the Walmart; I heard no other customers or employees speaking English on any of my visits. Everyone else spoke exclusively Spanish.

I found two grams of crystal in my car one day while sorting through my belongings. I added it to my ever-dwindling supply of methamphetamine. I walked around the strip mall complex when I couldn't stand sitting in my hot car any longer. I shopped at dollar stores, and I ate food from a food truck set up in the Walmart parking lot. I did laundry at the laundromat down the street. Sometimes I pushed my car to different parking spaces. My chemically enhanced and sleep deprived mind was ever paranoid.

I found an auto supply store, and I bought yet another new car battery. I then carried that battery down the street and all the way back across the Walmart parking lot; to the far side space where my car was parked. The battery worked. My car started. I couldn't drive it, though. The previous air intake hose arrangement, the one which I rebuilt and created, caused the car to idle at maximum rpm anytime the car was turned on. Idling in park barely kept the Subaru from uncontrollably lurching forward.

There was a new character in my proximity. Samuel spoke English, so I didn't have the language barrier as an excuse to avoid interaction. Samuel was a White gentleman in his late sixties. Samuel lived in his car in the Walmart parking lot in Tampa, Florida. According to Samuel, he had lived at that Walmart for a full three years when I arrived. I did what I could to keep exchanges with Samuel to a minimum. Patience with Samuel ran thin.

For the first time in days, I managed to fall asleep. The much-needed rest was interrupted. Samuel continued to knock on the window of my car. The knocking continued, even after I pulled down the shade to see who was outside the Subaru in the middle of the night. I flung open the car door. Anger replaced exhaustion as I engaged with Samuel. There was no avoiding that particular interaction. Samuel's sneak conversation attack as I slept required immediate and appropriate countermeasures.

"What? What do you want, Sam?"

"Here, here's some peanut butter and some..."

"You seriously woke me up to give me half a used jar of peanut butter?"

"Yeah, I also have some..."

"I haven't slept all week. Get out of here. I don't want that."

"The tow truck is gonna come back on Tuesday…"

"Sam, get out of here!"

Samuel was right. The tow truck came back on Tuesday. The driver stopped at each long-term vehicle in the shopping center. I was on edge already when the truck pulled up next to my Subaru. I had questions. The driver of the tow truck had answers. From that conversation, stress increased. Paranoia skyrocketed when I heard that the police were going to be cracking down on vehicles that long-term camped in the Walmart parking lot.

Hour by Hour

I had shelter in my car. I had all of my most important items secure with me in my car. The time came. My paranoia won. In the course of one day, I made a series of decisions; each markedly changed my life. Then, like that, I didn't have anything anymore. I lost everything in one day: my car, my belongings… Florida. They were gone.

2AM: Not again. I knew immediately what woke me up. Samuel was still knocking on the glass when I yanked the shade from my car window. Samuel looked startled, and he took a step back from the Subaru when he saw the look on my face.

"Never knock on my window again!"

"But the tow truck is coming for sure tomorrow."

"Sam! Never knock on my window again! If you don't see me outside my car, stay away from my car!"

I angrily put the shade back up in the window of my car. Samuel walked back across the Walmart parking lot towards his own vehicle. My anger was soon replaced with exhaustion. I had only been asleep for an hour when Samuel woke me up. I again fell asleep in my Subaru as sweat covered my body. Sleep was a relief from the hot Florida night.

3AM: Deep in sleep, I hadn't yet begun to dream. The hour passed; uneventful.

4AM: At peace, or as close to it as possible, I half awoke to roll over onto my other side. I was never able to sleep too long in one position.

5AM: The dreams began. Short and intense, their theme was brought on by Samuel's warning. A particular dream had jolted me awake just enough to be free of the particular nightmare. Once back asleep, a new nightmare took over my subconscious. Unrelenting; the nightmares pounded me in my slumber.

6AM: I quickly sat up and the dream disappeared from my mind. Instinctively, I started my car. The engine, at full RPM, shook the car quickly and violently. My body shook with the car and sweat dripped from my shaking body. I hadn't had a single clear thought since I woke. I mashed my foot on the brake pedal and struggled to yank the car into gear.

Even using all my strength to stand and push on the brake pedal, I couldn't hold my car from lurching forward once it was in gear. It took everything I could muster to steer the Subaru and maintain a controlled speed at full throttle. It was as if I were riding a bull. All the power of a full-bore engine was barely held in control on a vehicle wanting nothing more than to open up at the fastest speed possible.

I was fully physically drained in the few seconds it took me to frantically guide and govern my camper/car from its parking space to the dumpsters behind the shopping center. I managed to turn the car off as I collapsed in my seat, out of breath and overheated. That couple-hundred-yard drive was the test. It took all of my strength to maintain control of my Subaru at full throttle, but I managed it.

7AM: I finished the purge of unnecessary items from my vehicle. Anything I absolutely didn't need, or anything I felt I couldn't sell at a pawn shop, I tossed into the dumpsters behind the shopping center. My Subaru was half as packed as it had been before the trip to the dumpsters.

I sat in the Subaru and mentally sorted two items. First, I planned my route. Once I began driving, I knew I wouldn't have any time to make corrections or amendments. Once I was sure of the path to take, I began my next mental preparation. I had to psych myself up. What I was about to do, by any standard, was absolutely insane. I knew it, and I was scared.

There was no turning back once I committed to taking the action. I began a countdown from ten. I stopped at seven. After some deep breaths, I let out a scream as I gripped the steering wheel. I began to count down again. I stopped at four. I sat down in my driver's seat and caught my breath. I needed to mentally regroup. I wasn't ready. The moment was overwhelming. I shook as I prepared to begin the countdown again.

I reached the bottom of ten. As the word "zero" escaped my lips, I turned the key in the ignition of the Subaru. My foot stomped on the brake pedal as the car jumped into drive. My mind exploded as the absolutely most hectic five minutes of my life began right there next to those dumpsters, behind that shopping center, in Florida on a summer morning in 2021.

I couldn't help but let out a scream as the Subaru ripped from park and tore down the pavement behind the shopping center. It was all I could do to turn the wheel enough to stay out of the pond behind the crux at the backside of the shopping center. I managed to swerve around the right angle to continue down the other side, behind the buildings. A couple hundred yards ahead in the distance, the pavement opened up to the six-lane road adjacent to the shopping center. I barely managed to turn the wheel enough to not jump the median once I rocketed out onto the public street. My car was smoking, and the noise was almost unbearable.

Everything shook as I pushed my body from the roof of the car as I stomped, with all my might, continuously on the brake pedal to fight the open throttle. My camper/car screamed down the road, shaking violently as I used all of my strength to barely control the vehicle. I made it eight tenths of a mile down that road. I crossed six intersections of four-way traffic. Three of those intersections had traffic lights which were red; I had no option but to run those red lights and dodge traffic the entire way. I bombed across six lanes, and multiple curbs, to end up in the parking lot of the pawn shop which I had set as my goal. I collapsed into my seat again as I turned off my violently shaking and smoking vehicle. Those couple minutes of traveling, just shy of a mile, were the most extreme moments I had ever experienced.

8AM: It was eight o'clock in the morning when I finally had enough energy to step from my car and walk up to the pawn shop door. The store was closed. I didn't want to sit in that parking lot and wait for the store to open. I prepared myself to fight my car again.

That drive from Walmart to the pawn shop had burned up my transmission. The Subaru only worked in reverse. I drove backward into the neighborhood behind the pawn shop. I crossed two streets. At the third street, I spun the wheel and lurched back to a stop a hundred feet from the stop sign at the intersection; deep into the neighborhood. The car cut off. Birds chirped in the quiet morning air. The sun was well into heating up the day.

9AM: My car was finished. Smoke dissipated from underneath the hood. The smell of burning material was thick in the air. I knew I wasn't going to be driving it any farther than that street in that neighborhood. I emptied out all of the used syringes and garbage drug paraphernalia from one of my safes. I double bagged all of the unneeded drug items and stashed the bag under a seat. I then began sorting out other items from my car. I needed to separate what I wanted to keep, what I wanted to sell, and what I needed to throw away.

10AM: Suddenly, there was a random guy standing right

next to me. Question after question, the guy talked incessantly. There were obvious mental deficiencies. I was extremely suspicious. I had never heard anyone fit the stereotypical mental handicap as perfectly as had that guy. Twenty minutes later, the guy walked down the road to the house where he said he lived.

11AM: Police showed up. It had been a bit since I last told my story to the police. I filled in the female officer; up to the part where I was sorting out items to pawn so I could afford a tow.

12PM: The weird guy came back again and asked more questions. I remained busy sorting through items in my car. My answers became short. My tone became curt. The guy, tired of the interaction, wandered down the road in the direction opposite the house where he said he lived.

1PM: After failing multiple times, I abandoned the idea of making a cart out of floor jacks to pull items to the pawn shop. The wheels were too small. The load was precarious and unstable. I would never be able to pull the floor jacks a quarter mile to the pawn shop. Instead, I unbolted the hood from my Subaru. I tied ratchet straps to the corners of the hood, and I loaded items on top of the improvised sled I had made from my car's hood.

2PM: I wrapped the rope around my midsection. In the heat and sunlight, I pulled the hood along behind me, through the neighborhood, and across the strip of shops facing the main road. The quarter mile of extreme cardio wrecked me physically. A pawn shop employee saw my collapse at the front of the store. She brought me two bottles of cold water. I had trouble drinking the water as I desperately tried to catch my breath, barely on the edge of consciousness.

3PM: The trip was a disappointment. The pawn shop was uninterested in many of the items which I had with me on the hood of my car. The shop wanted fun items like my flame thrower and the drone a friend of mine gave me back in Detroit, but they didn't buy three quarters of the items I had with me. That meant I didn't make much money. It also meant the weight of the items on the car hood was going to prove to be another challenge to drag the quarter mile back to my car.

4PM: I strapped my gun on my ankle. I put my laptop in my backpack, along with my backup drive, and the very little drugs I had left. I made sure my toiletries and small items I frequently used were in my duffle bag. I locked up my car and walked with my backpack and duffle bag back towards the main road to find a restaurant to get some food to eat.

5PM: I sat in the air-conditioned dark of the Jamaican restaurant. I thoroughly enjoyed my meal and drink. It was the first time I had eaten food all day. I appreciated the moment; a relief from all that was going on around me. It was a reprieve from the stress of the day.

6PM: As I turned the corner, my heart dropped. Panic overtook me. No clear thoughts made any sense in my brain. My car was gone. All of my belongings were gone. Suddenly, I had nothing. I no longer had a place to sleep. I no longer had a home. I had the clothes I was wearing, a backpack, a duffle bag, and a handgun. I was alone, without shelter from the weather and the bugs.

7PM: After a brief conversation with a homeowner down the street from where my car had last sat, I walked out of the neighborhood. I then walked, with my duffle bag and backpack, the mile back to the Walmart parking lot.

8PM: All the other cars camped in the Walmart parking lot were still parked in the same spaces. The tow truck never came. Samuel's words had instigated my paranoia, and nothing had come of it for anyone but me: my car and belongings were gone, my home and shelter had disappeared. My clothes, collectables, electronics, everything. I lost the last of my supply of tadalafil; the drug I used to stay hard when crystal interfered with intimacy. I lost flash drives full of videos and pictures, documented memories from my travels. I lost the letters my mom wrote me over twenty-five years, the letters she gave me before she died. I had them in a safe in my Subaru, and they were gone, along with everything else.

9PM: I walked past Samuel's car. I aggressively confronted Samuel. Soon, I decided it wasn't worth it. I insulted Samuel one last time before walking across the parking lot and down another street.

10PM: I found a gas station with a picnic table behind it. I called Lyla. I knew Lyla from the website. We had been in contact for a few years. We had talked frequently about me coming to be with her in San Antonio, Texas when the time was right.

"Lyla?"

"Hi, baby."

"I think the time is right…"

Over the next hour, the two of us caught up with each other on what was going on in each of our lives. Before the phone conversation ended, Lyla and I reached a mutual conclusion. I was going to be with Lyla in San Antonio.

11PM: I fell asleep for an hour under the night sky as I sat on the picnic table behind the gas station.

12AM: I reached out to Lex. I explained my situation in a text message. A half hour passed by as I remained seated at the picnic table. My phone notification went off. Lex sent me money for a bus ticket to San Antonio.

1AM: I booked the bus trip. The bus was scheduled to leave at three o'clock the following afternoon. The bus was set to depart from the bus station in downtown Tampa. I texted Lyla the information. I then set up a ride service to pick me up from the Walmart parking lot and drive me to downtown Tampa at six o'clock in the morning.

Once I finished making arrangements, I stood up from the picnic table behind the gas station. I strapped my backpack over my shoulders and picked up my duffle bag. I then walked a quarter mile across the Walmart shopping center, back to the far side where the ride service was scheduled to meet me five hours later.

The Bus Did

With my backpack as a pillow, I laid on the sidewalk at the very end of the strip mall in the Walmart parking lot. The next hours, I spent in contemplation. I couldn't believe I had lost everything. I was tired, both mentally and physically. I knew I wasn't going to sleep anymore that night. All I could do was lean against the bricks of the strip mall and wait on my ride to whisk me away from the parking lot which I had called home for the prior month. I had no home. I was sad. 2021 had proven hard to navigate. Life was difficult to manage.

The sun came up as I gazed out the back window of the car. The driver suddenly realized he was about to miss his exit. He jerked the steering wheel hard and shot across two lanes of traffic, narrowly avoiding the cement barricade at the top of the interstate exit. I didn't even flinch. I didn't care in the least about what was going on in the world outside my head. I continued to gaze to the Tampa skyline. The car took surface streets on the way to the bus station in downtown Tampa.

It was seven thirty in the morning when I stepped into the bus station. I had almost eight hours ahead of me to wait before I could board my bus to another part of the country. Florida was about to be in my past. Texas was my future. My first ever trip by bus was about to begin later that day. I had time to kill, and I had a plan for how to spend my last hours in Tampa.

I was sore from all the walking the previous day. My backpack and duffle bag, though I was happy I at least had those items with me, were both heavy items to carry everywhere. The straps cut into my neck as I walked. The strain on my back required frequent moments of rest. One block over from the bus station, I found a restaurant.

I took my bags off from around my body and set them in a seat at the only open table in the deli. The restaurant was full. Over half of the customers were police. I left my bags and stepped over to queue up in line. I ordered some food. The lady in line in front of me must have inferred that I was having a difficult day. She bought me breakfast. I thanked her. I sat down and quietly ate my breakfast at the deli in downtown Tampa.

Feeling full and as rested as I could possibly feel in my predicament, I slung my bags over my back and stepped out into the already sweltering summer morning. On the approach with the ride service, I had seen row after row of cars as I gazed out the back window on the drive to the bus station; hundreds of cars filling in underneath bridges in any paved sections of downtown Tampa. I had hours to kill. I decided I may as well see if I could find my impounded Subaru and my belongings.

The hours went by painfully. My neck, back, and feet hurt constantly. The heat of the day was almost unbearable; it radiated from the pavement as I walked up and down the streets downtown. It was a valiant effort, but I never found my car. I stumbled back to the bus station an hour before I was scheduled to leave Florida. Sore and exhausted, I collapsed into a rigid plastic seat inside the bus station.

I listened carefully to make sure I didn't miss my boarding call. I lined up at the proper gate when the announcement came. I handed over my ticket, and I kept my two bags with me when I stepped onto the bus. Sweat poured from my body as I took a seat near the back of the bus. Once the bus began moving, I removed my tattoo equipment from my backpack. As the bus slowly meandered westward down the highways and byways of the Gulf coast of Florida, I tattooed eyeballs on the back of my left hand.

Since I hadn't taken a trip by bus before climbing on the bus in Tampa, I didn't know how the trips worked. I didn't know about the scheduled stops and breaks. I didn't know about the bus switches. I didn't know the difference in time between a bus ride and a car trip. The bus was going to be my home on the journey to San Antonio for the next three days.

Bus vibes were weird. I felt an odd sort of comradery with the others on the bus. We were all on a cross-country trip together. We had a mission; it would end in the middle of Texas, fifty hours and almost two thousand miles after it began. The driver and all us passengers had the same goal in mind; arrive safely in San Antonio with minimal discomfort and issues.

When the bus stopped at certain gas station parking lots, people got off to smoke, buy food, and use the restroom. When the bus pulled into various bus stations, a person or two would step off, other passengers from the station would take their places on the bus. In Mississippi, everyone was required, along with all their luggage, to vacate the bus. An hour later, another bus arrived in the parking lot to carry everyone the rest of the way to Texas. The stops were frequent, the drive was long, but the seats were surprisingly comfortable. It was a unique and interesting experience. I had never known such a scene prior to that first bus trip.

The bus screeched and jerked as the driver applied the brakes when he docked it in downtown Houston. It was the middle of the day, and I could see the heat in the air outside, through the bus windows. Houston was another station where I was going to completely switch to another bus. There was a four-hour layover at the downtown Houston station before the next bus was set to arrive and board.

The food kiosks within security boundaries inside the bus station were all closed. I was hungry. I saw a McDonald's restaurant across the street, through the wall of windows of the bus station. I saw the metal detector I would be required to walk through on my way back into the terminal. I paid it no mind. I figured I could easily get my handgun and a bit of drug paraphernalia back inside despite the security search upon my re-entry. Food was more of a concern in that moment; no way was I waiting to eat for four more hours at the station and however else long I would be on the next bus before the driver stopped for a break.

The heat instantly enveloped me in an uncomfortable embrace. Sweat began to pour from my body as soon as I stepped outside into the day. It was so bright. I had to squint as I continuously wiped sweat from my brow. I guessed Texas was going to be less humid than Florida. I was wrong. I stepped into a literal urban jungle. The extreme moisture in the air made it ever so much worse than if it had been a dry heat.

The next thing I noticed was the absurd number of people all over downtown Houston. There were people congregated in groups smoking cigarettes. There were shady and shifty characters scurrying about the streets and sidewalks. Makeshift tents and tarps sheltered others from the sun. There were sleeping derelicts lined up directly on the cement of the sidewalk, lying across the walkway. As I walked towards the McDonald's, I stepped over four sleeping bums in a row. It was like a sort-of homeless hurdles.

I passed by the armed guard in the McDonald's parking lot. At a glance, I wasn't sure if the guy was security or an actual police officer. When I looked again, I saw he was Houston police. The McDonald's lobby wasn't open to the public. Instead, there was a wooden door fastened in place. The door had a hole cut in it. I changed my mind when I saw the setup. I decided not to hand my last few dollars of cash through the door to possibly get food in return. I passed by the officer again as I left the parking lot.

I was sore again. Carrying my bags around my neck and on my back was hurting my back and neck. I took a second to remove the bags at an intersection and set them on the sidewalk for a brief moment to rest. A guy from across the street walked directly up to me as I stood on the corner to rest. The guy began to talk.

"Hey, buddy. Yo, you got like a dollar I can get from you?"

I was instantly mad. My answer conveyed my anger.

"What? Do YOU have a dollar for ME? You probably have more money than me! How about you give me a dollar? Give me a dollar!"

The guy looked bewildered. He hadn't expected me to reply as I had. The guy held up his hand and apologized as he quickly walked away from me and went about his day. I shook it off, and I picked up my bags again. I walked around the block and weaved through the people of downtown Houston. The look on my face from that point until I reached the door to the bus terminal on the other side of the block went a long way to keep anyone else from approaching me to ask for anything.

As soon as I stepped back into the bus station, I saw that the food kiosks were open for business. I also saw the line ahead of me as people waited to pass through security and the metal detector leading back inside the terminal. The same angry lady was on point as she searched through bags at the metal detector. I waited as the line moved closer to the checkpoint.

I lucked out as I reached the metal detector. The security lady, as soon as my non-problematic bag reached her, got tossed a question from someone already through the detector. I slid my hot bag through to the other side as I walked through the metal detector. I quickly put my backpack on my shoulders as the security lady was distracted and pointing to something on the other side of the terminal; answering the question of the other commuter.

The lady searched through my other bag as her interaction with the commuter came to an end. I could see in her eyes that she knew something was amiss. She couldn't pinpoint what it was, and she handed me my bag once she finished the search. I walked away from her as I put my duffle bag over the strap to my backpack on my right shoulder. I smiled as I walked across the terminal to the pizza stand.

After all that hassle outside the terminal and coming back inside, I bought a pizza just twenty feet from where I had stepped off the bus two hours prior. After I ate, I patiently waited until my next bus arrived, unloaded, and was then ready to re-board. I smiled as I sank down into my seat on the crowded bus to San Antonio. I recorded video from the window. Houston became smaller behind the departing bus.

Angel Lust

As the bus pulled into downtown San Antonio, I took my phone from my pocket. I sent Lyla a text. The San Antonio bus station occupied a large building in the middle of downtown. I walked through the terminal, and I stepped outside into the hot Texas sunlight. When I found a bench on the sidewalk, I took my bags off of my shoulders and sat down. Again, sweat poured, and I continuously wiped my eyes and face.

Fifteen minutes later, Lyla pulled up in front of the bench. I gathered up my bags and loaded them into the back of Lyla's car. I hopped into the passenger seat of Lyla's PT Cruiser. When I looked over at Lyla, she was already smiling as she gazed back at me. I asked a question as I smiled back.

"What?"

"You look exactly as you do online. I'm so happy!"

"Did you think I was catfishing you? We've video talked a hundred times…"

"I'm just happy that you are who I hoped you would be. Are you hungry?"

"Absolutely. I haven't eaten since Houston."

"Well, I know a great place to pick up tacos. It's on the way home."

"Bet. That's my favorite food."

I hadn't bathed in a month. I apologized to Lyla for possibly smelling offensive from the past month I spent in my car. Lyla said I smelled fine. She confirmed that I had no smell at all. I had wondered if, after a certain point, the bacteria on skin reaches a homeostasis. I noticed, after the first week of not bathing, that the smell of sweat seemed to disappear. I wasn't sure if I had gotten used to the smell of sweat or if that homeostasis was an actual thing. Lyla confirmed the latter. She told me that I could relax while she bathed me once we got back to her house. Lyla also informed me that she owned a massage table.

Freshly bathed and massaged, I began my clean life as a Texas resident. I was clean from drugs as well. I had run out of crystal just before boarding the bus in Tampa earlier in the week. That was about to change, though. Lyla had a crystal habit of her own. Lyla wanted to get high before she had sex with me. A slight smile crept onto my face when I noticed Lyla was trying to bring up the subject of introducing drugs to our dynamic. Usually, it was me attempting to broach the subject. I welcomed the situation with open arms.

"I thought you'd never ask."

Though it had only been a few days drug free, a wave of relief washed over me when I realized Lyla wanted to do drugs. A bigger wave of relief washed over me when Lyla pulled out a shoe box of supplies from under her bed. Lyla didn't just have the urge to do drugs, she didn't just have the equipment with which to do the drugs, she had the drugs. Lyla's shoe box contained multiple pipes, a few razor blades, a mirror, and no less than four separate bags of crystal.

From the time I ran out of drugs in Florida earlier in the week, I wondered when I would next have the opportunity to get high. The opportunity was there in Lyla's bedroom as the two of us sat naked on Lyla's bed and prepared our works. Lyla loaded an oil burner pipe. Her preferred route of administration was smoking. I lined up a big pile of crystal on the mirror using a razor blade. I was going to use another oil burner as a hotrail stem by heating the tube end with a torch and putting the bubble end up to my nostril.

"Watch this."

Lyla's eyes widened and her mouth dropped open slightly as I exhaled the hotrail.

"That's the most smoke I've ever seen…"

"I told ya. Dragon smoke. I'm f'n lit!" My body began to tingle as I spoke.

"Good. Now, come here. We have bedroom promises to keep to each other."

Lyla was a top. She climbed on top and took me from behind. I felt the firmness of her large silicone breasts against my back as the two of us rhythmically moved together. I was feeling wonderful in the moment. I was happy to be back on crystal again after the multi-day break from the drug. Everything else was inconsequential.

Lyla worked as a volunteer at a local youth center during the weekdays. Thursday through Saturday nights, Lyla worked as a performer at a show bar. Lyla also worked brunch hours at a different show bar each Sunday. I had a lot of time to myself, which I filled with work of my own. Fueled by crystal, I worked around the clock most days. I taught myself as I went. I learned with Lyla's home as my canvas.

For a full month, I gave my all to the task at hand. Lyla

bought supplies and gave me freedom to be as creative as I wished within some broad guidelines and stipulations. I had never before remodeled a home, but the time and place was right: Lyla's mobile home in a San Antonio trailer park in the summer of 2021.

The project began outside. In the awful heat and nearly one hundred percent humidity, I swung a hammer into bricks for hours to create the material needed for a rock garden around the entire trailer. The kitchen and dining room were completely remodeled. A floor was replaced in one of the bedrooms and in the living room. Two other bedrooms were combined into one large dressing room/closet. I barely slept. I worked through all hours, day and night. I took breaks to get high and video interact. At the end, I was proud of the work I had done. At the end, Lyla and I were barely on speaking terms. At the end, Lyla bought me a bus ticket.

...

The San Antonio scenery passed by as I gazed out from the passenger side window of Lyla's car. Not much was said on the half-hour ride from Lyla's house to the show bar downtown. It was still light outside, but the sky had that beginning darkness as the evening began. I wasn't focused on anything outside as Lyla drove down the congested interstate highway. It was my last evening in San Antonio. My thoughts weighed heavily on me as memories of 2021 played out in my mind. My eyes began to water. I felt a disbelief for what had become of my life. Texas, like Florida, was about to be behind me. 2021 was only halfway over. I silently sulked as I rode with Lyla on the interstate highway.

Lyla was scheduled to perform two shows at the downtown show bar. I waited in Lyla's car as she went inside the club for two hours. I was fine with the time alone. I cracked the windows in the car, and I thought about life while sitting in that parking lot in downtown San Antonio, Texas. Much had gone wrong. I lost control of my life a while back. I was fine with it when I was at the high points. Those high points had been washed away with the memories of times no longer tangible.

I felt scared as I wondered what came next. Each time I thought things were going to turn around for the better, they somehow managed to become worse. When I thought I had nothing left to lose, I found I was able to lose more. Each time I thought I had nothing left, I was pushed down to a new bottom where I dragged along at the lowest point.

It was ten o'clock at night when Lyla pulled into the parking lot across the street from the bus station. I gathered up my small amount of belongings and stepped from the PT Cruiser. Though happy to be away from the tension I felt anytime I was in Lyla's presence, I suddenly felt fully exposed and vulnerable to the world around me. Again, I was truly homeless. In two hours, I was about to begin another trip across the country.

Like my first bus ride from Florida to Texas, I wasn't going to be in control of anything: not the stops or the route, not the people with me or the time the trip took. I was again putting my faith in fate; I was going to literally be along for the ride. As I stepped from the darkness of the San Antonio night, into the surprisingly crowded bus terminal, I felt I had reached a particularly low point in life. I was alone. I was about to cross the country alone.

Earlier in the week, I took my friend Jane up on an offer which I realized she had made in haste one night after a couple of drinks. My experience renting a room from Jane when I left my house at the end of 2018 had been a mutually positive situation. Jane had recently offered me a place to stay when I explained to her that my time at Lyla's house in Texas had run its course.

A couple of days later, I wasn't sure Jane's offer stood when I discussed with her how I had a bus ticket to Toledo. In retrospect, I realized Jane had probably invited me back to her house while intoxicated after an evening at the bar. I had no other options in that moment, so I stayed on course and let Jane know to expect me within a week.

I sat in the bus terminal and contemplated all which had gone wrong in Texas. I had again reached a new rock bottom. The steps downward were blatant and clearly visible in retrospect. I found where my car was being held in impound, but I had no means to get back to Florida to recover my belongings. Everything was gone forever; forfeited to a destiny of loss.

My dynamic with Lyla progressed as had other dynamics in my life. I lost interest in intimacy, and I closed off emotionally. I distanced myself and retreated into myself, sleeping in a separate room and avoiding interaction with Lyla by busying myself constantly with the remodeling of Lyla's home. Lyla and I seemed to avoid each other, which was difficult to do inside of a mobile home.

Without a vehicle, I spent all of my time at Lyla's house. Tension and resentment built on both sides of the dynamic. The month I spent in San Antonio felt so much longer. While stranded in my car in Florida, I still felt a sense of freedom. In Texas, I felt all I did was at the mercy of another. I kept my head down, and I focused on my work on the house. Despite feeling lost and alone, I felt some relief as I sat at the bus terminal and waited to begin yet another chapter of my life.

I thought of something else as I sat at the bus terminal in downtown San Antonio. I had one twenty-ounce bottle of water with me. That was fine; I could keep it and refill it at different stops along the way. I had two granola bars with me. That was all the food I had. I also had no money at all.

The bus trip, with all stops and layovers, was going to take four days. I knew I was in a bad spot with regard to food. What I didn't know was how things were going to be worse than I could have ever imagined…far worse. I thought my second bus trip across the country was going to progress without incident. Already at a low point, I figured I was due for some good fortune. I had no idea how much farther down I could go. 2021 had shown me hardship and tribulation…and I hadn't seen anything yet.

Vast Difference

I jerked awake. A moment later, my thoughts came online. The events of the previous five minutes played out in my brain. My eyes opened wide, and my jaw dropped open. I ran. I ran from the bathroom. I ran through the store. I ran out into the parking lot and froze. The parking lot was empty.

"Oh, no! NO!"

The sun was just beginning to rise. I stared across the parking lot; eyes wide and jaw hanging open. By leaps and bounds, my life had instantly become much, much worse. I never imagined that moment even being a possibility. I had sat in pity for myself back at the bus terminal in San Antonio three days earlier. I thought I had it bad while I was still in Texas. I never imagined the possibility which then became my reality three days down the road.

I replayed the events of the previous five minutes as I frantically searched for a phone number in my phone. Those prior events played out, step by step, like a horror movie in my brain. Though my thoughts were all over the place, those previous five minutes of activity were clear and concise; it was as if fate was taunting me with clarity and awareness.

-I jerked awake; it had been the sound of the bus as it stopped in the parking lot of a Love's truck stop in central Illinois which woke me up.

-Due to exhaustion, I acted without thinking when I

awoke to the bus's brakes.

-The situation failed to register since I was barely awake; I wasn't at a scheduled bus stop, but rather a short stop for just the driver to exit the bus early in the morning.

-I grabbed my bag, I pushed past the gate on the bus, and I wandered into the bathroom at the truck stop. Nobody else from the bus was inside the truck stop.

-As I sat in the bathroom, the realization that I had just messed up hit me the second I was awake enough to comprehend my situation. That was when I ran from the bathroom.

The driver of that bus had taken over somewhere in the Midwest a day prior. She was a stern older woman who specifically mentioned multiple times that she wasn't going to wait for anyone at stops. She absolutely proved her point that morning in Kankakee, Illinois. To make matters worse, she had forced me to store my duffle bag in a compartment underneath the bus earlier, when it first departed. She told me that I was alright with the backpack, but the duffle bag was too large for the seats. It was the first time I was made to check either of my bags. The bus had left me in the dust...and it had taken my duffle bag to Chicago without me.

I was hungry. I hadn't eaten since that last granola bar two days prior. In that moment, I didn't care about that. I tried and tried, but I could not reach anyone to get in contact with that bus driver. Though I had already lost everything before that morning, I somehow managed to lose half of the nothing I had hung onto. Again, I reached a new low; one which I hadn't thought possible until it happened. I was alone in the middle of nowhere with nothing; no food, no money, no transportation, and no plan to survive the day.

My duffle bag had been full of what little I had left to my name; toiletries, some clothes Lyla had bought me in Texas, a digital scale which doubled as a power bank for charging my cell phone, some various adult novelties which managed to outlast the loss of my car, my old, expired driver's license, and a container of foot powder. The container of foot powder had something inside it; I had placed a small plastic bag in it prior to beginning the bus trip from Texas to Ohio. The plastic bag had almost an eightball of crystal inside of it. My duffle bag was gone.

I still had my backpack. Fortunately, other items weren't lost when the bus left me in the middle of Illinois. My backpack had my laptop, my phone, my tattoo equipment, my handgun, and a glass oil burner. The pipe had a melted gram of crystal inside of it. I still had drugs. I walked back inside the truck stop. I locked myself in a stall in the bathroom and pulled out the oil burner. I heated the glass bubble with a small torch, and I got high on crystal as I attempted to evaluate my current situation. I was in trouble, and I knew it.

Kankakee, Illinois wasn't a big city at all. It was a rundown town in the middle of Midwest farmland. That meant there wasn't even a real bus terminal. I sorted out the situation, and I received some information on how to proceed. The "bus station" was ran from a seedy hotel across the city. The "bus station" was closed until mid-day. There was a local route that the city buses circled. The first bus was due to stop by the bus stop a quarter mile down the road from the truck stop in forty-five minutes. I packed up my drug paraphernalia and began to walk. I needed to get on the local bus so I could get to the bus hotel across the city when it opened later in the day.

I also began the frustrating and arduous process of reaching customer service for the bus line, explaining my situation, and being put on another bus to Chicago. I realized something else in that moment; once in Chicago, I will already have missed my next bus to Toledo. I put that dilemma on the backburner, and I focused on guaranteeing a bus from the middle of nowhere.

As I rode local buses around the city, as I randomly got off at bus stops in various locations to walk around, I began to sort out my situation with the bus line. I had to speak with multiple people to try to find who could secure me a trip from Kankakee to Chicago. Frustration built as I repeated my story to each person they transferred me to. I hated everything about that morning in that city where I had been dropped. I hated being hungry.

I hated that customer service wasn't sure if I had been left behind or kicked off the bus due to bad behavior. I hated circling the city with nowhere to go. I hated being yelled at by some redneck lady for not wearing a mask on one of the local buses. I hated being told that the only bus out of Kankakee to Chicago wasn't until six o'clock in the evening. I hated life as I wandered through shady places and did my best to avoid interactions with shady people.

The hotel, which doubled as a bus stop in the evenings, also doubled as a den of drugs and prostitution. I spent most of the afternoon watching customers and suppliers go in and out of various rooms at the rundown hotel. I was thankful that I had my handgun. I fully expected someone to try to separate me from my backpack, but that situation never materialized.

My next bus, the bus to Chicago, showed up forty-five minutes late. At seven o'clock in the evening, twelve hours after being left in Kankakee, I departed from the hotel in the middle of nowhere. I settled in for the next couple of hours. I had new bus tickets. They were confusing to me, but I figured I knew where to get off and where to board the next bus in Chicago. Yes...I knew which stop.

Well...I had a fifty-fifty shot at it. I knew it was the current terminal or the next one. Both were in downtown Chicago. I knew I needed to be at the main terminal downtown. When the bus stopped at what appeared to be a main terminal, I grabbed my bag and stepped off with ten other people.

The bus pulled away from the stop. It joined the traffic pattern with multiple other buses, pulling out into the congested Chicago city traffic. People were everywhere. It was the opposite of the scene in Kankakee. I began to realize a terrible fact as I wandered through the sea of pedestrians; though I was for sure in Chicago, I had gotten off at the wrong bus terminal. A whole new world of problems opened up for me that evening in downtown Chicago.

For a half hour, I split my time between reading bus maps on the walls in the outside heat of summer and wandering through the underground terminal to find anyone who could help me find my bearings. At the bottom of some cement steps, there was a metal cage-style gate which led into the Chicago subway system. Guarding the gate was a female Chicago police officer. I told my story to the officer, and she took pity on me.

Since I had no money, the officer bought me an all-expenses-paid trip on the Chicago subway. She even took the time to write down the three locations where I needed to switch trains. The officer explained where my subway journey was going to end and where I would need to walk to reach the main bus terminal in another part of downtown Chicago. I almost cried as I thanked the officer for her help. She wished me luck as I headed through the metal gates and into the massive and crowded subway system of Chicago, Illinois.

After the train rides and the multi-block walk through downtown, I waited in a line inside the main Chicago bus terminal. Once I reached the worker at the front of the line, I again told my story. It was already past the time my connecting bus to Ohio had departed the station. I needed to find my duffle bag and secure a new trip to Ohio.

I secured a new trip. I found out I was about to spend the night in the bus terminal in downtown Chicago. My new bus was scheduled to arrive at six o'clock in the morning. My duffle bag was not recovered in Chicago. Employees suggested it could be waiting for me when I reached Toledo. I doubted I would ever see it again.

I settled in at the crowded bus terminal. The metal seats were too uncomfortable for me to sleep. The noise from the crowd in the bus station was excessive. On two separate occasions through the course of the night, police had to break up fist fights amongst the commuters in the terminal. I knew I wasn't going to sleep, so I locked myself in a bathroom stall and smoked crystal for a short while. I carefully blew the smoke into a handful of toilet paper after each hit, and I felt chemically refreshed from the drug consumption.

At six o'clock the next morning, I took my place in the proper line to wait to board the bus to Toledo. A half an hour later, I was on a seat in the back of the bus. That bus, unlike all the previous buses, was only half full. I was the only person in the back half of the bus. It was a relief to have some room to myself. I was on the last bus of my multi-state trip from the bottom to the top of the country, and I had just a few hours before I would arrive in Ohio.

I engaged with one of the females from the website as the bus drove between Chicago and Gary, Indiana. The two of us had shared a sexual dynamic during the previous three years. As the two of us interacted, I considered the fact that I was the only person in the back half of the bus. The woman encouraged me to act on it. I complied. As the bus passed from Illinois to Indiana, I recorded video as I used my hand to climax while I sat on the bus. I sent the video. It was met with approval.

I cleaned myself up and sat back for the remainder of the bus trip. It had been almost a week since I left Texas. I was hungry, frustrated, and exhausted. I was stressed from the events along the way. I was worried about my missing duffle bag, and I was worried for what was about to become my life the moment I stepped from the bus in Toledo.

When I left the Midwest at the beginning of the year, I was full of hope and optimism. On my return, I was broken; I had lost my vehicle, my home, and almost all of my belongings I traveled the country with. I had lost my freedom to go where I wanted when I wanted, to do what I wished when I wished. I had lost all my money, and I was again almost out of drugs.

I was in a bad spot, and I no longer looked forward to the future. Instead, I feared more bad luck. Each time I thought I had hit rock bottom; I somehow went down lower. I was scared to think of what could be lower than my current situation. I learned I was never truly at rock bottom. I knew things could always get worse. That much had been proven multiple times.

Another Life, Another Time

The familiar scenery outside the window of the bus weighed heavily on my mind. A sense of sadness and defeat washed over me as the bus made its way down Broadway in south Toledo. Though the scenery was familiar from a life long gone, the situation was new. I remembered being in the car with my parents and sister as we drove down Broadway when I was a child. My grandparents, my father's parents, lived on a street four miles away from the Toledo bus terminal. Their house, where my father was raised, was visible from Broadway. Holidays were spent with my extended family at that house near the other end of Broadway in Toledo.

I was alone on the bus as it pulled into the terminal on that sweltering summer day in Toledo, Ohio. As I thought back to my childhood, I felt memories of a life with which I no longer had any connection. My mom had died ten years prior. Except for that time when I stopped at my dad's house before I left for Florida at the beginning of 2021, I had no interaction with my father in the years prior. I last spoke with my sister back in 2020, while I was in Colorado. She had her own life hundreds of miles away from Ohio.

Though my grandfather on my dad's side had passed away, my grandmother still lived four miles away at the other end of Broadway in south Toledo. I thought about what I was going to do as the bus unloaded, and I stepped into the terminal. My first order of business was to again attempt to recover my duffle bag of belongings. Once I thought beyond that task, I came to a conclusion; I had no other immediate option but to walk the four miles through south Toledo to my grandmother's house.

As I had assumed, my bag was not at the Toledo terminal. It hadn't made it to Ohio to await my arrival. There was no sign of it anywhere. The Toledo terminal contacted the Chicago station; it still hadn't shown up there. Toledo took my information, and the manager of the bus station assured me that he would contact me if it showed up. I knew I wouldn't be hearing from them. I knew my bag was gone forever. Later, I figured I would have to make a complaint to the bus company.

With backpack on my shoulders and handgun strapped to the shoulder strap of the backpack, I stepped out into the hot sunlight in south Toledo. I began to walk. I was sore and tired, hungry and depressed. As sweat dripped into my eyes and soaked my clothing, I mentally prepared for a four mile walk in the heat of summer. I had no other option; I walked. The scenery, though familiar, was completely different. The buildings I had seen so many times before, they all seemed foreign to me. For the next couple of hours, I walked down a street which I had been down many times before but never in the way I existed in that moment. My old life was long gone. My current life was precarious and uncertain. I walked.

Around the corner of the cross-street, right before the viaduct, the house still looked as it had lifetimes ago. The front porch was glassed in. I was probably around ten years old when the porch was enclosed. There were three cement steps leading up to the thin glass door on the front of the porch. I stepped up and knocked on the door. I waited. I didn't see any movement inside. I knocked again. That time, the knocking elicited a response from inside the house.

I hadn't seen my grandmother in years. I was slightly surprised to see her approaching the door on an electric scooter. The surprise wore off fast; she had always been a larger woman. The scooter made sense. I smiled as my grandma unlocked the door and pushed it open. Having no clue if I was close to recognizable, I spoke to that effect.

"Hi Grandma, it's Doug...Joe and Marie's son."

Upon receipt of those words, recognition crossed my grandmother's face. She smiled at her grandson. She invited me inside. I was thankful for the hospitality. Soaked in sweat and exhausted, I collapsed on the floor next to a chair in the living room; my backpack dropped alongside the chair. Observing my current state, my grandmother offered me food. She told me of items in the kitchen refrigerator. Though I was exhausted from the walk in the heat, my hunger far outweighed my exhaustion. I quickly headed to the kitchen.

Back on the floor in the living room, halfway through my second sandwich, someone walked in the front door. It was my aunt. I waved as I chugged down a glass of juice. My aunt and uncle lived a few houses down from my grandma. My uncle was at work, but my aunt stopped by after grandma called to let her know that I was there. I saw relief in my aunt's eyes when she recognized me. She had stopped over to be sure that it really was me who showed up out of nowhere that summer day in 2021.

Another half of a sandwich, a bowl of chips, and a second glass of juice later, my aunt stood up to head back home. She was happy I was alright after my recent ordeal, and she was glad to see me again after years apart. The two of us hugged, and my aunt told me that she hoped to see me again soon. She let me know one more thing on her way out the door.

"I let your uncle Rich know you were here. He told me to tell you he will be over once he's off work. Love ya."

Once my focus returned to my grandma, I saw she was on the phone. The land line phone was on a table, next to a lamp in the opposite corner of the living room. Grandma, still seated in her scooter, had the phone up to her ear. It only took a few seconds before I knew who was on the other end of the phone. My grandma then spoke a sentence into the phone which confirmed I had been correct in my assumption.

"Joey, he doesn't have anything…"

My mood switched. I knew what was being discussed, and I knew I had been right about something back in January when I stopped over at my dad's house on my way to Florida. I had no agenda back then, and I had no agenda as I sat on my grandma's living room floor months later. I was tired, exhausted, and lost. I knew I had been within walking distance when I departed the bus station in Toledo earlier that afternoon. I had no other options. I decided to stop over at my grandma's house.

In the moment I heard my grandma speaking with my dad on the phone, I knew my dad was not anymore connected to my life in any way. I had seen disappointment in my dad's face back in January. I felt disappointment in my own heart that summer day as I sat on the floor at my grandma's house. I hadn't asked my grandma for anything, but I knew my dad was on the phone with her, telling her not to give me anything. I saw my grandma reach the phone out to me. I stood up and walked over to take the phone from her.

"I'm not here trying to get money. I had nowhere else to go."

"What happened? You said you were on your way to Florida."

As I had done many times in the previous couple of days, I told my story. I spoke of what had happened since January. I explained hardships and disappointment. I conveyed the details of my journey to that point in 2021. I also spoke of the positives, such as my discovered ability for home renovation, which I put to work successfully in Texas.

My dad, as figured, remained stuck on the point that I needed to get a job. I expressed that I understood, but what happened had happened. There was no changing the past, and job advice for the future wasn't going to fix my current situation. I knew my dad had zero insight into my life and who I was as a person. The conversation went in a direction which showed me that my dad was done with me in this life.

"Do not ask your grandma for money."

"What are you talking about? I told you I don't want anything from her." I turned to face my grandma. I spoke to her. "Grandma, I don't want anything from you."

The phone conversation ended. I hung up the phone. I knew my thoughts back in January had been accurate. That conversation confirmed it. My mom was long gone. My dad was long gone as well.

"Sorry about that, grandma. I seriously don't want anything from you."

"It's ok, hon. Rich should be able to give you a ride wherever you need to go once he gets home from work."

A half hour later, my uncle Rich walked into the house. Rich and I hugged. The two of us caught up for a bit. Rich offered to give me a ride. I accepted the offer. I had an idea. My uncle insisted that I take the cash he had on him; forty dollars. I accepted the money and thanked my uncle for the help. After I hugged my grandma goodbye for the last time, I hopped into Rich's car. The two of us hit the road.

"So, where am I takin' ya?"

"Head to Perrysburg."

I felt a lump form in my throat. I typed out a text message. I knew the situation wasn't ideal, but I had no other option. Yes,

Jane had previously told me that I was welcome to come stay with her again. I knew, deep down, that Jane had only made that offer on a superficial level. I wasn't comfortable making good on the offer...but it was all I had.

Surface Knowledge and Delusions

Amongst the gridded country roads, crisscrossing the farm fields on the outskirts of Perrysburg, I was again back at Jane's house. The scene in summer of 2021 was a far cry from my experience in the winter of 2018/2019. I had no room of my own; I slept on the couch. Without a car, I no longer came and went as I pleased. No longer being immersed in the drug game, I had no money, and no money was coming in. My life had come full circle; flushed down a death spiral. Life, in the same place, was so much different.

Three quarters of a mile down one road, a right turn, and another mile down another road was the entrance to my storage unit complex. The road, the first road from Jane's house, had only fields of crops along the way. The second road, once past the railroad tracks and police station, had more fields with random warehousing and industry on both sides. The speed limit on both of the roads was fifty-five miles per hour.

Traffic was sparse on the first country road, the road leading from Jane's house. Traffic was heavy on the second road leading to the storage complex; it was the main thoroughfare between Perrysburg and smaller rural cities to the east of the metro Toledo area. There were deep runoffs and ditches running alongside the roads. There were crops, mostly corn and soybeans, in the fields; fields which were cut into square grids by the country roads.

The walk back and forth was unpleasant; the heat from the pavement burnt the bottoms of my shoes. Due to traffic, especially on that second road, much of the walking was spent navigating the uneven gravel and bumpy ground between the pavement and the steep drop-offs into the ditches. The excursions were further complicated by anything I carried with me, either to, or from my storage unit.

Jane worked every day; she already seemed put out by my presence. I never asked for a ride. I chose to walk each time i felt the need to visit the storage unit. I spent many hours of each visit sorting through my storage unit in an attempt to locate items of need and items I could sell for any sort of money. My time at the storage unit was also a relief from the tension I felt. Tension was building the longer I remained at Jane's house.

On a hot summer day in the first week of July, my shoes wore out from all the walking through the farmland on the outskirts of Perrysburg. By late afternoon, I had walked close to fifteen miles that day. As I walked back towards Jane's house, down the busy road from my storage unit, a police cruiser pulled up and stopped in front of me. After a brief conversation, I hopped in the cruiser and took a ride another mile down the road and into the city limits of Perrysburg. The fields around me were replaced with strip malls and the large stores of the city. I thanked the officer for the ride and got back to walking again.

I came across the parking lot of the Kroger grocery store. I had a few dollars, so I walked into the store and bought a small box of fried chicken. Instead of then walking the two miles back to Jane's house, I decided to rest on a picnic table outside of the store and eat the chicken.

As I sat and ate, I noticed my ex-wife walking from her car to the store. I didn't say anything as she walked inside. It was the first time I had seen her in years. I was happy to see that she looked well. Moments later, she left the store and walked back to her car. Again, I said nothing. She drove away. She hadn't noticed me. I sat and ate the rest of my chicken. I threw away the box once I finished eating.

I walked around to the other side of the Kroger entrance. I bought a cigar from the gas station on the side of the Kroger. I sat at the picnic table between the gas station and the store entrance. I lit the cigar. It was the first I had used any tobacco since back when I began using crystal meth. Since I was no longer on crystal, the desire to use tobacco had returned.

I squinted my eyes. Was that Jane? I saw the silver car pull up and stop at the curb in front of the store. Was Jane there to pick me up and give me a ride back to her house? I saw the blonde ponytail, worn on top of the driver's head, exactly the way Jane wore her hair. It had to be her. I could see that I was being waved over to the car. It was her. I was saved. I didn't have to walk two more miles in the heat to get back to Jane's house. I was rescued.

I reached for the door handle of the car. That was when I saw it. The car wasn't Jane's car. The driver of the car was not Jane. What was going on? Confused, I leaned down to look into the open passenger window of the car. The driver of the car was a pretty, blonde-haired girl in her early twenties. I began the exchange of words.

"Oh, man. I thought you were my friend Jane. You have the same car. Your hair looks exactly like hers…"

The girl was intoxicated on something, I could see it before she even replied. "Is there an ice cream place around here? I'm supposed to meet some friends at an ice cream place around here."

"That's why you waved me over? I thought you were my friend, here to pick me up."

The conversation progressed. A moment later, I was in the passenger seat of Alyssa's car, thanking her for giving me a ride. The situation blew my mind; a girl who looked just like Jane, in a car which looked just like Jane's car, had motioned me over to her car. I was then riding with a complete stranger back to Jane's house, the same as I would have been doing if it were actually Jane who stopped to pick me up at Kroger.

Alyssa pulled into Jane's driveway. Jane pulled up right after Alyssa, and she waited in her matching car in the street while Alyssa and I exchanged phone numbers. Alyssa did drugs, as I assumed upon first speaking with her. Alyssa did drugs, and the two of us planned to hang out in the near future. I thanked Alyssa for the ride, and I looked at Jane as I stepped back from Alyssa's car. Jane looked annoyed that she had to wait to pull into her own driveway. Alyssa pulled out to leave, and Jane pulled in her driveway to park.

"Who was that? She was messed up. I was behind you guys the whole way down the road, and she was swerving all over the place."

"Her name's Alyssa. I just met her. I wouldn't have even met her if I hadn't thought it was you. That was so weird."

Evergreen

I stared at the words on my phone as I sat alone in Jane's living room. Jane was back at work after her lunch break that afternoon. Since Jane had stopped back at her house that day for lunch, I had been waiting for it; I could tell. Then, the message came through.

"Dude, I'm sorry. You have to go."

I made a phone call. Jacob and I had been in random communication while I traveled the country, but my focus had been on travel, new dynamics, and drugs. When I returned to northwest Ohio in the summer of 2021, I reached out to my old friend Jacob. When Jane gave me the boot, I reached out to Jacob again.

I needed help, and Jacob offered to come pick me up from Jane's house in Perrysburg. Jacob showed up to Jane's house before Jane got back from work that afternoon. I grabbed my belongings. Jacob helped me carry a couple of my bags out to the car.

Though I was close with Jacob, I knew he wasn't right in the head. I had always listened as Jacob went on about all sorts of delusions of grandeur. Upon reconnection in the summer of 2021, I listened as Jacob picked up where he had left off. As Jacob drove the two of us from Perrysburg to Toledo, the familiar diatribe flowed from his mouth. I sat back and listened. I didn't have the energy to add to the conversation.

Three tumultuous days went by as I stayed with Jacob. The two of us took trips to pawn shops so I could attempt to sell items from my storage unit. I managed to make enough money to have my storage unit bill paid for the next month and the unit subsequentially unlocked again so I could regain access. I sorted out more items for sale. The pawn shops around Toledo weren't biting. I tattooed my hand in Jacob's basement while he argued with his sister and parents upstairs in the house. I slept two nights in Jacob's car as it was parked in the street in front of his house. The entire situation was stressful. I knew I needed to figure out something else. Jacob's mental state, as always, was very unstable. Jacob's moods switched instantly and frequently. He was unpredictable and slipping farther off the deep end of sanity.

On that third day with Jacob, I knew my time was done. The two of us returned to west Toledo after I rode along to a metro park on the Maumee River where Jacob "needed" to test out his new electric skateboard. The skateboard arrived that morning at Jacob's house; much to his delight. Though I tried my best to understand the importance of the skateboard to Jacob's plans of infamy, I only understood two points of the diatribe he spewed to me on the ride: the skateboard was somehow going to complete Jacob's martial arts training, and that was going to lead him to internet domination. Jacob didn't even use crystal.

As Jacob drove me and my two suitcases' worth of belongings down Alexis Road in west Toledo, his mood instantly changed to aggressive and confrontational. It came out of nowhere. The two of us had been talking peacefully as we rode in the car back towards Jacob's house. Suddenly, I realized his paranoid delusions were in control. As Jacob began yelling about kicking me out of the car, I calmly thanked him for helping me out over the prior three days. I tried to diffuse the situation, but Jacob continued to become angrier and more irrational. I guessed what was coming before it happened. I knew Jacob would never be violent towards me, but I also knew he had reached his limit.

"I'll kick you out right here if you say that to me again!"

"I love you, man. I appreciate your help. If you want me to, I'll get out."

"I mean it! If you keep saying that…"

"Seriously dude…thanks for your help. If that's what you want to do, it's ok."

Jacob took a right, onto a side street on the north side of Alexis Road. He pulled to a stop across the street from the General Motors Powertrain factory in the middle of the west Toledo area. Jacob stomped his foot down on the brake pedal. His car screeched to a halt. Jacob, with wide unblinking eyes, turned his head to stare at me from the driver's seat of his car. I gazed back to him from the opposite side of the car. After five tense seconds of silence, I spoke.

"As I said, I sincerely thank you for your help. I'm fine here. I love ya, man. I wish you the best."

Jacob sat and stared as I stepped to the ground and opened the back car door to grab my two suitcases. He hopped out from his side and walked around the car to face me. The two of us hugged briefly and Jacob spoke once more before he got back in his car and left me in the middle of west Toledo.

"I…love ya too, man. I hope things work out for you. You just can't be talking like that."

I stood in the road in a random neighborhood across the street from the auto plant, and I watched as Jacob drove away. With a suitcase handle in each hand, I began to walk into the neighborhood and away from the main road. Sweat poured from me as I began to drag the heavy luggage down the road. I made it fifty feet into the neighborhood. A wheel on my larger and much heavier suitcase snapped off at the base. My belongings weighed too much for the wheel. All it took was fifty feet for the wheel to break, leaving me in an unfamiliar neighborhood, unable to go any farther.

It was afternoon in summer. I was exhausted, hot, and defeated. I pulled my two suitcases up onto the grass beyond the curb, and I collapsed next to them. As sweat poured down my face, I laid back and gave up. I had nowhere to go and no way to get there. As I lay on my back in the grass in that neighborhood, I didn't even have the energy to care.

A half hour passed, then an hour. Clouds came in, and rain began to sprinkle down from the sky. I sat up in the grass in the center median where the roads split off into three directions of streets lined with houses. The rain continued, but it remained light as the afternoon grew later. Then, like something out of a made for tv movie, a scene played out in real life which I never considered. Outside of lore and urban legend, I had never heard of it in an actual real-world instance.

As I sat there in the grass where the neighborhood streets converged, I adjusted my hand, giving me a firm grip on the gun in my front pocket. The windowless white van pulled up on the street in front of me. I took in the details of the vehicle as it came to a stop at the intersection in the neighborhood. There were no windows on the side of the van behind the driver's window. The van was full-sized and older. It was white, with some rust and missing paint. Two metal ladders were strapped onto the roof. Smoke escaped from the van's exhaust as it sat and loudly idled.

I couldn't see into the driver's window. Though it wasn't sunny outside, the angle of the light, as it reflected on the glass, obscured view of anyone inside. I felt my heartbeat increase. I didn't stand up, but I sat at full attention as I faced the van directly. I felt sweat on my hand as I held my handgun in my pocket. I watched, and the driver's window rolled down. I could see at least two people in the front seats of the white van. Neither had shirts. Both had full beards. I continued to watch. The driver of the van turned to me and spoke.

"Hey!"

I stared at the van. I didn't reply. I didn't move. Short, tense seconds seemed to pass in slow motion. The driver spoke again.

"Hey!"

As I considered how to respond, the driver of the van leaned farther out of his window, staring directly into my eyes.

"Do you wanna work?"

That sentence caught me off guard. As the words reached my ears, I had to consider the question. I rearranged my thought process. I thought on the question for only a split second before I replied. I yelled one word back across the street to those strangers in the windowless van, a van where I then saw at least three people inside.

"Yes."

"Well, grab your stuff and come on. Jesse will help you load your suitcases in the back on the other side. We gotta hurry. It's supposed to rain hard in a few hours."

Against every bit of childhood advice ever spoken about stranger danger, not taking rides from strangers...and windowless vans, I stood up and dragged my luggage across the street. Between the light rain and my own sweat, I was soaked. I passed my two suitcases up to the man in the back of the van, the only of the three wearing a shirt and not sporting a beard. I climbed in the side door and sat on a bucket amongst the tools and equipment which filled the back of the van. I had surprised myself with how quickly I happily accepted the offer from the three van guys. I was no longer stranded on the side of the road in the summer rain. I suddenly had the chance to earn some much-needed cash. I had something to do for the evening, and I was ready for whatever that entailed.

For the next five hours, I worked alongside the three van guys as we roofed a house on the opposite side of Toledo. I took instruction as I went, being unfamiliar with the process. The men were in a race against night and the weather to finish the job they had been working the previous week. I learned how to hold shingles as they were nailed in place. I carried supplies up and down a ladder at the base of the steep roof. I threw debris from the roof, and I gathered up piles of old roof to carry to the dumpster in the driveway.

I worked hard that evening. The opportunity was a blessing, and I did my best to keep up. I only took one break to sit and drink water by my suitcases next to the neighbor's wooden fence. My break was cut short, and I jumped backward as a large angry head of a pit bull suddenly appeared at my feet. From underneath the fence, barking and snarling aggressively, the dog seemed angry enough to squeeze through the hole on effort alone. I caught my breath as I put my gun back in my pocket, not even realizing I had pulled it out as I jumped backward in reaction to the dog.

The three roofers and I finished the job as the sky grew dark and the rain began to come down harder. I looked online for a hotel. I couldn't find any vacancies anywhere in that part of Toledo. The roofers assured me that they knew a hotel close-by with vacancies. Half an hour later, I hopped from the van in a hotel parking lot.

As two of the guys unloaded my suitcases for me, the third guy pulled a stack of bills from his pocket. As the third guy, the driver of the van, counted out money, he thanked me for my help finishing the roof. The van pulled away as I walked towards the lobby of the hotel. I had a hundred and fifty dollars in my hand;

money I didn't have before I accepted the ride in the windowless van.

Online, the hotel showed no vacancy. The parking lot was full. People were out and about everywhere. I had a bad feeling as I worked my way to the lobby entrance. I pulled one suitcase and lifted the suitcase with the broken wheel, step by step, as I attempted to get inside the building. Again, I was exhausted and soaked in sweat. The roofing job, though worth it, had taken a lot out of me.

I finally reached the desk in the front lobby, and I rang the bell. As I waited, I collapsed into a seat next to the desk. People were everywhere. I didn't care. With my bags in each of my hands, I closed my eyes to wait for a hotel employee to show up to the desk. I had a bad feeling. The internet showed no vacancy…

"Sir. Sir, may I help you?"

I opened my eyes. "Yeah, please tell me you have a room available."

"No sir, we do not. We are all booked up for the night."

My heart sank. Just as I took in the words from the Indian guy at the desk, someone else spoke from the other side of the coffee pot in the lobby. It was a younger Mexican guy, clean cut and dressed well. I turned to face him.

"I overheard you can't get a room. I've got a room for the night. I'm waiting to get picked up. You can come hang out in my room while I wait, and then you can stay in it once I leave."

"Dude, thank you so much. That's…"

The hotel clerk cut me off mid-sentence. "There's no

shared rooms. It is not allowed."

It took some convincing, but I managed to talk the hotel clerk into allowing me to hang out in the room. I told the clerk I was only going to be there until I found someone to pick me up. It was that, or I would have to sit with my bags in the lobby for the evening. The clerk made the exception, and I walked outside with the young Mexican guy.

That particular hotel had entrance doors to the rooms from the inside hallways and also from outside in the parking lot. The room which the two of us were headed to was halfway down the parking lot. As I walked with my luggage, I took in the scene around me. The hotel was seedy, for sure. Seedy people were out and about everywhere. I didn't care. I was grateful for a place to rest.

Two hours later, the moderate rain began to pick up to a full-on storm. The hotel clerk had been to the room once earlier to remind me that I needed to be out of the room that evening. Once the rain began to fall hard, I knew the clerk wouldn't be by again. I was set for the night. I was concerned, though. Checkout was at eleven o'clock the next morning. Whether Derrick's ride picked him up that night or the next morning, I was still on a timer. I needed to rest, so I put the stress of finding somewhere else to go on the back burner.

Derrick's phone rang. It was his ride. They weren't going to pick him up until check-out the next morning. Derrick was from Toledo, but he just got back from Cincinnati shortly before I was dropped off at the hotel. Derrick had just completed a two-week stint in a rehab facility down in Cincinnati. Derrick, though only nineteen years old, had a half-decade long fentanyl addiction which landed him in some trouble with the law. That two-week period in rehabilitation was the first time he had been clean from the drug since he was fifteen years old.

Derrick stepped out of the room after answering a phone call once it was dark outside. When he returned, I knew his short-lived sobriety was about to come to an end. I set up my tattoo equipment. Derrick pulled a cigarette cellophane from his pocket and set it on the table. My mood switched from exhausted to anticipatory. The cellophane on the table was wrapped around twenty little white pills. I didn't need to ask, but I did anyhow. Derrick confirmed that the two of them were about to sniff fentanyl.

I set up my tattoo ink while Derrick used a credit card to smash up some of the pills. The two of us took turns sniffing lines of the powder before I began tattooing. After two lines, I was high. Derrick did three more lines of fentanyl before he sat down in front of me. As I began to tattoo his wrist, Derrick spoke.

"I have a Narcan nasal spray right here. Just make sure to use it if I overdose."

I finished tattooing as Derrick nodded in and out of consciousness. I was high, but I was able to stay awake. After I cleaned up my tattoo equipment, I periodically checked to be sure that Derrick was still breathing. Derrick was seated upright in a chair in the hotel room, his head leaning backward. He was fully unconscious, but his breathing was steady. I spent that time on my phone. I needed to figure out what I was going to do when I had to leave the hotel the next morning.

I walked with my two suitcases through Toledo, down Alexis Road. It was noon. The rain from the night before was gone. The sunlight forced me to squint as I walked. I had a half hour. I was a quarter mile from a Taco Bell. I wanted to eat before my ride picked me up. I had money from the roofing job. I looked forward to eating at my favorite fast-food restaurant. Though my luggage was weighing me down, with frequent stops to catch my breath, I knew I was going to make it to the restaurant.

An hour earlier, I had solved the problem of where I was going to go once Derrick checked out from the hotel. On a website of classified ads, a particular post stood out amongst the others. The ad, though written to appear innocent and straightforward to the standard viewer, had blatant nefarious undertones to anyone on the level. Being an astute adult hookup practitioner, I noticed the true nature of the online ad. It was perfect, and I knew I had found what I was looking for. I replied to the post. I was soon in a text conversation with a man from a suburb on the other side of the river, south of Toledo.

"M seeking M. Offering room and board for a younger male who is good with his hands. I'm looking for a guy to do handy work and various tasks around my home. I live in a house by myself, and I will provide a private bedroom and meals for a male who fits what I seek. Be young, fit and attractive, 18 to 25. Send picture."

"Hi, I saw your ad. I'm not in your age range. I think if I send you a few pictures, you will make the exception."

"Send pictures."

And like that, I was off and running. I knew what it was that the man in Rossford sought. I also knew I had just done a respectable job down in Texas remodeling Lyla's mobile home. If there was any real work to be done at the house, I had those skills with which to bargain. If not...well, I would cross that bridge when I got there.

Bits and Pieces

I washed the massage oil from my hands in the upstairs bathroom sink. Down the hallway was my new bedroom. On the bed, I sorted out the items from my two suitcases. I knew I was going to need Harrold to drive me to my storage unit within the next couple of days. I had items to drop off and other items I wanted to pick up. I sat down on the edge of my new bed, and I thought in silence for a moment. I was lost; my life seemed so unfamiliar. Though I was a mere ten minutes from my old house in Perrysburg, I felt a lifetime away from everything. Whatever I had gotten myself into, it was an improvement from where I was the day before. I had a roof over my head. Harrold was a nice guy…as far as I could tell.

Fortunately, over the next couple of weeks, there were plenty of home improvement projects to keep me busy and earning my keep away from Harrold's bedroom. That massage on the first day was the only time I had to bend to the agreement which was implied in the online classified ad. Harrold had many home projects, and I had the skills needed to put in the work. Digging up a cement fire pit, moving and leveling a shed, creating a rock garden, redoing the glassed-in front porch, painting and tiling the kitchen wall and floor, any other random item which came up; I stayed busy while I lived with Harrold in Rossford.

I went above and beyond. Harrold saw the work and paid me cash on top of room and board. Harrold farmed me out to his mother. Harrold's mother lived across the city, and Harrold dropped me off at her house for three full workdays. At the end of those three days, I had removed two large trees from her yard and cleared out the overgrowth around the garage in the backyard. Harrold's mom was pleased with my work. She paid seven hundred dollars for my effort. With that and the money Harrold paid to me for work on his house, I had over a grand which I didn't have before.

I was at a pivotal point. Though I hadn't done crystal in a while, I knew I wanted to get back in the scene. I knew I finally had enough money to buy a quantity worth buying. Though I was no longer in contact with my sources, I knew someone who could put me on. Since I first met Meg on the website, back when I was staying in Michigan and building my Subaru camper/car, Meg always had substantial amounts of crystal from a source independent of me. I remained in touch with Meg through all my tribulations and travel during 2021. Meg wanted to see me again if I ever returned to the Midwest. I knew it was time to let Meg know that I was back…and that I was looking to party.

"So where are we headed?"

"Well, my guy won't be around for a few more hours. I have a place by my house I want to take you."

McCourtie Park, in Somerset Center, Michigan, was a wonderful experience. I held hands with Meg as she showed me around. The seventeen bridges, wooden in appearance, were all actually cement sculptures. The bridges, sculpted by Mexican immigrant expert cement artists George Cardoso and Ralph Corona in the 1930s, spanned the various creeks and waterways which meandered through the park. Meg shared the history of the place, having grown up and having lived a stone's throw away. There were mafia connections and rumors of underground passages. There were rumors of bodies entombed beneath the cement structures on the grounds.

I took in the sights and the moments with Meg. I expressed my appreciation for her and for sharing the experience with me. Though my year was not going anything like I had hoped, my time that day with Meg was a welcome reprieve. With the flowers of the botanical gardens as a backdrop, Meg and I shared a kiss which took me away from all the negativity I had experienced in 2021. For that afternoon, I forgot about everything which wasn't that moment in time. For that afternoon, I was happy. In that moment, life was again amazing.

As Meg and I explored the park together, we took note of the various groups of well-dressed high school aged kids walking around and posing for pictures together. The kids were dressed formally, dresses and tuxedos. I remembered being that age; my whole life ahead of me. I smiled at the thought. I gazed at Meg. She seemed to be deep in thought as well, maybe thinking the same thing. Meg's phone rang. It was her guy. We had to go. The afternoon at the park was done.

I sat in a bedroom with a twitchy guy. We conversed while we passed a mirror back and forth to do hotrails. Meg and another guy had left the house to make a run to score drugs. The twitchy guy shared his personal supply of crystal with me as we waited for the two others to return. I was high again. It had been a minute. I was content. I knew I was about to have a large quantity of crystal to get me through.

It was raining hard later that night when Meg and I arrived at Meg's parents' house in Hillsdale, Michigan. The house was huge. It was divided into two sections, connected by a section of hallways in the middle. The rain was flooding the grounds of the farm property outside the house. Meg found a place to park amongst the mud and puddles. The two of us ran through the rain and dark to reach the section of the house where Meg was living. Though Meg told me to be quiet once we got inside, I wasn't too worried about waking Meg's parents; they were fast asleep and far away, upstairs in the other section of the house.

Once inside, I cooked food. The two of us took off our wet

clothes and ate before we went upstairs to do drugs in Meg's section of the home. Though Meg and I kissed throughout the night as we did methamphetamine, we never took it any farther. Meg painted pictures while I explored the large room. Both of us ended up falling asleep in an entertainment room, amongst storage items and below the vaulted ceiling. I had two ounces of crystal, enough to keep me high for a long time. I slept well that night at Meg's house.

The next morning, the house was alive with people. I met Meg's parents. I also met her sister, her brothers, and their children, all of whom had stopped over to the house for a cookout. After eating, Meg took me back to Ohio. Outside Harrold's house, we hugged and kissed.

"Thank you. This is gonna last me a minute. I hope to see ya again soon."

...

As with previous dynamics, I knew my time at Harrold's house was coming to an end. I finished all the home improvement projects. I wasn't paying for my room and board with any sexual favors. I saw that Harrold felt it was getting to be time we parted ways. Though I ate meals with Harrold, and sometimes some of Harrold's friends who came over for dinner, I mainly kept to myself at all other times. I worked out with Harrold's weights in the basement. I wore the clothes Harrold had given me. I interacted online from my bedroom, and Alyssa, Jane's doppelganger, picked me up on occasion to get high at her house.

Alyssa dropped me off one afternoon. When I walked inside, Harrold began the conversation which I had been expecting.

"So, it looks like all the work around here is done."

"Unless you have anything else…"

"Do you think you can find a place to go by the end of the week?"

"I'll do what I can. I should be able to. Harrold, thank you for the hospitality."

"Well, thank you for the hard work you did around here. I'm grateful for it. I hope staying here helped you out."

"It did, for sure. I really appreciate it. I'll work on getting out of here."

When the next week began, Harrold helped me load my belongings into the car. I hadn't found a place to go, but I knew I wasn't able to stay at Harrold's house any longer. As Harrold dropped me off at my storage unit, I assured him that I would figure something out from there.

"Are you sure you'll be alright from here."

"No worries, man. I'll get it sorted. Again, thank you for having me and paying me for working."

"Thank you. You did a great job."

"Well, who knows what the future holds. We were meant to cross paths. Maybe we will again down the road."

"Take care."

I watched Harrold's car pull out of the storage complex and disappear into the morning. As I unlocked my storage unit, I truly didn't know what I was going to do. I was alone with all

I owned in the entire world. I was at a storage unit outside of Perrysburg, Ohio, the city where I grew up and spent most of my life.

My storage unit was facing out of the complex. Across the auxiliary road on the other side of the fence were the township softball diamonds. At the far end of the complex, the auxiliary road ended at two factories. Down the other end of the road, past the building where the offices to the storage company were housed, was the entrance to the main road which ran two miles down to Perrysburg. On the backside of the particular building which housed my unit, there were four other rows of storage unit buildings which ran parallel to my particular unit, all the way down to the factories at the end of the road.

My unit was only six units deep on the front side, facing the auxiliary road and softball diamonds. Dozens of other units lined the building and the next building down from me, all the way to the fence dividing the complex from the factories at the end of the road. Along the fences on the far side and opposite side of the complex, boats and vehicles were parked for storage.

It was late summer, almost the beginning of fall. It was hot outside, both day and night. The heat from inside the metal storage unit hit me as I opened the roll-up door to place my items inside. Harrold was gone. The softball diamonds were empty. It was still too early in the year for softball season. I hadn't seen anyone at the storage complex when I punched in the gate code and Harrold drove me to my unit inside the complex.

The sun was shining brightly that morning. Birds were randomly chirping from locations close by. As I stood on the pavement in front of my open storage unit, I gazed past the fence which lined the outside of the paved ground of the complex. I was alone, a million miles away from where I grew up: just down the street.

In the moment, my mind was elsewhere. My storage unit, loaded up with furniture, weights, and everything I had accumulated in a lifetime on Earth, was filled from top to bottom, front to back. There was a small area of cement floor, three feet by three feet, in the front of the unit. The floor space was void of my belongings. I climbed up on a stack of my belongings and retrieved a folding chair.

I opened the chair and placed it in the small open spot on the pavement. Despite the heat, I rolled down the metal door to my unit with me inside. The light inside the unit, coming in from gaps above, was enough to see what I was doing. Sweat poured from me as I sat down on the folding chair, surrounded by my belongings in my closed-up storage unit. I removed my drug equipment and my bag of crystal from my backpack. As I sat alone, pouring sweat in the almost dark storage unit, while amongst everything I had collected in a lifetime no longer seeming my own, I blew down hotrails for the next hour without break.

There's No Place Like Home

That first night was a mental journey through negativity. As the sun went down, a storm swept in. It seemed fitting. A storm was raging in my mind, as well. With the metal roller-door fully shut, and a screwdriver jammed in the side rail to effectively lock the door, I frantically sorted through my belongings. I hurried to move whatever I could away from the base of the door. Water from the severe thunderstorm began to wash underneath the metal and onto the cement floor.

The hard rain's relentless pounding on the metal storage structure was deafening. Once I climbed over some couches, with a flashlight in my mouth, I found some old ear plugs in the drawer of a dresser. Up high in the towers of storage, the smaller dresser was stacked closer to the ceiling, on top of another dresser. I put in the ear plugs. With the plugs blocking out most of the noise from the rain, my thoughts seemed only louder.

The remnants of a life lost, stacked and packed all around me. Floor to ceiling high, front to back; everything I had accumulated and held onto from the beginning of my existence. Boxes of family picture albums, the baby book my mom began keeping at the end of 1979, stacks of totes containing what was left of my childhood; action figures, games, figurines, everything in the entire world which still belonged to me.

There were appliances and furniture, there were collections of books, music, and movies. In every available gap between tables and gym equipment, there was box after box, each filled with random items such as electronics and dishes. Car parts were strewn about on stacks of other items. There was a living room set in the front. There was a disassembled queen-sized bed in the back corner. An old, floor-model projection television held two wall-sized mirrors against the side of the metal storage unit. A washing machine in the back corner was stuffed full of fake plants from my old office. The matching dryer, long gone; given to my friend Jane back when I rented a room from her long ago.

I was there inside the metal box, amongst four decades of everything. I had time, I had treasures to uncover and sort, and I had enough crystal to fuel the exploratory mission for the unforeseeable future. That was it; my mind was breaking down and my distraction was my tomb. I was relegated to reside amongst ghosts and memories of a life no longer my own.

I was entombed with all I possessed in the world, but I was still breathing as I lay alone on piles of my own history. There was so much there with me in the contained chaos and disorganization of what once made sense. All of it meant nothing and was nothing, distractions and tasks to occupy time as the crystal dictated, how the crystal dictated. I floated there in suspended animation, reunited with my past belongings in petrified time and space.

I was in Hell; I was living my rock bottom. It was a realization which was blatant and obvious from that stormy first night. I no longer wondered when my luck was going to turn around. I no longer wondered what else was going to go wrong. I knew I was in it.

My mind broke as I poured sweat, locked in my metal box of everything which I had spent the previous years trying to escape. My mind, my Hell. My storage unit; a reminder of the mess inside my brain. A reminder which had become my entire world, all which was in my immediate presence, surrounding me at every moment of every day and night. It was no longer a storage unit of my belongings; it was my entire world. There was no line where the inner turmoil ended and the outside clutter began. My mind and my world around me: it was all one big mess.

There was so much packed into such a small area around me. As the clouds of crystal smoke dissipated through the cracks of the metal ceiling grating and into the adjacent units, I poured sweat while frantically sorting through remnants of my former life. Full days were spent on individual missions to locate and organize. Other days were spent shifting ceiling-high stacks of my belongings to try to create new places to rest. Countless boxes were emptied and reloaded with other items. Each attempt to organize left more of a mess than before. The pile of belongings appeared to have been bulldozed into the unit. Floor to ceiling, all the way from the door to the back wall, the enclosed disaster consumed me physically and mentally.

There was a day when I figured I couldn't make progress because there was nowhere to move anything to begin any real organization. I began at six o'clock in the morning. By midday, seventy-five percent of my hoard was on the pavement outside my unit. From two units down, on either side, and all the way to the fence on the side of the storage complex, my belongings filled the ground. That disaster caught the attention of the front office. I was visited by employees at three separate times that morning.

At noon, the owner of the complex drove up to the outside of the fence on the auxiliary road between the complex and the softball diamond. The complex owner jumped from his pickup truck and angrily walked over to the fence. After some choice words, he hopped back in his truck and sped off. I agreed to have the mess cleaned up by the end of the day, but I knew that meant I was going to be working well into the night. I had planned to do that anyhow. I had nowhere to go, and crystal was fueling my actions.

It ended up taking until three o'clock the following morning for me to use a snow shovel to finally shovel the last of my belongings off the pavement outside. All the broken items and garbage with nowhere else to go were loaded back into the storage unit along with the items I sorted out over that entire day. The wall of debris was barely contained when I tried to roll down the overhead door. It took another hour of attempting to push the pile back away from the track of the door at the front of the unit before I was finally able to close myself and my belongings inside to remain for the rest of the work week. That morning, I slept for a few hours three quarters of the way up the side of a stack of my belongings.

"Imagine loading all your belongings from your entire house and garage into a large semi-trailer. Then imagine the trailer being turned up on its end and everything dumped out into a pile; some items break, some boxes break open, nothing in any semblance of order. Imagine then living there with the mess, enclosed in four metal walls and a metal roof, creating garbage daily from biproducts of life…in extreme heat, and with no bathroom, barely able to fit."

I sent the text to Lex, and I included a picture from my current vantage point where I sat in the passenger seat from my old BMW, on top of a dresser which was balanced on a table, with boxes and debris piled up to that top layer of hoard. I turned to reach up to remove a drawer from a nightstand above me to my right. As I pulled out the drawer, the weight from the contents caused it to slide out quicker than I was able to react.

The corner of the drawer hit me and split the bridge of my nose. Everything from inside the drawer fell around me and tumbled down the piles of hoard. Seeing stars, I fell backward down the pile where I had been perched. Luckily, I managed to grab onto some gym equipment as I fell. I carefully slid the rest of the way to a stop on top of a stack of boxes. I reached my hand to my face. Blood steadily trickled from my face, and drops of blood rained down to the hoard below.

When one of the wall-length mirrors shattered, there were suddenly shards of glass to contend with, mixed in amongst the hoard which was my life. A glass end table broke one day when I was climbing to the back of the pile; more glass to manage on the excursions of discovery. Especially in the dark, I was prone to catching a glass shard in a hand or a leg. The terrain was treacherous, but the treasures found were worth the injuries.

There was no electricity in my unit, but I had a solution. In the evenings, after the office workers went home for the day, I took walks. I walked to the end of the building. Around the corner, on the short side of the building, there were electrical outlets. I had multiple extension cords, forty feet long and twenty feet long. After connecting six of the cords, I was able to reach my unit from the power outlets.

I plugged in a box fan, a lamp, and a power strip to the end of the cords inside of my unit. I was able to charge my phone in the middle of the night. I had light to see what I was perpetually sorting, and the breeze from the fan was a relief from the hot and stale air of the metal box. Each morning, at five o'clock, I made sure to unplug and wind up my cords so when the staff arrived for the day, they were none the wiser.

There were many things which were only able to be done in the middle of the night when nobody else was anywhere close. The streetlamps at the far end of the complex, all the way down by the factories at the end of the road; underneath those was the only place bright enough to manage certain tasks. I took two broken pieces of the wall mirror and my electric shaver to that far end of the complex. In the middle of the night, I used those items to line myself up. Homemade haircuts took place at three in the morning.

In the middle of one of the nights, I was far into a journey inside my metal box. I was up high, close to the roller door, on a precarious stack of my belongings. Items shifted beneath my feet. I struggled for stability, and I hopped up another level closer to the top. A heavy glass coffee table shifted below me. Suddenly, the coffee table fell. The table caught on the closed roller door. Seconds later, an avalanche cascaded down the pile to rest on top of the coffee table. The weight was too much, and the roller door broke free from the metal which fastened it to the top of the unit.

The door and the roller on the side of the unit all dropped from up by the ceiling. The hoard and I were instantly exposed. As I stared out to the night sky beyond the storage building, my heart began to race. Not only had I just broken the roller door, but I had exposed everything to the outside world. The door was still hanging from the other side, but there was a gap of emptiness from the ceiling to the ground. The hoard and I were exposed to the world.

It ended up taking eight hours. Eight hours after the door fell, I secured it back in position. I could barely catch my breath. I was physically exhausted. I sacrificed two belts and three ratchet straps, but I fixed it. Standing high up against the ceiling of the storage unit, I managed to tie off the heavy metal roller door. It still functioned, and it again shielded me from the outside world. Straps and belts were tied from the top of the door to various metal beams along the corner of the ceiling. The roller was then bolted back into place. I had done it, and just in time. Moments later, the staff began to arrive at the facility for their morning work shifts.

Some evenings and nights, I ventured out. It was two miles down the main road to reach the shopping strips on the outskirts of Perrysburg proper. I prepared for each journey. With my headphones and phone charged, I strapped my gun to my ankle for the walk. At night, I carried a flashlight. The walks were arduous, but they were breaks from the monotony of being alone and closed-up in a metal cube.

Some days, I made trips to eat at my favorite Greek restaurant. Only one pizza place delivered all the way out to my storage unit, so I was perpetually sick of it. The walks to the Greek restaurant were a welcomed change. Walmart and Meijer were two miles away. Certain toiletries were needed, as imagined. I wore a backpack on those trips. It made it easier to carry purchased items the two miles back down the road. I felt I had accomplished something on those days when I made the four-mile round trip.

Some days, the storms rolled in. Northwest Ohio, in the Midwest, was prone to severe weather. I loved storms, even when I was immediately facing the elements. If I had my belongings strewn about outside my storage unit while sorting them through, I kept an eye out for clouds rolling in. Sometimes, Lex would text me warnings of impending extreme weather.

I then did all I could to re-load my belongings back into storage before the rain and wind hit. Sometimes I made it, closed up in my metal box with all my belongings to wait out the weather. Other times, I got soaked as I finished loading my sopping wet treasures into my home, hoping I managed to get any water-soluble belongings away from the threat.

The lightning in the distance was always a beautiful sign of immediate peril. The dark clouds on the horizon gave me a feeling of excitement. As the sky grew black, the wind picked up, and the ominous feeling of what was to come was blatant. I prepared myself to wait it out. I knew when to move things off of the inside ground near the roller door, and I knew when I was about to be closed in for the duration. There was a peacefulness amongst the weather's chaos. I knew I was alone for the duration of any extreme storm which swept through.

I was always on alert. The factories at the end of the auxiliary road seemed to operate around the clock. I watched through binoculars as the workers took breaks incrementally around the clock. I did my best to go unnoticed. I did my best to not exist. On occasions, police cruisers patrolled down the auxiliary road, between storage and the softball diamond, to the far end of industry. If I was outside, I acted nonchalant. If I was in my unit with the door cracked for ventilation, I closed the door completely and dealt with the stale air until the police were gone.

One night, at one o'clock in the morning, I was caught off guard. My crystal-fueled brain was too preoccupied as I sorted out car speaker components. As I stood just inside the threshold of storage, a police officer was suddenly standing right behind me. I wasn't ready for the interaction. I instantly covered my drug paraphernalia as the officer made his presence known.

"Hi, sir. We got a call of some activity here tonight…"

"Well, yeah. I guarantee you it was my activity."

"What are you…wait a minute. I remember you. Last month…"

"Yes. Wow, that was you, wasn't it?"

"You told me your story; how you're sorting your storage unit. Well, you sure are. Still going, huh?"

Fortune was in my favor that night. That same officer, the one who was so cool despite me having a handgun on my ankle and pulling my luggage through a parking lot a mile away. It was the same officer. I had rapport, and I was put at ease from the familiar face. The two of us conversed for the next ten minutes. I was actually happy to have some company. After some parting words, the officer left me to my project. I shook my head. I was amazed that I saw that same officer again.

There were days when direct storage neighbors spent time at their units. It was usually on Sundays. Once in a while, both next door neighbors showed up at the same time. I was effectively surrounded on those days. I did what I could to blend in, just another guy, randomly at my storage unit. Some days, I was closed inside when my neighbors arrived. I remained silent until they left, whether it was minutes or hours.

Other times, there wasn't any way to avoid being seen. I

did all I could to appear to be going about normal activities at my unit. I interacted with my neighbors, typical greetings and small talk. I worked while the neighbors pulled out their jet-skis and hooked them to their trucks. I acted busy when my neighbors stopped by to load items into their storage units.

It was dark in the unit. The sunlight coming in from the gaps, up by the front of the ceiling where it met the roller, was enough to see. The heat was almost unbearable when I woke up. Though I continuously wiped away the sweat with a towel, I couldn't keep up. I touched the inside of the metal rollup door. I pulled my hand back instantly in reaction to the burn. I wiped sweat from my body one more time, and I began gathering up items from the cramped space around me.

Within an hour, I had two bags packed. Tattoo equipment, drug paraphernalia, and adult novelty items filled my backpack. My suitcase was filled with clothes and toiletries, enough to cover the three days I was about to spend in a hotel. I also had a stack of totes and boxes separated out from the rest of my hoard. The containers were filled with all of my books, my DVDs and Blue rays, my video games and multiple game consoles, and a couple of old laptops. My entire collections of media; all I had carefully curated over four decades, nine large boxes and totes, hundreds of pounds from a lifetime of collection, everything was stacked there in the front corner of the storage unit.

Over the previous week, I was in contact with a friend of mine from Toledo. My friend had recently opened a store in the city. The store was a second-hand video and bookstore. I knew what I had to do. Though I wished I could avoid it, I needed the money and the extra space in my storage unit. My friend was expecting me in the upcoming week. I was going to sell my complete collection. Over the week, I had spent hours locating, sorting, and packing all of it into those nine totes and boxes. My opportunity to transport my belongings was coming.

I met Shannon at the gate to the storage complex. I

punched in the gate code, and Shannon drove around to the front of my storage unit. Shannon was in town from Florida for four days. She had business obligations and family to see. I was about to get a reprieve from the storage unit. I hadn't showered in weeks, I hadn't had air conditioning, and I hadn't slept in a bed. I was overdue for all of it.

After Shannon helped me load my media into the trunk and back seats of her rental car, I grabbed my two bags and hopped in the passenger seat. The air conditioning was instantly amazing. Shannon had a stop to make before she checked into her hotel. Shannon's mom's house was down the road in Perrysburg. Her mom was out of town, but Shannon needed to stop by and pick up some mail which was there for her.

I showered as Shannon sat in the bathroom and sorted through her mail. It was a luxury which I hadn't realized I had been missing as much as I had. While in the shower, I blew down hotrails. Shannon walked over to me after each hit. I kissed the smoke from my lungs into her mouth. By the end of the shower, Shannon was higher than she had been since I last saw her in Florida in spring.

Once Shannon checked into the hotel in Rossford, the two of us continued our dynamic up in the hotel room. I remained unclothed and in the room for the duration. When Shannon left for work and family obligations, I used the time to tattoo myself, make videos for her, and craft new adult toys with hot glue sticks and a blowtorch. I stayed high the entire time, same as I had been doing in my storage unit. When Shannon returned from each excursion, I quickly got her high again, and the two of us put my newly created adult novelty items to work together.

On our last day together, Shannon drove me to my friend's store in Toledo. I used a hand cart to lug all of my boxes and totes from Shannon's car into the store. After a few moments of catching up with my friend, I left my lifetime of media items at the store in Toledo. I left with no money because all of my items needed to be sorted and priced. I was told to expect payment by the end of the week. It was a lot to sort out, and I understood it was going to take some time.

    I wasn't happy when I left the store. I felt a sadness of loss. I felt as if I had just parted with a huge component of a long-lost life. I was then even further removed from my current situation. Those items, especially my book collection, represented a simpler time, a more innocent and carefree part of a previous life. I told Shannon of the hole I felt as we drove back to Perrysburg. Shannon said she understood, but I doubted she actually knew.

    Unloading media items sparked a new crystal-fueled obsession in my cooked brain: clearing out space in the storage unit. Though I sold off much of my gym equipment back when I left my house at the end of 2018, I still had many more fitness items in storage. I had two benches, a squat rack, a universal gym with every attachment, Olympic bars, dumbbells, Olympic plates, a weight tree, a dumbbell rack, and a leg-press machine. A lot of space was occupied by equipment which was not getting used. I posted an ad online. I knew my equipment was going to sell fast, especially at the price point I set in the ad.

    Within minutes, I began fielding responses to my post. A man in Michigan told me he would be there at six in the morning with a trailer and the money for the gym equipment. I told the guy to call me when he arrived the next morning, and I closed out of the app. I had been awake for a couple of days at that point, so I spent the rest of the day smoking crystal inside my storage unit. My goal was to stay awake so I could meet the guy the next morning at six o'clock. I did the last hotrail at four in the morning. My body carried me no further. I fell asleep on a fold-out loveseat amongst my gym equipment and all of my other possessions.

    At ten o'clock the next morning, I woke up with a jolt. I saw the light coming in around the gap between the roller door and the ceiling. As when I used to sleep through my alarm and see my room lit up on days when I should have been at work well before the sun came up, I knew I missed the six o'clock transaction with the guy from Michigan. I quickly did a hotrail, and I checked my phone. Sure enough, I missed calls from the guy. I sent an apology message, and I assured the guy I was there and able to sell my equipment. It was too late. The guy was back up in Michigan, unable to make a return trip.

    I opened the app where my ad was still posted. I replied to the next message. An hour later, a man and his wife pulled into the complex in a pickup truck which was pulling a flatbed trailer. After another hour, I located the last dumbbell amongst the hoard in the storage unit. The benches and universal gym had been strapped down to the trailer. The dumbbells and plates had been loaded into the back of the pickup truck. I ironically got in a last pump from the workout caused by loading up all of the gym equipment which I no longer owned. That same hollow feeling which I felt when parted with my books and movies was back. I was dismantling my former life, pieces at a time.

Accidental Art

My time in my storage unit was winding down. I didn't know how I would leave, but I knew I wasn't going to be there forever. The nights were getting cold. My paranoia had me always thinking people knew I was living there. The staff of the complex, the daily softball players and crowds, the workers at the factories at the end of the auxiliary road, the construction workers building a new structure up by the main road; I was conspicuous, and I knew it. The problem: I still had nowhere else to go.

In the dark one night, my glasses broke. The frame broke in the middle, and the pieces dropped to the floor below me. Without my glasses, I had trouble finding my glasses. After an hour, I located both pieces of the frame and one of my lenses. There was no fixing the frame. I only had one of my lenses anyhow. Things went from worst to beyond worst. All I saw was blur in front of my face. To see anything, I had to hold my remaining lens up to my right eye.

Unable to see anything, I made the two-mile walk to Walmart the next afternoon. I bought a pair of reading glasses and some epoxy. As I sat outside of Walmart, I popped out the right lens of the readers and glued my old lens in place. The lens was all scratched up, but at least I could see again out of one eye.

On the walk back to storage, the wind picked up as I traversed the terrain on the side of the state highway which led out of town. As I stumbled back home, a gust of wind blew my new glasses off of my face. The grass was long, and I was again unable to see. It took me twenty minutes, as the rain intensified, for me to finally locate my homemade glasses amongst the grass and weeds on the side of the road. Mosquitos were terrible that evening. I did all I could to bat them away as I continued on the return journey to my storage home.

When I reached the railroad tracks by the crossroad to Jane's house, a police cruiser flashed lights and pulled up in front of me. I threw my backpack in the trunk and caught a ride back to the storage complex. When the officer typed in the gate code I supplied, the code didn't work. I realized, in that moment, that I was a day late on my monthly payment.

The officer retrieved my backpack from her trunk. As the cruiser sat at the gate, I put my backpack on and began walking. I thanked the officer for the ride, and I squeezed through the gap between the fence and the gate. That was when I was abruptly told to stop.

"Are you kidding me? You can't do that right in front of me. If the code doesn't work, you don't have access. You can't go in there, that's trespassing."

"Alright, I won't. I'll sit right here and make some phone calls."

The officer drove away. It was nighttime at that point. There was no way I could pay my bill until the next business day. In that moment, I was effectively banned from the storage unit;,my only home at the end of the 2021 summer.

"Okay, baby. I'll be there in about twenty minutes."

I hung up the phone. A reprieve. I had an out. Barb, an older White woman from north Toledo, was on her way to pick me up from the pavement where I sat, outside the gate to the storage complex. I had met Barb on an app back in 2019. The two of us had hung out, but I hadn't seen her in two years. Back in the day, the two of us made a couple of videos together. I was relieved that Barb was able and willing to come pick me up.

The rain stopped as I sat in wait on the pavement in the night. Me, my backpack, and my one-lens homemade glasses were moving to Toledo. I could pay my storage bill when the staff arrive on Monday morning. Barb could then bring me back to grab supplies. She had a spare room. I had plenty to furnish the room. Barb was my guardian angel that night. I prepared for a change of scenery. It was long overdue. Though my vision was only through a scratched single lens, I finally had a vision for a future away from the metal box.

Over the next couple of weeks, Barb and I made multiple trips to retrieve items from the storage unit. I spent much time in the detached garage in Barb's backyard. I cleaned it out and organized it. I did yardwork, and I did work around the house. I redid the glassed-in front porch. I pulled up the carpet on the main floor of the house to expose the hardwood floor underneath. I fixed the stove in the kitchen. I deep cleaned and organized all the cupboards. I arranged for a nonworking car to be sold for scrap.

Customizing my new bedroom with countless items from my storage unit; I painted walls and hung shelves. I set up a living space similar to my old room back at Jane's house. I cleaned out the shed behind the pool in the backyard. Trip after trip to Perrysburg resulted in Barb's shed being filled with items from my storage unit. The point arrived where my payments lapsed, and I lost my storage unit. Though it was still full of my belongings, my most treasured items had been moved to my room, the garage, and the shed at Barb's house.

Lex came through for me once again in the first couple weeks I was living at Barb's house. She set me up an eye doctor's appointment and bought me two pairs of much needed new glasses. I waited on pins and needles for three days between the appointment and the call to inform me that my glasses were ready for pickup. I literally cried as Barb drove me back to the house after going to pick them up. I could finally see again. My life had changed for the better.

Barb had another car parked in her driveway, her old daily-driver. It had issues running. I got it working, and I began driving again. Barb put me on her car insurance, and it somehow lowered her monthly payment. Since I was driving again, I began donating plasma at the donation center in north Toledo. I was able to donate twice a week and get paid for it.

I began a new regimen of working out while staying with Barb. I had saved four dumbbells from storage, four dumbbells I never sold. Daily, I went out to the glassed-in front porch, turned on music, and lifted weights for a while. I felt better than I had in quite some time. Though I always maintained top shape, the new consistent workout routine added a noticeable change in a noticeably brief time.

I picked up a cough in mid-November. Prone to bronchitis as a child, I figured I caught bronchitis from living in Barb's home, where cigarettes were smoked indoors. I hadn't been sick in any other way in six years, so the chronic cough bugged me to no end. I also hadn't drunk alcohol since mid-2016. I made a choice one night. I wanted to cure my cough. I had a plan. I downed an entire mid-sized bottle of vodka. When I woke up the next morning, my cough was gone. It worked, but it also opened a gate which had been closed long ago.

Remaining high was important during those days at Barb's house. I had set into motion my thoughts of travel. I had new plans in place, and I needed the extra energy from crystal to manage what I needed to get done. Online, I had met a girl on an app. She was a twenty-six-year-old Asian woman who lived in Fresno, California. Mia and I grew extremely close in a brief period of time. We texted, we talked on the phone, and we shared video calls.

Weeks passed; the holiday season of 2021 became the dawn of 2022. I was drinking beer one evening with Barb, and I spilled out my plans for the future. Barb hadn't expected to hear what I told her, and I hadn't planned to tell her in that way. I was going to tell her eventually, but alcohol may have preemptively loosened my tongue that evening. I was happy to put the words out there. It was another weight lifted from my shoulders.

"So, here's the thing; I'm gonna be leaving soon. My friend Lex bought me an airline ticket. I'm heading out to California."

"What, really? You have people out there?"

"Yeah, I'm going to see how it goes. I can't shake the urge to travel. I appreciate being able to stay here. You literally rescued me from the side of the road, and I'll be grateful forever. I also appreciate being able to keep my belongings in your shed out back."

"Well, thank you for the work you did around here. Having you here was...interesting, to say the least."

"I love ya, Barb."

"Love you, too..."

I hugged Barb. I could feel the awkwardness in the air despite having a buzz from the alcohol. The two of us continued to drink together that evening, but Barb was quieter than usual. I felt bad for unloading that new information on her like that, but I knew I needed to tell her sooner rather than later.

I had a lot to do before I left. I needed to completely clear out my bedroom, stocked full of belongings. I then needed to paint the walls and fill in all the holes from the shelves and decorations I had hung up. I needed to pack as carefully as I could for the flight to California, and I needed to put everything else in the shed out back. My bedroom at Barb's house, same as my storage unit had been, was overloaded with way too many items. I was going to need the crystal my friend David had given me. It was going to be the fuel to work around the clock until it was time to leave. I knew I needed as much time as possible because of how much work I needed to complete.

Barb had many projects around the house when I moved in. I completed every one of them in my time there...except for one. The old ceiling fan was broken long before my arrival. The new ceiling fan was packed in the closet of my bedroom. Though I made attempts to replace the old fan with the new one, I never successfully finished out the job. The wiring and the brackets seemed straightforward. High on crystal, I needed to give it one more try. Still high on crystal and having been electrocuted twice, I decided to settle for installing the fan in the ceiling without connecting the wires.

The fan ended up in place, bracketed securely to the ceiling. The wiring was capped off. I left it at that, form over function. It looked better than the previous fan, and it functioned exactly the same as the old fan functioned; it didn't. Twice, the house went dark as I fell off of a chair in the middle of the bedroom. Twice, I received burns to my fingers. Twice, I thought that the electricity to the room was turned off, and I still got shocked. Twice, I had to flip the circuit breaker to restore power to the house. There was not going to be a strike three. My crystal-inspired need to finish the job was cooked out of me. It was the only job I failed to complete for Barb.

As for the rest of the room, I felt as overwhelmed as I had when I began sorting my old storage unit. I knew the irony of the situation. All of the items I was about to pack up and remove from my bedroom, they were all items I had repeatedly sorted, time and time again, back in my storage unit. The same items, just less of them. The same belongings, just with less garbage and broken things. The same task, just with a definite and limited timeline. The hoard was inescapable. When I left the hoard, the hoard relocated with me, trip by trip and carload by carload.

During that last week in Ohio at Barb's house, as expected, crystal was an absolute requirement for the around-the-clock work that was needed to wrap up my stay at the house. Days and nights passed in a blur. Half of the time, I wasn't even sure if it was light outside or dark. I would find out when I managed to get boxes sorted out enough to run them out to the shed in the backyard. Sorting, packing, painting; I barely took breaks to eat, and I never slept.

My focus, obsessive and compulsive, bordered on destructive to my physical health. I felt my body breaking down from lack of food and rest, but I kept going. At one point, I suddenly lost my senses of smell and taste. Lex had texted me that she had contracted coronavirus, so had David. I assumed I did too, but I pressed on. I didn't care about anything except the task at hand, and I was going to finish before my flight.

I finally completed the work. The room was empty. The walls were freshly painted. I curled up on the floor and fell asleep. My small supply of crystal had lasted through the job, but it ran out right at the end. It was good timing, and I didn't care. I planned to head to California drug-free, anyhow. I had two suitcases and a backpack in the corner of my empty room. It was all I was going to take with me across the country. It was enough, and the rest of my belongings, the items saved from my doomed storage unit, were loaded into the shed behind Barb's pool. The shed, like the storage unit, was filled completely. I was done.

After some issues with the airline the day before I was planning to leave, Lex sent me the money to cover the difference in ticket prices. I spent that entire day on the phone with the airline. The stress was high as I tried to sort out the situation. Though I had confirmation that I previously purchased my ticket, nothing was showing up for my flight when I looked up the details. My earlier purchase, unbeknownst to me, hadn't been confirmed by the airline. I then needed the money to cover the difference for a short-notice ticket.

After that ordeal, and Lex coming to the rescue again, I was finally in the clear. All the work around the house had been completed. My flight was guaranteed. All I had to do was wait. With nothing to do to stay busy, my mind went to dark places. Whether it was my depression, withdrawal from drugs, or a combination of the two, I was in a bad place mentally.

I drank alcohol alone in the empty bedroom on the day I was to leave for the airport. Barb was at work until three thirty that afternoon. I drank as I waited for her to get home. I stared at the walls and wondered about the uncertainty ahead. I thought about all that could go wrong. I thought about all of the negative which befell me over the previous year. Though I was excited for a new adventure, fear of my life once again falling apart was at the forefront of my mind. However ready I thought I was, I knew, deep down, that I wasn't.

It was gray and depressing outside when Barb walked in from work. While she changed into different clothes, I loaded my luggage into her car. It was freezing outside, and snow was falling lightly. I looked around. It was the last day I was going to be at Barb's home in Ohio. I was about to face the unknown. I closed up the car door and walked back inside. I had some beer I was planning to drink on the ride. I needed to step back into Barb's house to grab it.

"You ready? Did you get all your stuff loaded up? Even with weather and traffic, we should make good time to Detroit."

"I just need to grab these beers…There, I'm ready."

I wasn't ready, and I knew it.

Anhedonia

"Well...this is it."

"Barb, seriously, thank you for everything. Thanks for saving me that night, thanks for the storage shed, thanks for letting me stay at your home."

"Well, I wish you the best out there. Stay on the right path."

"I will. I don't know what's about to happen, but it's my time. Be safe driving back."

I wiped a tear from my eye, and I closed the door to Barb's car. The snow was falling hard and the wind had picked up as I walked into the terminal of the Detroit airport. It was almost dark outside. I looked around for a clock. It was just past six o'clock in the evening. I was hungry, and the effects of the beers I drank had all but worn off, leaving me tired and groggy. I knew how my night was about to go. I had accepted my fate well before I stepped into the terminal at the airport. I had a long night ahead of me. My flight didn't depart until eleven o'clock the following morning.

I checked in at the airline desk. I asked where I could get some food. The woman behind the counter told me that all the places which sold food outside of the gates had closed at six o'clock. I asked if I could get through the gates so I could eat. I found out that I had to wait until two hours prior to takeoff to cross through the gates. Once the woman behind the counter saw the time when my flight was scheduled to depart, she took pity on me.

"Tell ya what. I get an employee meal on my shift. You can have it. I'll run inside at get it for you. Is a chicken Caesar salad alright?"

"Yes, absolutely. Thank you so much."

I rolled my two new suitcases over to a row of seats along a wall of glass windows. I took off my jacket to use as a pillow, and I put my feet up on my bags. I took my headphones and my phone out of my backpack. Moments later, true to her word, I had a large plastic bowl in front of me. Still deep in a downward spiral of thought, I ate my meal as I glanced around at all the people inside the airport. Everyone living their own unique lives, people heading from here to there, wrapped up in everything consuming their own unique worlds; I was so different from everyone else I saw, and everyone else was so different from all the others.

Through the night, I watched movies on my phone. I remained in a constant battle with getting comfortable. The rigid plastic seats and armrests left little room to find a position which was comfortable for more than a few minutes. The longer I sat, the harder it was to stay seated. New people came and went around me. Workers behind the counter, in the distance, were replaced with the next shift of airline employees. Commuters hurrying past were soon gone, out of my life on their own journeys through the world. New people passed by in other directions, on to their own unique life experiences. I sat and watched, seated there for the duration.

I jolted awake the next morning. Sunlight from the early morning had begun to fill the terminal where I sat. I was amazed that I had managed to get some sleep, but it wasn't much. My neck hurt from sleeping upright in a chair. It was still early; I could tell from the light. I checked my phone; it was eight thirty.

In half an hour, I would be able to head through the gates and into the inner terminal.

I waited in line with my bags at the main security checkpoint. Slowly, the line moved forward. As people placed their personal effects on the conveyor belt to the x-ray machine, others stepped through the body scanner. I reached the point where I had to remove my shoes. I put them in a bin with my backpack. I put the smaller of my two suitcases up on the belt behind my backpack. I had bag-checked my larger suitcase before I stepped into the security line.

I stepped through the body scanner. I then walked back over to the belt to take my belongings from the other side of the x-ray machine. My items came out on the belt. As I pulled my backpack and suitcase from the belt, an employee took the bin with my shoes and wallet. Security again placed the bin in front of the x-ray machine to run it through a second time. I wondered what was going on. After the third time, I asked what was happening.

I felt a jolt of adrenaline as I remembered something from long ago. My mind flashed back to an extremely specific moment in time. It was almost Halloween in 2020. The sparkle of the Sun's reflection caught my attention as I stood outside of my Subaru on the side of the road in Aurora, Colorado. I walked back to my Lexus, parked behind my Subaru. I opened the door on the driver's side and reached in to remove the source of the light's reflection.

In that moment, as I stood next to security at the airport in Detroit, I knew what was going on. I looked toward the offices beyond the far wall of the security checkpoint. As I watched, an airline security employee pointed back in my direction. I saw a Detroit police officer step out from the office and follow the security worker back over to where I was standing. The oversight, clear as day in retrospect, was burning in my mind as I waited for the inevitable police interaction.

"Oh, my God. I know what's going on. I'm so sorry. I forgot

that it was even in there. It's been in my wallet since I had to leave my car in Colorado last year. I'm moving to California right now. I…"

I once again began to explain my situation to yet another police officer at rapid-fire speed. The officer held up a finger as he opened up my wallet. I couldn't believe what was happening. I was so close, so close to being on my way. I had made it through being stranded in Florida, then stuck in Texas, then I was left for a day in the middle of Illinois. I made it through the worst point in my life, stranded in a storage unit in my hometown for weeks on end. I just spent the previous week wrapping up loose ends at Barb's house. I spent a day on the phone with the airline to fix issues with my booking, and I spent a full night on a plastic seat in the airport.

I was so close. All I had to do was walk through the terminal to reach my gate, sit down, and wait for the airline to announce boarding of the aircraft. I was less than two hours away from beginning a new chapter of my life. I had come so far to reach that moment. It was less than two hours away…and an easily avoidable oversight may have just ruined everything.

The last item I retrieved from my Lexus on the side of the road in Aurora, Colorado in late 2020; I had forgotten about it. I bought it at a mall in Toledo back when I was a teenager. From the time I began driving, I always had it with me. Anytime I switched cars, I made sure that it was hung from the rearview mirror of my latest vehicle. It was nothing that caught any negative attention in a car. I hadn't thought twice about it since I took it from my Lexus and slipped it into my wallet. I forgot about it after that.

I never hung it in my Subaru because I forgot I had it. It stayed with me, in my wallet, as I traveled the country by car and bus in 2021. It stayed in my wallet as I spent the night in the airport in Detroit, and it was with me as I waited in the security line to enter the terminal gates. It went through the metal detector when I tossed my wallet in the bin on the conveyor belt...and then it was run through the machine two more times by a security worker. That third time through the x-ray machine was what prompted my memory. At that point, it was out of my control.

When that Detroit police officer pulled it from my wallet, all I could do was nod. There, held up in front of me, was the little metal ninja star I bought at the mall as a teenager. I knew it wasn't an appropriate airline carry-on item. I knew I was potentially facing an issue. I decided to open my big fat mouth.

"Dude, I seriously forgot that was even in there. I took it from my car when it broke down in Colorado. I haven't even thought about it since then. It's not a weapon, I promise."

"Well, this could be an issue...but I don't think it's a weapon..."

On autopilot, I began to recite my story another time. "Seriously, it's not. I'm moving to California right now. I've been here in the airport since last night. I'm down on my luck. I'm headed out there to start over..."

The officer cut me off. "I have to take this from you. I need you to sign this paper stating you acknowledge we confiscated this item from you while you were entering through security. This could catch you a charge. I could take you to jail, but I don't think all that needs to happen."

"Thank you, sir. I'm sorry I had that with me. I seriously forgot."

I stepped off to the side and put my shoes on as quickly as I could. The fog of the embarrassment and the adrenaline of the situation slowly wore off as I walked through the airport terminal. I was through that last hurdle before the new life ahead of me. I found the proper gate, and I sat down to wait for my flight.

Hours later, on Mountain Time, I stepped into the terminal of the airport in Denver, Colorado. The winter weather was horrible; the short walk down the steps of the airplane, across the runway, and into the building froze me to my core. Instantly, I was able to warm up. I had under an hour until my next flight, so I had to pick up the pace to reach the far side of the Denver terminal. There was a lot of ground to cover, and I was dripping sweat just moments after I escaped the outside cold of Colorado in January. Though I wasn't running, my pace was fast enough that I had to frequently stop and catch my breath.

On one of my short breaks, I stripped off my coat. As I wiped sweat from my forehead, I checked my location. I made it. After crossing the airport, I found my departure gate. Just as I slumped down into a seat to wait, the call to board my flight came across the intercom. I wasn't going to be able to pick up any food to satiate my growing hunger, but I was at least going to make my connecting flight to California.

On Pacific Time, hours later, I arrived in Fresno, California. The airport was decorated to showcase the wilderness of the Yosemite National Forrest. I walked through the terminal, amongst the large fake sequoia trees lining the inside of the terminal walkways. Just before I entered the baggage claim area, I walked through a massive base of a fake sequoia tree; a tunnel designed to replicate the real tunnels for vehicles on the roads in the area.

The actual tree tunnels were carved through real sequoia trees growing in that part of California. Even the scaled-down walking tunnel through the fake tree in the airport was impressive. I did a little research on my phone. Yosemite National Park was a mere half hour from where Mia lived. I hoped I would get the chance to see the actual sequoia trees in the near future. Though the nature artwork inside the airport in Fresno was impressive, I had no energy left in me to truly appreciate my situation.

I wanted to be away from airports for a while. Fresno, the third and final airport of the day, was almost just a memory. I reached baggage claim. After some waiting, I scooped up my suitcase as it popped out on the conveyor belt. With all of my luggage, I stepped out into the warm California night. The weather was perfect: no precipitation, a nice temperature, a cool breeze.

The cold winter of the Midwest was gone. The freezing Colorado snowstorm was behind me. There were no more airports in my immediate future. I took a deep breath. I exhaled slowly as I looked around at the line of cars waiting to pick people up from the terminal. All I had to do was locate Mia's car, and my latest journey would be complete. As I began to walk towards the cars, I felt something else. Originally, I first thought it was just stress. I realized what it was as I looked for Mia; I was in the first stages of drug withdrawal.

California Knows How to Party

I knew Mia was drug free. I wanted to live drug free with her in California. The ghosts from my immediate past were interfering with my goals. From the time I ran out of drugs when I finished packing up my room at Barb's house, I was distracted by immediate concerns. It wasn't until I stepped out from the airport and into the California night that all of those stressors were suddenly lifted. At that moment, with a clear mind, I knew I was about to face a horrible mental and physical transition to sobriety.

Timing doomed me from the very beginning. All those things which should have been magical first moments: meeting Mia for the first time, our first hug and kiss, riding with her back to her house, seeing the decorations Mia set up to welcome me into her home; all of the magic from those first experiences was shrouded in an ever-growing fog of drug withdrawal. I knew that if I could just wait for it to pass over the next couple of days, I would come out on the other side and be able to progress my new dynamic. From what I knew from my exchanges with Mia, I was fairly certain that she wouldn't understand. In that moment, I decided I was going to keep the drug withdrawal to myself.

Mental and physical exhaustion, with no chemicals to boost energy, left me in a constant fog of lethargy. I could barely complete thoughts. I slept while Mia went to work. I slept while she was home. Mia went about her days while I remained in bed. Depression, when I was awake, caused me to wish I was asleep. Thoughts were hard to keep in my head; I didn't have the energy to try to think.

Mia checked on me, and I responded with new complaints of aches and pains. I never let Mia know what was going on. I just hoped it would pass before she had enough of me. Mia tried to initiate intimacy. I brushed off any advances. If she lay down on the bed next to me, I rolled over to face the other direction. All of Mia's efforts caused her frustration, I could tell. I wasn't in any condition to fix my failing dynamic.

Four days passed. I was miserable. I knew Mia was unhappy. I heard her on the phone with her parents, arguing about moving back into their house to help take care of her father. I just needed to get through the withdrawal. I thought of ways to help. I picked a terrible way to try and remedy the situation.

I made a suggestion to Mia. I told her that I wanted to get drunk with her. Mia was all for it. She didn't know my history with alcohol. She thought it was going to be fun. I just wanted some relief from my withdrawal symptoms. I figured my time was almost up. Having heard Mia discussing her move back to her parents' house, I knew she had an excuse to give me the boot. I knew that my stay was coming to an end. I knew alcohol wasn't going to be a good thing, but I had lost all hope of making that situation with Mia work. I felt terrible in every way, and I wanted it to end.

The January days in Fresno, California were seventy degrees and sunny. I squinted as I stepped out of Mia's front door. It was the first time I had left the house since I showed up. Mia lived in a neighborhood of townhouses in the middle of fields. Mia lived in wine country. Mia's block, a collection of similar townhouses, was visible in all directions from the fields of grapes; one square block of homes which seemed to be placed in the middle of nowhere.

When Mia and I reached the grocery store, she led me to the back of the store. There in the back, amongst the beverage coolers, was the alcohol section. In that moment, I made a bad decision. The small bottles of whisky were ten dollars apiece. I silently debated for a moment with myself. First, I had two bottles in my hands. I picked up a third bottle. I looked at the three bottles in my hands. Three was the magic number. I walked over to Mia. She had a pack of four hard seltzers. The two of us paid for our alcohol and left the store.

Back at the house, my mind was all over the place. The sense of impending doom was with me from the drug withdrawal, and it was amplified by my knowledge that Mia planned to move back home with her parents. I opened the first pint of whiskey. Five seconds later, it was empty. Before the alcohol hit, I opened the second bottle. I downed that second bottle just as fast as I had the first. As the effects of the alcohol began to take hold, I opened the third bottle of liquor...

It was dark outside. What time was it? I saw the digital readout from a clock. I squinted to read it; it was four o'clock in the morning. I was lying naked in a bed. It was Mia's bed, but I was alone. What day was it? I felt like I had been out for multiple days. I reached my hand around me on the bed to try to find my phone. When my fingers brushed over my phone, I picked it up and looked at the screen. I saw the date on my phone screen. It was, in fact, two days later; two days had passed since I last remembered opening that third bottle of whiskey. With one eye open, I checked my text messages. I had a new message from Mia.

"We need to talk when I get home from work."

As I set my phone down again, I closed my eyes. I felt bad from the hangover, but I also felt better; I was on the other side of the drug withdrawal. I knew I was too late. I knew the conversation was coming. Bits and pieces of memories from the previous two days flashed through my mind as I lay alone in Mia's bed. I recalled tattooing myself in Mia's kitchen. I remembered kissing Mia while we were in the shower together.

Maybe nothing crazy happened while I was blacked out. Oh, no...another memory flashed through my head; I remembered a quick snippet of taking my shirt off while inside a fast-food restaurant. Then another flash of memory: walking shirtless along the fields of grapes in the California countryside. I was shirtless in that recollection...but was I also without pants? I was fully naked when I awoke in Mia's bed...

The talk with Mia went exactly as I had expected. Mia filled in the gaps in my timeline where my own drunken memory lapsed. A feeling washed over me as I listened to Mia recount the events of the previous two days. It was that same feeling which I last felt in mid-2016, a mix of embarrassment and recollection. That feeling was one of the main reasons I knew, all those years prior, that I had to completely stop drinking.

I hated those conversations; each time someone told me of a drunken act, my brain suddenly registered the scene and remembered more of what had been lost in the blackout. My embarrassment grew with each newly recovered, assisted memory. As the conversation continued, as more memories were brought to the surface, my regret and embarrassment intensified.

After Mia helped me piece together my two-day drunken misadventure, she followed up with the other part to the conversation. I had been awaiting that inevitable piece of information. I had been correct; Mia's parents had convinced her to move back into their home to help out; amidst the failing health of her father. In my situation, I wasn't even able to blame timing for the failure. I rightfully blamed myself for my failure in California.

It was my misguided wishful thinking which led me across the country as 2022 began. I couldn't have seriously thought the dynamic was possible had I considered anything beyond the desire to leave northwest Ohio yet again. It wasn't the timing with Mia's family situation, it wasn't the drug withdrawal upon my arrival, and it wasn't the drunken blackout over the prior two days.

It was me; I had no good plan to make anything work, and I had no hope of that particular life becoming a reality in California...and I knew it as I flew out to Mia anyhow. I had acted impulsively. I had acted in reaction to my unhappiness in northwest Ohio, and however I managed to escape that unhappiness was as far of a plan as I put in place. I manipulated a way out from the Midwest, and I never bothered to consider anything besides changing my immediate situation.

I had failed again, and I very much deserved to fail. I was through the withdrawal. I was out the other side. My hangover had worn off by the time Mia arrived home from work. All that remained was the shame and embarrassment of my entire time spent with Mia since she picked me up from the airport. I failed her since I first saw her in the line of cars outside of baggage claim. I had failed her from the moment the dynamic began online at the end of 2021.

My first real-world interaction with Mia had been on the half-hour car ride from the airport to her house. My last interaction with Mia was on that same drive, but in the opposite direction. No, I didn't have a flight departing from that airport, but I also knew I was in no position to protest the return drive through the fields of grapes.

I remained silent on that ride to the far side of Fresno. I had my two suitcases in the back seat. Mia parked in a parking space at a hotel, along the road to the airport. She stepped from her car as I got out on my side. I pulled my suitcase from the back seat. Mia walked around to my side and handed me the handle to my other suitcase. Mia spoke as she gave me a hug.

"Get a room here. Figure out what you are going to do."

"No, I'm not getting a room. I have no money, and I don't want a room."

As Mia began to protest, I broke off the hug and turned

my back on her. With one suitcase rolling on either side of me, I walked away from Mia's car. Though I didn't hear Mia start her car or leave, I didn't bother to turn back. I knew it was my own failure which resulted in the end of that short dynamic.

I was alone in California. I had no money. I had no shelter. I had nowhere to go…so I just walked.

The Last Great American Adventure

Sunny and cloudless with a light breeze; a January morning in Fresno, California. The taco truck was open for business in the gas station parking lot; the usual trickle of customers came and went. Some people walked up from their cars while they fueled. Others pulled into the parking lot specifically for the truck. I wandered over from the lot next door. As I stepped in line behind an older couple, my mind raced. I stood there, lost in thought as the couple stepped aside. It was my turn to order.

"Sir? Sir, what can I get for you?"

Seated at the picnic table behind the gas station, I took another bite of a chorizo taco. My luggage rested atop the table while I ate. I wondered what was next; thoughts swirled in my mind. Thousands of miles from where I began the week, nothing around me was familiar. Alone on the street, I had a few dollars, two suitcases of belongings, and no plan for the future.

When 2022 began, I was a newly forty-two years old. My life, after the recent four years of extreme living, had fallen apart around me. I sat at that picnic table, and I thought about everything. The things I had seen, what I had done, where I had been; so many memories came to me from those previous four years. I'd been everywhere. I'd met so many new people. I'd experienced more than I could have ever imagined.

It was my first day homeless, countless miles from comfort or familiarity. No house or career…as was life since 2018. No car, no money, no drugs…those were new factors, suddenly my reality. Fresno, California; completely foreign despite all previous travels. Life, through all which had happened since the adventure began…everything was so different. So much had been lost to unforgiving time. So many opportunities had slipped away to memories. Trajectory, once only upward, reached a drastically new low point as 2022 began.

I snapped out of it. I shook the thoughts from my mind. It wasn't time to wonder how I got there. It wasn't time for the "what ifs" and what could have been. My goal, back in 2018, was to truly live. As I abandoned all that was familiar, I wanted to feel alive. Nothing could be more life-affirming than basic survival. My situation was immediate. It was time to act. I was alone, on streets unfamiliar.

Fresno Yosemite National Airport; it was where I had touched down the week before. From where I sat at the picnic table behind the gas station, I could see the airport in the distance. A thought crossed my mind as I gazed down the road to the vast airport parking lot; I felt some relief from the immediacy of my situation. No matter what happened that day, as long as I stayed somewhat close, I had a place to sleep.

I turned around to survey the scenery behind me. Beyond the gas station and taco truck, there was a busy intersection. At that intersection, on the corner of the sidewalk, there was a bus stop. I still had a few dollars left after buying those tacos. With a suitcase handle in each hand, I walked towards the bus stop. My suitcases rolled along behind me.

I knew nothing about the city of Fresno, but I figured there would be some businesses which offered free wi-fi. Without phone service, wi-fi was going to be my only option to contact anyone. I thought things through as I rode the local bus. I quickly realized that riding the bus had been a mistake. Without wi-fi, I was afraid of where the bus would take me. The airport, further behind me the longer I remained on the bus, was a point of safety. I had been there before, unlike anywhere else in the city. After just two stops, I pulled the rope. I needed off the bus. I needed to remain close to my homebase.

When I stepped off of the bus, I spotted a bus stop bench across the street. It was a block behind me. Another bus was three blocks down the street and headed my way, back in the direction of the airport. My heartbeat sped up. I needed to be on the other side of the street. The traffic was unrelenting. The bus approached the stop. My two suitcases, though on wheels, were both heavy. I chose my moment. I ran.

Horns honked; tires screeched against the pavement of the road. I kept going. Just as the bus began to pull away from the stop, I made it to the other side of the street. The bus was unable to pull away without me. I was standing in the way, directly in front of it. I pointed to indicate that I needed a ride. The driver, with an angry look, motioned me around to the door.

I opened my eyes. It was five o'clock in the morning. I could see the digital readout on the clock, high up on the wall across the terminal. As I lifted my head from my suitcase, I adjusted my glasses. The room around me was full of noise. People were everywhere. The fake sequoia trees in the terminal, resembling the national forest a short distance from Fresno, were providing backdrop for many of the commuters' pictures and videos as they scurried through the airport.

My neck hurt from using my suitcase as a pillow. My back hurt from the rigid plastic seat in the airport terminal. I'd done it; I'd masqueraded as a commuter to allow for some quality sleep inside the airport. Nobody was the wiser. As I gazed around the entirety of the terminal, I froze. From the other end of the long row of seats, an airport security guard faced my direction. The guard didn't move; he just stood and stared. That was all the prompting I needed to get up and on with my day.

Hours went by as I worked out a plan. I sat on a bench in the sunshine, typing away on my phone. I was close enough to the terminal that the airport wi-fi had good reception. I sent Mary another text. Over the previous year, Mary and I had built an intimate dynamic online. Through all of my travel around the country, the two of us remained in contact. Timing had never lined up, and I hadn't visited Mary in Milwaukee. Multiple times, Mary had mentioned to me that she wished for me to come live with her in Wisconsin. Until I was suddenly homeless in California, the thought of making good on that idea was never a serious consideration. Suddenly, the idea to be with Mary in Milwaukee became the logical conclusion; a way for me to escape the streets of Fresno.

My friend Lex, a friend I had known my entire life, a friend who had helped me out of many jams in the previous four years; Lex was the final piece in the plan to escape homelessness in California. Once Mary and I finalized plans to be together on the opposite side of the country, I needed a way to get to her. I messaged back and forth with Lex as I sat on the bench in the California sunlight. I wasn't looking for a plane ticket to Milwaukee. Lex and I settled on another option.

I was familiar with that other option, having used the service twice in 2021: Florida to Texas and Texas to Ohio. Both of those trips proved to be challenging ordeals, especially the second trip; the trip which left me stranded in the middle of nowhere, Illinois. I had a credit with the bus company. I was awarded compensation after being left behind at a truck stop in central Illinois. The bus traveled on to Chicago with my luggage; luggage which was never recovered. It was luggage which accounted for half of my belongings. When I finally finished the week-long journey from San Antonio to Toledo, I was never reunited with my belongings.

Though I wasn't awarded nearly enough to compensate fairly, I had been given enough to cover half of a bus trip across the country. Lex let me know that she was willing to cover the other half of my ticket from Fresno to Milwaukee. Though I had arrived in Fresno on an airplane, and though I was currently seated on a bench outside of the airport, I used the airport's wi-fi to book the trip by bus.

I booked the next available bus trip, set to depart from downtown Fresno at six o'clock the following evening. I had another day and a half to be homeless in Fresno. I just had to get through the day, make it through the night, manage the following day, and arrive at the bus station in time to board the bus the following evening.

I sat in the beautiful California morning. I remembered the complications of the two prior cross-country bus trips. They were both ordeals, time-consuming and stress-inducing. I knew my coming trip, covering many miles, had much more potential for problems. Some stress was lifted, though. I had a plan. I wasn't going to be lost to the streets of Fresno. Life was going to change.

As I sat there on the airport bench, I had no idea how soon things were set to be different. I heard footsteps. I was suddenly sitting in someone's shadow. I looked up to see a man standing in front of me. In that moment, life again became interesting.

"Hey, man. How you doin'? You smoke?"

"No, man. Not pot."

"What's your name?"

The conversation with the middle-aged Black man progressed over the next ten minutes. I could quickly tell that my new friend was on the level. Through the guy's rapid-fire delivery of his life story, his paranoid delusions, and his reason for being at the airport, I immediately knew that methamphetamine was fueling Donny's brain. I had been free from crystal since leaving the Midwest the week before. It was only the second week I hadn't been high on methamphetamine in almost five years.

I listened as Donny explained how his ex-wife was casting spells on him to destroy his life. I nodded as Donny told me that he was about to catch a flight to North Carolina. Donny's brother lived in North Carolina, and Donny was headed there to escape the evil magic which caused his life to fall apart. I could tell where the conversation was headed. I eagerly anticipated those next words; and then Donny said what I had been expecting.

"You said you don't smoke pot. What about other things? I need to be inside to board a plane in an hour. I can't take anything with me. I need to get out of California before my ex knows I'm gone. That way, it'll be too late to cast a spell on me to keep me here."

"I hear ya. I understand. We should take a walk."

I stood up. With a suitcase handle in each hand, I fell into step alongside Donny. Somehow, thousands of miles and a week removed from crystal meth, the drug found me again. I contained my anticipation as we put distance between us and the entrance to the airport. We walked. We crossed the parking lot. I saw the gas station and taco truck up ahead. Next to that, I saw the hotel.

The hotel: a day earlier, I had been dropped off in that hotel parking lot. As Donny and I walked, I couldn't suppress a smile. Once amongst a small group of trees on the back side of the hotel, Donny pulled out his torch and a glass bubble pipe. When I saw the pipe, my smile amplified; the entire oil burner was filled with crystal. I was back in action.

Donny and I walked around the roads adjacent to the airport for the next half hour. As we walked, we found out-of-the-way spots to smoke crystal. The time came when Donny needed to head inside the airport to board his flight. I thanked Donny for smoking with me. Out of courtesy, I reached out to hand the still-full pipe back to him. Knowing the situation, I received the expected response.

"Keep it. I can't take it with me."

"Again, man...much appreciated. You don't know how much you just helped me out. I'll be able to handle the bus trip this coming week. You're a lifesaver."

As Donny headed back towards the airport entrance, I turned to walk the rest of the way to the taco truck. I still had a few dollars. I also had a new torch. I even had a new pipe…and it was almost completely full of rocket fuel. My drug of choice; methamphetamine had been the drug which shaped and guided my entire world since 2017.

In early 2018, crystal had been my inspiration to drop out of the corporate world and leave northwest Ohio; my home for the first thirty-eight years of my life. Crystal had been my driving force when I suddenly found popularity, on a large scale, in the adult social media hookup universe. Crystal had helped fund my travel as I crisscrossed the country, countless times over, meeting new people and sharing new intimate experiences with lovers, fans, and friends everywhere in the United States.

Since 2018, I had led a life of extraordinary note. I had seen so much, done so much, and been to so many places. Before all which happened, I had made a deal with myself. Back in 2018, while still in my house, while still connected to my former life, and before I truly stepped from the edge, I held onto just one notion. Whether it was an excuse to put off the inevitable, or it was a way to find meaning, my only plan for my future was that deal.

No matter what happens, I can't kill myself until I write a book.

2022 had begun. I had made it through extreme circumstances which landed me on the streets of Fresno, a city of which I knew nothing. Two weeks into the year, and I had already traveled from the Midwest to the West Coast, briefly stopping in Colorado along the way. I was already planning to cross the country again in the second half of January. All of my hardships, all of my triumphs, and all in between; all I had done, and all which I hadn't...it all led me to where I was in that moment. In that moment, as I hit that crystal meth pipe, I thought I was ready for anything 2022 could throw at me.

Coming In Hot

There was that bus stop again, on the corner of that busy intersection. I watched a local bus pull up to the corner. Two people stepped onto the bus, and it pulled away. Repeating what I had done the previous day, I ate chorizo tacos on the picnic table. With crystal flowing through me, I had some exploration to do. There was no longer any apprehension about ending up too far from the airport. I realized I most likely wasn't going to sleep that night, anyhow. It was only mid-afternoon. I still had well over a full day until I needed to be at the downtown bus terminal. Maybe I would take a practice run downtown to gauge the next day's travel time. Maybe I should see what was happening in downtown Fresno. I looked into my crystal ball. My future was clear…with a hazy white tint.

Tweaking out and pulling my two suitcases, I stepped off of a local bus somewhere in a busy section of the city. After riding around on multiple local buses in the afternoon, I was hungry. People were out, walking everywhere. Multiple-lane streets were congested with traffic in every direction. I didn't expect to see the sheer number of people everywhere around me. Fresno was hopping. The crystal helped me maintain my pace as I pulled my suitcases through the city. As I walked, I found a feature I hadn't encountered before.

On the corner of a busy intersection, cars rolled by with stereo systems bumping loud music. People scurried in all directions on foot; to, and from the strips of stores and businesses. There, on that corner, was my solution to my hunger. There was a large flat cement slab, easily the size of a standard gas station parking lot. Rows of picnic tables were lined up underneath a roof structure. The roof was secured to the tops of cement poles, jutting upward from all sides of the cement floor. Condiments and napkin holders were placed incrementally along the picnic tables. A DJ booth was anchored to one corner of the cement slab. Music was blasting from the open-air restaurant. Three sides of the cement slab had what appeared to be permanent taco trucks as walls: different businesses, different employees.

I found where I was going to eat. I walked onto the cement slab through a turnstile at the one side of the slab which lacked a taco truck. There was an issue when I approached the window of the middle taco truck; the employees didn't speak English, and I spoke no Spanish. After pointing to pictures on the menu, I paid for my food. While I sat alone at a table in the middle of the taco truck open-air restaurant, I noticed everyone else in my vicinity watching me closely while I ate. I began to chew faster. I began to feel uneasy. I knew I had to leave.

Back on another bus, I was on my practice ride to the downtown area. I wanted to be left alone. When a younger White guy asked me for spare change, I replied honestly. I had just spent the last of my money at the taco truck complex, a couple of miles back. The White guy continued down the aisle, asking others for spare change. When he reached the Mexican man seated in the second row from the front, the conversation intensified. A fight broke out. Fists flew as the bus driver pulled to a stop in downtown Fresno. The police were already waiting outside.

I stepped from the bus. I was as close as that bus route would take me. I worked my way beyond the ruckus. I started my walk to the bus terminal, almost a mile up the street. I walked across downtown Fresno as the evening sunlight began to fade away, suitcases rolled alongside of me. The farther I walked, the heavier my luggage felt. The crystal was fueling me, but I had reached a point where exhaustion outweighed chemical enhancement.

Startled outside the courtyard square in downtown

Fresno, I stopped when the disheveled White homeless man jumped onto the sidewalk in front of me. The man had dirty ripped clothes. He carried two plastic bags of what I assumed were more clothes. Zooted from the crystal and overheated from the walk, I stared at the man in front of me. I didn't have the patience for whatever was happening. I didn't have any money or any drugs to spare. After what seemed like an impromptu staring contest, it was the disheveled homeless man who spoke first.

"I saw you on TV. Your sister, how is she after the accident? I saw you on the news on TV. I was there. I met with Pickles. It was Pickles and Harry Potter. I was at their house. We're famous, me and you. Pickles and Harry Potter were there…"

And just like that, I was no longer annoyed that the man had jumped in front of me. I took interest in the conversation. I agreed with the man. Anytime the man spoke of events in his life, I nodded my reassurance. Slowly, I stepped forward, doing my best to inform the man that I was late to an appointment down the street. Though I continued to engage, I made my way past the gentleman and put some distance between us. I had physically broken free, but my new friend had more to say.

"It's us! We're famous! We did it!"

"I know. I'll see you later. Thanks for talking with me."

It was almost nighttime as I bid that final farewell to my new friend. I waved goodbye. I walked on, pulling my suitcases up the street. I was almost to the bus terminal. Though I had sorted out the ticket situation online earlier that morning, I hadn't been able to receive an electronic ticket on my phone. Due to using the credits, I was told I needed to pick up the ticket in person.

I collapsed into a chair at the bus station. Pouring sweat from the drugs and the physical exertion, I could only hold up a finger when I was asked what I needed. Seeing my condition, the lady behind the counter retrieved a bottle of water. As I chugged the water, the lady explained that the terminal was closing in ten minutes. I caught my breath in that time, and I presented my information to the woman behind the counter. Moments later, as the lights of the terminal shut off, my tickets printed from the front desk.

As I stepped out into the darkness of the downtown Fresno evening, I looked over the papers in my hand. My meth-saturated mind raced. I saw how many stops and switches the bus was going to make as I traveled across the country over the course of the upcoming week. Eighteen cities in twelve states, and those were just the manifested locations printed on the tickets. In 2021, I had journeyed on two cross-country bus rides. Those two trips, even including the extra day when I was abandoned in the middle of the country, didn't add up to the time and distance of the coming bus trip.

I had twenty-four hours to wait before my bus was scheduled to depart from the street where I was standing. I looked around. It was dark outside, and I knew I needed to be somewhere else besides that part of town overnight. I walked farther on, beyond the bus station. Though I arrived from the center of downtown, the airport was in the opposite direction. After passing through a group of sidewalk loiterers who eyed my suitcases, I stepped into an alley between two buildings. As I hit the crystal, I decided I was going to walk straight up the road, in the unfamiliar direction, until I inevitably came across a bus stop. I didn't know when I would reach the next bus stop. My hope fueled me as I pulled my suitcases behind me. If my hopes eventually ran out, drugs would fuel me the rest of the way.

There it was up ahead, on the corner of an intersection. It was a bus stop. My labored breathing was deep and heavy. My steps: slow as I dragged my feet along the sidewalk. No more breaks until I reached the bus stop. I could make it. I was miles beyond the downtown bus terminal where I picked up my ticket that evening. All the walking had paid off. Just two more blocks, and I could sit and rest while I waited for the next bus. My feet hurt, my hands were cramped from pulling my suitcases, my eyes burned from the constant sweat from my forehead.

I made it. A wooden bench had never looked so inviting. With a suitcase on either side of me, I sank down on the bench. Before I shut my eyes, I looked to the horizon in each of the four directions from the intersection. I saw traffic everywhere, but no buses were in the immediate vicinity. With no energy to keep my eyes open, I fell asleep on the bus stop bench.

What was that?

I opened my eyes as that question entered my mind. Something caused me to wake. It wasn't the traffic on the Fresno streets which woke me that night. Something seemed off. I shook off the fog of my post-sleep mindset. As I did, the scenery around me came into focus. What was it? I looked to my left; nothing unusual. I slowly scanned the streets as I turned my head and began to scan to the right of where I sat. As soon as I turned slightly to the right, I froze. I found what woke me from my nap on the bus stop bench that evening. As I saw it, I fully snapped awake. Adrenaline hit, and it mixed with the crystal in my system. Time suddenly moved in slow motion.

There in front of me, in the road just ten feet away, was a new and immediate concern. I had previously considered that I was likely to face some sort of dangerous interactions from shady people on the street. I knew I had to keep an eye out for seedy strangers and suspicious activity. I had thought ahead to situations involving others on the streets in the dark of night. An oversight: what I saw just ten feet in front of me, I had no way to prepare. I was caught, as vulnerable as could be. There in front of me, staring directly at me and facing me, was a large pit bull.

Silence hung in the air for what seemed like an eternity. As I sat there, frozen in place, thoughts bounced around in my brain. The dog, as if in the same trance as I, didn't move. It just stood there, staring. I snapped out of it and opened my mouth. My voice, loud and firm as words escaped into the air.

"Hey buddy...go away!"

The dog cocked its head to the side. An ear lifted in response. The longest seconds of my life passed by, lost to eternity. Suddenly, as if called away by another force, the dog turned and trotted past me, through the intersection, and down the road beyond the traffic lights.

As I kept my eyes on the departing animal, the front of a bus appeared in the distance. I watched as the dog hopped into the grass to avoid the bus. I heard the bus's brakes as it began to slow. It passed through the intersection to the left of me. The bus stopped, and I stepped aboard. Once I confirmed my route to the airport, I took a seat. The bus, at that time of night, was empty besides me. After breathing a sigh of relief, I settled in for my ride to the airport.

After a repeat of the night before, I stepped out into the morning. Again, the airport had been sanctuary when I had nowhere else to sleep. The weather was the same as the day before, as was the scene outside the airport. Again, I smoked crystal while I rode the local buses around the city and ate tacos. When late afternoon arrived, I began my trip downtown. I knew I was going to have to walk from the center of downtown again, so I added that length of time to my departure from the general vicinity near the airport.

Even with the extra time factored in, I had to hurry once I reached downtown. One of my bus transfers in the city had been incorrect. Once sorted, I had to get off one of the buses and walk, with my heavy suitcases, to a bus stop down the road. The time I spent on the wrong bus and the time it took to reach the next proper bus stop put me behind schedule. I had to run from the square in downtown Fresno, pulling my suitcases over bumps, curbs, and grass, almost all of that last mile to the bus terminal. The same vagrant again stopped me. I had no time for any delusional stories. I handed the guy a lighter, and I continued my exhausting run through downtown Fresno.

As the sky grew dark as night began, I reached the bus terminal. Unlike the day before, the terminal was packed with people; all waiting for the same bus as me. Once the bus arrived, everyone boarded. The bus was full. I had a window seat towards the back. One suitcase was between my feet. The other, the larger suitcase, had to be checked. It was loaded in the luggage compartment underneath the passenger cabin.

I looked at my ticket. The first leg of the trip was set to cross California. The bus, headed south, was scheduled to reach Bakersfield late that night. The first leg of the trip was scheduled to end, early in the morning, in Los Angeles. That was where that first bus terminated its route. I would then have four hours to wait at the terminal in Los Angeles before I departed on my first eastbound bus. After a full night of travel, I would still be in California. Eleven more states to go once I finally left California.

I heard stories of the Los Angeles bus terminal from other riders as everyone boarded the bus in Fresno. I settled in, fully expecting an adventure. It was going to be a long week, no matter what happened. Once again, I was completely starting my life over. If all went according to plan, I would be living in Milwaukee, thousands of miles away, by the beginning of the next week. If all went according to plan...

Cross Country Fish Boot

"I'm on the first bus. Leaving Fresno now. I'll be in Los Angeles at two o'clock."

"Looking forward to seeing you. Keep me posted."

I turned off my phone after I read Mary's reply. The bus pulled away from the terminal. The rows of lights above the passengers' heads faded out. The interior of the bus went dark, matching the California night sky. People shuffled around in their seats, adjusting their belongings to get comfortable for the southbound trip through California. I tried my best to clear some room at my feet. With my suitcase between my legs on the floor, there wasn't much I could do. Settled in the best I could, I closed my eyes. The bumps and engine noise of the bus blended with the random conversations of other passengers. I drifted off to sleep.

The stop in Bakersfield was uneventful. I woke when the bus pulled into the terminal. The passengers had time for a quick bathroom break while a couple people transferred buses. The break gave me an opportunity to hit the pipe. Once everyone was back on the bus, the interior lights again faded to black. The meth infusion in the Bakersfield bus terminal had me zooted up. I knew I wasn't going to get any more sleep as the bus continued the journey to Los Angeles. It was hard to sit still. Sweat began to drip from my face.

When the bus docked in Los Angeles, I put my phone away. I had been recording videos out of the window since the bus exited the interstate. As I waited to claim my bag from underneath the bus, I researched the Los Angeles bus terminal on my phone. I was in a bad area of the city. I read warnings from previous travelers; reviews which included property theft and personal safety concerns. As I collected my luggage, I looked around my immediate area. Armed security guards inside the facility were visible from the parking lot. With my two suitcases rolling beside me, I walked towards the entrance to the terminal.

I spent four hours in the terminal. Anytime I managed to fall asleep for a minute, with my smaller suitcase as an uncomfortable pillow, I was almost immediately woken up by commotion somewhere nearby. Homeless people kept sneaking into the terminal, and security kept removing them from inside. Some yelled at the guards, others became physically aggressive. I got no quality sleep. I occasionally stepped outside to smoke. Shady people loitered around outside the doors to the terminal. After the final unpleasant interaction with a man asking for money, I decided I wasn't going to step outside anymore.

The cafeteria opened before it was time to board the next bus. I sat and ate my overpriced, dry chicken strips. A beautiful blonde girl walked past to queue up in the proper line for her bus. I threw away my trash and stepped in line behind the girl, at the gate specified over the intercom. I made small talk with the blonde girl as we waited to board the bus. Kay was a twenty-two-year-old White girl. She was about to head across the country on the same route as me. Her year in Santa Monica was at an end. She was headed to Michigan to start a new life. Just before six o'clock in the morning, I watched through the windows of the terminal as a bus pulled into its parking space in the lot outside.

"Looks like that's us."

"Will you sit next to me? We can share headphones. I've got good music."

Kay was right. Her musical taste was in line with the music I enjoyed. As the sky began to turn purple, just before sunrise, I handed Kay's headphone back to her. The bus pulled into a gas station in the desert of Arizona. I recorded video of the sunrise beyond the Arizona mountains. Kay and I shared a magical moment as we stood outside together in the early morning. From the gas station parking lot, while Kay and I ate food and drank soft drinks, the sun crested the mountains and cast light to the desert below.

It was those small moments of nothing which felt pure and life-affirming. I lived for moments such as the moment I shared with Kay that morning outside in the desert. Fleeting, but in those brief moments, nothing mattered beyond what was immediate. The past: everything led up to that exact moment in time. The future; inconsequential. All that mattered, all that meant anything, was the present. The present; and nothing more. In those brief moments, life made sense. I smiled; I had someone to share that moment with me.

It was a long ride across the desert of the Southwest that day in late January 2022. The bus made frequent stops as it rolled its way across the lower United States. I stretched my legs and bought food at various locations. I also stayed high on crystal. Each stop was an opportunity to lock myself in a bathroom stall at a rest stop and fire up the torch. The pipe maintained its supply of melted crystal, despite my frequent methamphetamine breaks.

After each bathroom break, I hurried back to the bus. Paranoia was instant, even though I was careful. The second I stepped from a bathroom, I figured everyone inside the rest stops knew I had just smoked crystal. Once the bus pulled away from each stop, my paranoia subsided. I was still too paranoid to attempt to smoke crystal in the small restroom aboard the bus, at least not while the bus was full to capacity. The bus remained at capacity for the entire trip across the desert.

When the bus reached Flagstaff, Arizona, I experienced a surprise. I didn't know that it snowed in Arizona. The heat in Phoenix, earlier that same day, was expected. The weather in Flagstaff, which I attributed to the elevation and time of year, was the opposite of Phoenix. The layover in Flagstaff was only forty-five minutes, but there was nowhere indoors to wait. I wrapped my arms around Kay, and the two of us struggled to stay warm in the wind and snow.

Crossing over to New Mexico, Kay and I picked up a stray. The two of us, sitting together in the very back row of the bus, were attempting to listen to music through Kay's headphones. The kid seated directly in front of Kay continuously turned around to talk to us over the back of his seat. Kay and I learned much about the kid, though none of the information was requested. He just kept talking, sharing his strange story and all sorts of useless information. Jason was sixteen years old and traveling by himself. He was a big White kid; he could have easily passed for a man in his mid-twenties. His haircut was ridiculous; dark brown, it was the most uneven and choppy bowl cut, shaved down to the skin below the bowl, with bangs cut high up on his forehead.

There was no possibility that Kay and I could avoid the barrage of useless information. On breaks at rest stops, Jason followed us anywhere we went. He droned on and on about where he was headed: his aunt's house in Louisiana. Jason chain-smoked cigarettes, which gave me a chance to be alone in bathrooms to hit my pipe while Jason and Kay smoked cigarettes next to the bus. I wasn't sure of Jason's exact mental deficiency, but I knew something about Jason was very off. Kay and I had picked up a third wheel, and we weren't going to lose him until he switched buses in Texas.

The bus reached Albuquerque, New Mexico late in the night. As the bus unloaded outside of the terminal, I heard commotion from the intersection adjacent to the parking lot. As a blatantly homeless man yelled obscenities at another homeless gentleman across the street from where he stood, the recipient of the verbal assault decided to take it up a notch. Shirtless, the second man suddenly burst into a full sprint across the road. The two men met with fists as they assaulted one-another until the instigator ran off into the darkness.

The victor, the shirtless man from the other side of the street, raised his arms in celebration. It was he who then began to yell obscenities into the air. There was no target to his verbal tirade, but he didn't seem discouraged. He remained on the street corner, yelling all sorts of creative slurs. Kay and I retrieved our bags from under the bus. The two of us rolled our suitcases to the entrance of the terminal. Jason followed closely behind. We could still hear the man yelling through the glass when the doors closed behind us and the three of us were inside the bus terminal.

The bus terminal in Albuquerque had no food services. The vending machines in the terminal were all out of order. I had credit with a delivery service from a mistake on an order in Ohio at the end of 2021. As I smoked crystal in one of the bathrooms, I found a pizzeria which used the delivery service. The restaurant was open for another hour; it was the only open restaurant in the area. I had time, so I ordered a pizza.

"Is pepperoni okay? It was the only place open. It'll be here in thirty minutes."

"Oh, my God! You're my hero!"

Kay thanked me for placing the order. Jason, standing right next to us, asked a question.

"Can I have a piece?"

"Yeah, sure. All good, man. We can go meet the driver outside when he gets here."

When the three of us walked outside a half hour later, the shirtless man on the corner was still yelling at nobody. Kay and Jason stayed up by the door. I walked out to meet the pizza delivery driver in the street. The man on the corner noticed me. He stopped yelling and stared as the pizza transaction went down. When I walked back up to the doors of the bus terminal, the man resumed his incoherent screaming session.

The next bus to Texas was about to board. Kay, Jason, and I stood outside and ate pizza to the sounds of aggressive obscenities. Once the three of us got our fill, I told the other two that I would meet them back inside, in line at the gate. Kay and Jason went inside, I turned and walked back towards the street. The man on the corner saw me approaching. When I stepped onto the side of the street where the man was standing, his yelling abruptly stopped.

I walked directly up to the man while the man stared with wild eyes. I opened the pizza box; two pieces remained in the box. I held the box out to the man. Wild eyes focused directly on mine. I nodded to the man. The man reluctantly took the box from my hand. As I walked back across the street, I heard the man as he again screamed obscenities. I assumed those pieces of pizza were going to fuel a full night of street corner obscenity yelling. I met Kay and Jason in line inside the terminal as our next bus was boarding.

Hours passed on the dark and quiet bus. Again, Kay and I had the seats at the very back. Jason was seated on the other side, three rows closer to the front. Kay and I had a break from Jason's incessant pestering. Though Jason occasionally tried to yell things across the bus to us, we were able to ignore him. It was late, and other passengers were trying to sleep. When Jason tried to start conversations, other passengers told him to quiet down.

Kay and I sat and listened to music on Kay's headphones. We took turns sharing new music. Suddenly, Kay asked for her headphone back. She wanted to talk. I handed her the headphone, and Kay put it in her pocket. She leaned closely to me and looked at me with a serious expression. Quietly, she began to speak.

"Can I tell you a secret? I need to show you something. You can't tell anyone. You have to promise me."

"Okay...Yeah, sure. What is it?"

Kay had been carrying a pair of cowboy boots with her the entire trip. She made sure they were always upright and carefully placed next to her on all of the buses. Kay reached down and slowly lifted up her boots to set them between her and me. She looked around to make sure nobody else on the bus was paying any attention. Once she was sure that nobody would be able to see what she was about to do, she reached into one of the boots. Her hand slowly came up out of the boot. I could see that Kay had something in her hand. I watched; anticipation for the sudden secret which Kay was about to reveal. Right before Kay's hand cleared the top of the boot, she stopped. She again looked directly into my eyes.

"You promise you won't say anything? I'm trusting you."

"Yes, I promise."

Kay finished removing what was previously hidden away. Her hand cleared the top of her boot. What was in her hand was fully unexpected. It was Kay's big secret, the item she made me promise to keep to myself. My eyebrows raised, and I smiled. From inside of her boot, Kay pulled out a small round fishbowl. There was gravel at the bottom. It was filled to the top with water. Swimming in the water was a beta. A fish: Kay's pet fish.

"This is Joe. I couldn't leave him in California. He's my traveling buddy. He came out to California with me. I'm taking him to Michigan."

"Uhh...that's the big secret? You're so serious about

keeping it a secret?"

"Well, you're not allowed to have pets on the bus."

"Don't worry…you're secret's safe with me."

Parting Ways

The following night, there was no comfort in Amarillo. Again, my assumptions had been wrong about states in the southern part of the country. The snow in Arizona had been a surprising experience. Amarillo, Texas was something else altogether. It was thirteen degrees outside when the bus pulled into the dilapidated Amarillo bus station. Everyone had to vacate the bus for two hours, whether or not they were continuing on that same bus. Amarillo was a scheduled stop for cleaning and maintenance. Passengers stepped off the bus and retrieved their luggage.

There were no employees at the bus station. There was no electricity, no intercoms, no lights, no heat. It was as cold inside as it was outside. The Amarillo bus station looked as if it had been abandoned for years. It was dirty, it was run down, and it was horrible in every way. The bathrooms didn't have running water. The floor inside had a layer of ice on it, making each step treacherous. The wind, biting and frigid, blew in through gaps and open doors. The crystal I smoked in the bathroom did nothing to combat the deep freeze of winter in northern Texas.

Kay and I again cuddled up together to try to stay warm. Many others from the bus were doing the same thing on different seats around the dark and empty shell of the terminal. Not Jason, though. Jason stood directly behind us, talking enough to keep his core temperature warm. No complaints from Jason about the conditions, just nonstop words spilling from his mouth. I was reaching my limit, but I was too cold to say anything. I held Kay against me. The shared body heat was the only relief from the nightmare situation.

I began to notice something the longer I sat in that terminal. My bus was the only bus which had unloaded in Amarillo, but more and more people continued to trickle in around me. In groups of three or four at a time, the terminal began to fill up. Each new group of arrivals shared many similar qualities. They were all males, mostly appearing to be in their twenties. They all wore plain-colored button-down shirts in pastel colors. All of them had what appeared to be tied-off garbage bags of personal effects.

My assumptions were proven correct after brief conversations with a couple of the new arrivals. The terminal became crowded with people as the night wore on. I had heard other conversations in passing. I spoke directly with a few of the new people around me. That Amarillo bus terminal, in all of its lack of glory, was where prison inmates were sent back into the world.

Jason's ridiculous mouth continued to spout off obviously fake accomplishments and stories. Jason continued to brag about far-fetched feats and delusions of grandeur. Kay and I did our best to ignore him. Jason was loud. Others in the terminal randomly shot glances in his direction whenever they caught a small bit of the ridiculousness of Jason's never-ending diatribe. Jason, clueless to his place in the world, noticed none of the attention. Jason, a big and goofy sixteen-year-old White kid with a terrible bowl cut, suddenly added a new level to his buffoonery. As Jason told terrible stories at high volume, he suddenly started dropping random n-bombs. The first slur caught me by surprise.

"Dude…what? You need to shut up, right now."

Jason, paying no attention to anything besides his self-spewed stupidity, continued telling nonsense stories. It only took a minute before the next inadvertent slur slipped out. Jason wasn't using the word with a hard "r." It didn't matter, though. I took my moment. It was time to separate from Jason for good. Kay and I were boarding the same bus as before. Jason was taking another bus to Louisiana. Though there was still another thirty minutes until boarding, I turned to Kay.

"Alright, enough of this kid. You ready? Let's walk around to the other side."

Like that, Jason was no longer in my life. Once on the bus, Kay and I warmed up. The two hours in thirteen-degree weather were rough. My circulation, due to a combination of weather and crystal meth, was severely struggling. I managed some sleep. Kay laid her head on my shoulder, and she slept all the way to Oklahoma City.

Oklahoma was where my time with Kay came to an end. Though she was headed to Michigan, her ticket stopped in Oklahoma City. Kay was in her home city. She planned to get more money when she arrived in Oklahoma City, buy a ticket to Michigan, and head that way after briefly visiting her family. I had half an hour with Kay at the bus terminal while she waited for her ride to pick her up. Her fish made it that far in a bowl in her boot. Kay and I hugged outside the bus when my boarding was called. I was happy to share the journey with her. After making sure Kay was fine, I boarded my next bus to Chicago. I'd made it through the longer, warmer half of my bus journey. My colder, lonelier half began in Oklahoma. Kay was then in my past, only a memory of a girl and her fish.

As the trip progressed, I continued to send update texts to Mary when wi-fi permitted. When I reached Tulsa, I told Mary of a new development. I wasn't just switching buses in Tulsa, Oklahoma. I was switching bus companies completely. The next bus line had far lower standards. The seats were dusty and worn down. The electrical plugs didn't work. There was barely any leg room. With my smaller suitcase by my feet, I needed an aisle seat to put my legs down. The seats were not only less comfortable, but they were also noticeably smaller. The bus, as had been the situation on previous buses, was completely full. Though it was winter, the lack of airflow and congestion on the bus had me dripping sweat. The crystal I smoked before I stepped onto the bus only exacerbated the situation. I knew I was in for a miserable experience.

In the middle of the night, I awoke when my bus arrived at a terminal in Kansas City. The terminal for that new bus line was pure chaos as I stepped out into a snowstorm at two o'clock in the morning. I scrambled, amongst the falling snow and people everywhere, to recover my second suitcase from underneath the bus. I almost missed my connecting trip when the confusion in the winter weather caused me to line up outside for the wrong bus. As I sat on the correct bus, I saw my suitcase outside on the black top. It was covered in snow, but I knew it was mine. Just before my bus pulled away from the terminal, I caught the attention of the driver. The driver radioed to someone outside in the snowstorm. I watched as my suitcase was subsequently thrown into the compartment underneath the bus. I breathed a sigh of relief as I watched the luggage compartment close below me.

The snow was still falling heavily when the bus pulled into the downtown Chicago bus station. Weather through the night had caused delays, and I was too late to catch my connecting bus. My connection, back on the original bus line, was long gone when I arrived in Chicago. After sorting it out at customer service, I retired to the bathroom to warm up and smoke crystal. Hours later, I sent Mary another update to let her know I was in Chicago. Before sunrise that morning, I boarded the final bus of the cross-country journey to my new life in Milwaukee, Wisconsin.

That final bus, from Chicago to Milwaukee, was a new luxury. The first third of the seats contained commuters. The entire rear two-thirds of the bus was completely empty. I had peace and quiet. I had space. I had two-thirds of a bus to myself. The sky began to lighten as the early morning progressed. I had an idea. I knew, on that bus to Milwaukee, that I could pull it off. I locked myself in the bathroom at the back of the bus.

While other passengers slept in the front, I smoked crystal in the bathroom.

My pipe, full to the top in California, no longer looked limitless. When I put the torch's flame to the sides of the glass bubble, all the crystal melted and pooled at the bottom of the pipe. The heated liquid bubbled as I sucked the smoke into my lungs. I held in each hit as long as I could. Then I exhaled into a rolled-up ball of toilet paper. I made multiple trips to the bathroom to get high on that last bus. Only once was I interrupted with a knock on the door; a passenger from the front, needing to use the facilities. I sprayed cologne and stepped out to allow the commuter to use the bathroom. Once the woman finished, I locked myself inside again.

It was cloudy and cold when the bus pulled up to the terminal in Milwaukee. I exited the bus with my suitcase. I waited outside in the lightly falling snow. When the bus driver opened up the compartments underneath the bus, I grabbed my other suitcase. The weather, though cold and windy, was a slight improvement from that stretch between Amarillo and Chicago. I fought the wind, and I rolled my two suitcases into the bus terminal. It was the nicest terminal I had seen. It was huge, and everything looked brand new.

I sat down in a row of seats along the wall. As I warmed up, I sent Mary another text message. I made it. I had traveled from Fresno, California to Milwaukee, Wisconsin. A week had passed, along with thousands of miles. I was done, no more buses, such a relief. Crystal had my thoughts swirling around in my head. I checked my phone. Mary hadn't replied. Maybe she was asleep. I sent her another message. Again, I waited for a response.

My drug-saturated brain began an inner-dialogue of worry. I called Mary's phone; it went to voicemail. Time passed, nothing happened. Anxiety consumed me as I sat in the bus terminal in Milwaukee, Wisconsin. I wondered; I worried. Something was wrong. I was all the way across the country. I overcame challenges during the previous week, but I was there; right where I was supposed to be. Another half hour passed into memory. I paced back and forth. I finally felt my phone vibrate in my hand. Like that, in the space between breaths, my world fell apart.

"I talked with my brother-in-law, and he's not okay with this situation. I jumped ahead of things, and since he's paying for bills. My landlord has no idea about you. I didn't think you were serious about coming here. I made a mistake."

I read the message in disbelief. A year of building the dynamic, and I was just then learning about Mary's brother-in-law and landlord. Mary had previously told me that she owned her own house. Mary's text stated otherwise. I immediately replied; crystal fueled my response.

"Your 'mistake' left me, after all this travel which we communicated the whole time, and I asked you many times if you were sure. I updated you, all the time, where I was. At any point, you could have said you thought I wasn't serious, but I have no idea how all of that wasn't coming off as serious. I sent videos from the bus, saying where I was. We discussed this over the past year as a possibility. Then, from California, I made sure, in many questions, to get a 'for sure' answer from you. I said I needed to be sure, then I bought a ticket. I sent you a screenshot of the ticket. You could have said anything at any time about it. You let me buy the ticket, travel from last Wednesday to now, and now I'm stranded here with no money."

My mind was exploding in all directions. Messages continued to fly back and forth. In disbelief, I replied to everything Mary sent me. Mary texted again.

"People say all the time, 'I'm coming to see you,' yet never actually show up. I didn't think you were, for real, going to get on a bus and show up here. Are you still at the bus station?"

"I have no money or anywhere to go. I'm in a city I don't know, with nothing, so yes, I'm at the bus station."

"I'm stepping out of my comfort zone here…give me a few minutes to get ready."

"You're getting ready for what? I don't know what's going on."

Setup for Failure

I stepped from the bathroom. My pipe, though low, still had some crystal melted to the sides of the glass bubble. Lacking sleep, I was again chemically recharged. My last message to Mary was twenty minutes earlier. I was still in disbelief. I wandered through the terminal, in a daze as I weaved around other commuters. As I walked back to a row of seats, I saw a pickup truck pull up on the road outside. Through the glass wall of the bus station, I saw a girl step out from the passenger side of the pickup truck. It was Mary. She showed up at the bus station.

I waited in the middle of the large lobby, thirty feet in front of the entrance. Mary walked in. She looked around. When she recognized me, she immediately ran up to me. I stood still. I watched as Mary stepped into place two feet in front of me. Mary's thin body was draped in an oversized winter coat. Her glasses had fogged up from the heat inside the terminal. Mary cleaned her glasses with her shirt. Her dyed red hair hung over the sides of her face. I remained silent. Mary broke the silence.

"I can't believe you actually came to Milwaukee."

The conversation continued for ten minutes in the middle of the bus station. Suddenly, I saw the lobby door swing open from behind Mary. I nodded when the fit Black man walked up to us. I introduced myself. The man just stared back at me. The man turned to Mary and stared at her while she spoke to me. The man's eyes widened; his expression was far from pleasant. He finally spoke. His words, firm and demanding, were no suggestion.

"Mary. Let's go. Now."

After the man repeated himself two times, Mary hugged me tightly. The man walked back outside, and Mary followed behind him. Before she walked out the door, Mary looked back. Her look was apologetic. I just stood there in place, not knowing what had just happened. I watched, through the glass wall of the terminal, as Mary and the man disappeared from sight. A moment passed in silence. Though people were all around, though I was sure there were others talking near me, I heard none of it. My world, in that moment, was silent. I snapped out of it. I walked over to a row of seats along the glass wall, and I sat down.

Ten minutes slowly passed. I sat there alone. I didn't move at all for the duration of those ten minutes; my mind was blank. I was at a loss, and there was no way for me to act. From the corner of my eye, I saw the lobby door fly open again. I turned to face the door. It was the man who led Mary outside ten minutes earlier. The look on his face was the same; stern and wide-eyed. The man walked, with purpose, directly toward me. He covered the distance between us in no time. Soon, he stood directly in front of where I sat. I braced for a potential confrontation. The man had the advantage. I was seated. The man stared for what felt like an eternity. Abruptly, he stuck out his hand.

"I'm Dante. Mary just now told me what's going on. Let's talk."

I shook Dante's hand. Still confused, I engaged with Dante. Though Dante had no prior knowledge of my arrangement with Mary, he was sympathetic. Dante and I spoke for five minutes. I apologized for the surprise. Dante apologized for his demeanor.

"Come on. I bet you're hungry from the bus ride. Let's go eat breakfast."

"You sure? I'm not trying to put you out."

"Yes, come on. Let's go eat and sort out this situation."

The three of us squeezed into the pickup truck. Fully confused, I rode in the truck with the other two. Mary wrapped her arms around me. When we reached a favorite breakfast restaurant, the three of us ate food together and talked. Mary apologized again. Mary explained to Dante the extent of her dynamic with me.

I learned that Dante was ex-military, discharged for mental health reasons after a tour of combat. I also learned that Dante was the brother of Mary's ex-husband. The two of them lived together on the ground floor of a duplex in Milwaukee. The owner of the duplex, their landlord, lived directly above them. They were currently in a dispute with their landlord over remaining in the house. At the end of the meal, Dante invited me back to the house for what was a much-needed shower. I hadn't showered since I first arrived in California, earlier in the month. I accepted the offer.

I spent my first day in Milwaukee at Mary and Dante's home. Though Mary was extremely interested in me romantically, I wasn't sure what was up with the dynamic in the house. The scene was weird, for sure. I did the best I could to role with it. Whenever Mary was alone with me, she reiterated how Dante was in love with her; she insisted she didn't reciprocate. Dante functioned as Mary's protector. He spoke as if the two of them were a couple. I couldn't wrap my head around the situation.

Mary and Dante's nosey landlord had seen me enter the home with his tenants. Both received text messages. The landlord, an older gentleman, was still afraid of the pandemic. He made it clear that I was not to be there long-term. That added more to my confusion regarding my situation. I smoked the last of my crystal while I took a shower that first day in Milwaukee. I couldn't make my drugs last any longer than that first day. The situation was more stressful once I burned up the last of the crystal in my pipe. My mind, all day, was all over the place.

I tattooed Mary with equipment from my suitcase. Surprisingly, Dante had his own tattoo equipment. Dante's machine had sat in a drawer for over a year, never used. Dante thought it was missing pieces. I fixed Dante's situation for him. I had the ink cartridges needed to complete Dante's setup. I also had an extra power supply. I gifted those items to Dante as a way to thank him for the hospitality. Dante was thrilled. He spent hours tattooing himself for the first time. He was an artist. I gave Dante the items needed to create his art, his skin as his canvas. He learned fast, and his first tattoo on his arm looked as if done by a professional.

At nine o'clock that first night, Mary and Dante got dressed up to go out. They told me to do the same. Dante lent me a winter coat. After driving through a snowstorm in the pickup truck, the three of us reached the karaoke bar where Mary and Dante spent four nights each week. They knew everyone inside the hole-in-the-wall bar. Both of them were amazing singers. After one of the most chaotic days of a chaotic week, I had a surprisingly great time with the two of them at the bar. It was unexpected, but it was the first night I managed to enjoy myself in some time. When the three of us returned home, we watched a movie in the living room. Once Dante went to sleep in his room, Mary encouraged me to sleep with her in her bedroom. I slept on the couch in the living room, far too baffled by the abnormal dynamic in the house.

Extremely cold temperatures were all over the Midwest in early 2022. Milwaukee was no exception. The wind was constant and biting. From sunup to sundown, Mary, Dante, and I crammed into the pickup truck and drove everywhere in the city. I helped Mary and Dante grocery shop and deliver the groceries to people who ordered them from an app. It was a strenuous, cold, and odd existence. I froze in the wind as I carried bags of food to customers' doorsteps. Mary and Dante showed me around the city. At one point, the three of us sat in the pickup truck at a park in downtown Milwaukee. We were facing Lake Michigan. I noticed the lake had frozen over.

I thought I was done with bus rides. I was wrong. Once again, I had to move on. My presence at Mary and Dante's home had set off a flashpoint with their landlord. At six o'clock on my fourth evening in Milwaukee, I rolled my two suitcases into the Milwaukee bus station.

The snow was falling hard. I was barely able to see Dante's pickup truck as it pulled away. The temperature outside was well below zero. I wondered what that meant for the bus; on its way to pick me up and take me down to Chicago.

The customer service worker was posted up at the front desk; she told me the bad news. My bus was broken down from the cold, on the side of the interstate two hours north of Milwaukee. I again had no money, no food, and an unknown wait for a new bus. I hoped I wasn't waiting for the same bus as was the man pacing back and forth, preaching his unique religious sermon at the top of his lungs in the middle of the terminal.

The recovery bus arrived eight hours later. It was filled with the passengers who had been rescued from the side of the road. I knew I missed my next bus in Chicago. I knew I was going to have more issues sorting out my ride from Chicago to Dayton, Ohio. When the bus boarded, I knew I was traveling to Chicago with the bus station preacher.

Two full days later, I stepped off of my last connection. I was in Trotwood, Ohio. It was dark outside at six o'clock in the evening. I was still half an hour north of my destination. I had no phone service, so I hadn't been able to let my friend Maren know that I was a full day late to Ohio. The bus stop was closed when I stepped off of my final bus. The air temperature was already below zero. With the sunlight gone, the temperature was plummeting fast. Winds blew constantly between thirty and forty miles per hour, but intermittent, stronger gusts frequently cut through the air.

I was alone in the winter night with no shelter, a day beyond the original time I told my friend Maren to pick me up. I was on the side of the road in the dark. I had two suitcases to pull with me. I needed to make some quick decisions. There was a very real chance that my life was in immediate peril. In 2018, I had vowed to die somewhere other than Ohio. If I didn't figure out some way to escape the frigid winter night, I was going to freeze to death.

After trudging through the snow for half an hour, pulling two heavy suitcases and doing all I could to shield my face from the wind, I reached an area of town where restaurants and shops lined the busy highway. Barely able to move my fingers, I managed to open the door to a fast-food restaurant. As I collapsed into a seat in the lobby, a manager noticed me. I warmed up the best I could while I ate my free meal. The restaurant lobby closed while I sat and ate. I knew I had to leave.

It was twenty minutes later when I stepped back outside. As I again faced the frozen Hell, I feared for my life. I stood in a parking lot by the road, and I felt the weather overtaking me. My mind began to slow. I had no plan; I had no action to take. As the wind whipped against my face, as the cold began to settle into my bones, I began to give up. With nowhere to go, hopelessness sank in with the cold. The darkness of the night permeated my soul.

Four years of travel, four years of truly living; feeling alive. I knew it was coming to an end right there on the side of that road in Ohio. I was a mere thirty-minute drive from my destination, if only I had a car. I may as well have been a million miles away from everything. Hope, it faded away into the horrible and painfully cold winter night. Thousands of miles, and I was just twenty miles shy of my destination. In that moment, the only twenty miles that mattered were those miles untraveled; twenty miles I was never going to see.

It was over; everything was done. On the side of that horrible road in that horrible place, I had arrived in Hell. All my efforts, all I had done, and all I hadn't; everything led me to that exact point in space and time. I had been on a journey to find myself since I left my old life back in 2018. I had seen so much and done so much. In that moment, I had two thoughts; I believed I had finally lived, and I believed it was my moment to live no more. There was no doubt that the cold that night was going to be my end. After forty-two years of existence, my journey was over. As destiny was there in front of me, as I readied myself for the horrible and painful death from the cold, something happened which changed everything.

Below the Permafrost

As I resigned myself to fate while I stood alone in the night, fate showed me that I wasn't yet counted out; fate brought others to me. Others: in the same predicament, at the same time, in the same place, led to me through their own series of trials and tribulations. Divergence converged in space-time to save me at that lowest point…in the very moment I needed it most, a moment almost my last.

I wasn't the only one. I wasn't the only person in Trotwood, Ohio fighting for survival on one of the coldest nights on record. I wasn't the only traveler fresh off of a bus, without phone service, in an unfamiliar location, and desperately seeking protection against certain death from exposure. I wasn't the only one who had all but lost every sliver of hope, swept away by the blistering wind in the night. Not being the only one; that fact alone was enough to spark the tiniest hope in what had been a presumed bleak end.

The two wide-eyed teenagers appeared in front of me as if out of nowhere. The third companion, a forty-year-old man, walked up to add his presence to the group. The new group, four people, became a sudden force in the night. The two teenagers were boyfriend and girlfriend. They had also taken a bus to Trotwood. They were on their way across the country, to California. For whatever reason, their bus tickets ended in Ohio. The couple shared a phone, which was dead. They needed to reach a relative out West to buy them tickets the rest of the way. They had nowhere to go until they figured out their ticket issue.

The lone man had met up with the teenage couple just five minutes prior to their encounter with me. His eyebrows were shaved off. I could tell that the man was a heavy drug user. I assumed he latched onto the innocent teenage couple to use them for something. I wasn't sure what he sought, but the forty-year-old man was also on his way out West…or so he claimed. A hookup from a phone app had dropped the man off on the street shortly before he met up with the couple. There was no time to weed out seedy characters. Lives were legitimately in danger each minute the four of us remained exposed to the elements.

Our group chose to act so we all didn't freeze to death. The four of us thought to rent a moving van from a home improvement store down the road. Nobody had the money to cover the rental. A worker at the store told our group that the local buses ran routes around the Dayton metro area until midnight each night. Our group struggled through the cold night. We eventually reached the nearest roadside bus stop. The four of us rode the local bus loop for the remainder of the night, in circles to downtown Dayton and back to Trotwood.

Once the local busses stopped for the night, the four of us went back to the home improvement store. It was closed. We had no intentions of going inside the store anyhow. When we were sure nobody was around, we broke into the back of one of the box trucks in the parking lot. We needed an escape from the wind. Even with the door closed, it was too cold in the truck. All four of us were sure we were going to begin losing fingers and toes to frostbite. After only an hour inside the truck, we abandoned the idea. We needed somewhere warmer.

Braving the wind for a thirty-minute trek down the street, the four of us ran inside the only open gas station in the area. It was one thirty in the morning. After attempting to warm up in the back of the small store, the owner of the gas station took notice. He motioned me to the counter. The owner handed me a key. The four of us went outside again. Around the corner, I unlocked the bathroom door. It was cramped and cold, but we all fit into the bathroom for the remainder of the night. By six in the morning, all four of us were fading in and out of consciousness. By six thirty, the forty-year-old man was gone, along with the teenage couple's cellphone. The man stole it from them and disappeared into the cold morning while we slept on the floor of the bathroom.

Our group, down to just three, left the bathroom at seven in the morning. The local buses began their routes at seven, and the station was half a mile down the road. The teenage couple and I pushed through the cold and wind to reach the bus station. Still pulling two heavy suitcases behind me, I led the way. Once inside the station, we bought local bus passes to get us to downtown Dayton. Once we reached the main bus terminal in downtown Dayton, I began to search for someone who could help me finish my trip to my friend Maren's house. The couple stayed close to me. I knew I had to split off from them. I wasn't able to speak with anyone without the couple butting in to tell their stories. Anytime I felt I was making progress, the two teenagers interrupted my conversations. I knew I was better off alone.

I found a local bus which took me to another suburb, south of Dayton. I then walked the last mile to the city's shopping mall, pulling my two heavy suitcases through the bitter cold. The mall had wi-fi, which I needed to utilize so I could reach out to Maren. As I waited for Maren to pick me up, my eyes grew heavy. Mall security came by frequently to remind me that there was no sleeping in the food court. I dozed off a final time. I awoke to a phone call. Maren was pulling into the mall parking lot. I gathered my belongings, shuffled down the escalator, and made my way to the main entrance of the mall. Soon, I was outside. Through the falling snow, I saw Maren's car pull up to the curb.

I stayed at Maren's house for the first two weeks of February. While there, I reupped my crystal supply. I visited other friends in the area to share intimate encounters. I took part in a lesbian wedding which was held in Maren's living room. Maren's house was always filled with family and friends. I had shelter, and I had a chance to regroup. With wi-fi service at the house, I was able to reach out to friends and intimate partners online.

I was also able to log into the website. The adult hookup website had been a source of income since the end of 2017. Even though I hadn't been recently active on the site, money still came in. I cashed out on the website. My mind, prompted when I logged into my profile on the site, drifted back to recent years, years so different from 2022. I shook my head. The past was gone. I needed to bring my focus back from a shadowland of memories. I needed to sort out my present life.

I knew I wasn't going to stay at Maren's too long. She provided me with a reprieve, and I owed it to her to not overstay my welcome. My friend Marquisha offered me a place to live. Once again, I booked a trip by bus. I bought the ticket. One more bus trip. I was scheduled to leave Ohio on Valentine's Day. Before bringing me to my destination in the middle of Maryland, my bus was scheduled to take me to Philadelphia and Baltimore.

Besides the lady trying to steal my luggage in the Philadelphia bus terminal, my final bus trip was uneventful. Once I reached the terminal in Baltimore, I waited six hours for a shuttle van to arrive and take me on the final leg of my trip. I was completely drained. It was well into the night when I was dropped off in Hagerstown, Maryland. The weather was terrible, as expected.

My trip was almost over. The hardest mile was all that was left. Marquisha didn't have a car, so I had to walk that last mile from the middle of downtown. The walk, in the cold and wind, was all uphill. I still had my two heavy suitcases, requiring physical effort to pull behind me. An hour went by as I trudged through the city. Unable to take one more step, I passed out in Marquisha's front yard.

Final Resting Place

"I want to sit on your face."

I read the message from the phone on my living room table. I planned to reply, but I was in the middle of something. Two seconds after I fully depressed the plunger, I jumped up from my seat. I ran down the hallway, and into the bathroom on the left. As I hyperventilated, I ran to the vanity on the far side of my guest bathroom.

With my hands on the marble countertop, my wide eyes stared back from my mirror. Breathing began to slow as I came back to Earth. The heat on my palms and the soles of my feet began to fade away. I still had what I called "googly vision," but that was always the final side effect to wear off when I injected crystal meth.

As I stood naked in front of my bathroom mirror, I thought more on a subject which often, as of late, occupied my mind. Maybe it was the crystal, but I was becoming more discontent with life. All thirty-eight years of my life, I'd lived in northwest Ohio. Maybe it was time to leave. Maybe 2018 was to be the year when I set out for new horizons.

Back in my living room, I picked up my phone. I began replying to everyone who messaged me while I was in the process of injecting methamphetamine. I scrolled and replied. I reached the message I had seen as I was preparing the syringe. I replied with a single sentence.

"I guess we will have to make that happen."

...

As I traveled the country, I made it a point to stay with Marquisha anytime I passed through Maryland. It had been a while since I last visited my friend. Once I no longer had cars, I had no way to see Marquisha. I hadn't planned on all the bus trips in the beginning of 2022, but that final bus trip ended in a familiar location.

I spent two short weeks unwinding from the absurd trip around the country. While at Marquisha's house, I got back on the hookup apps. I began meeting people for hookups in Hagerstown. I met the owner of a hair salon on one of the apps. After a night of crystal fueled intimacy at the salon, I arrived back at Marquisha's house. When Marquisha opened the door to let me inside, something seemed off.

As the day progressed, I couldn't shake the weird vibe in the household. Afternoon gave way to evening. Marquisha walked into the living room. I was busy texting with a new person online. When I looked up, I saw the expression on my friend's face. I put down my phone. I braced myself. I knew I was about to learn what was going on with Marquisha. I gazed up at her. Marquisha stood still in the center of the room. After a moment of silence slipped away; she began to speak.

"I'm going to have to move in with my mom for the foreseeable future. I'm sure you've seen the bathroom floor. Remember when my landlord was here the other day? He's bringing in a construction crew on Monday to keep the floor from caving in on the neighbors below us. That's only two days from now, but you've seen how bad it is. The landlord is afraid anymore time and it will cave in."

Everywhere I went in 2022; everywhere came to an abrupt end in such a short time. I slowly shook my head. I was over it. 2022 was nothing but stress. Each time I almost found footing, the ground below me gave way. The bathroom floor at Marquisha's place; a literal example of the instability on which I stepped throughout 2022. Marquisha walked out of her living room, back towards her kitchen. I picked up my phone to continue the text conversation with my new online friend.

"Yeah, noon is good for me. I should be awake by then. Just text me when you're on your way."

I turned off my phone. It wasn't late in the night, but I hadn't been to sleep in two days. The salon owner's crystal had fueled me since the previous afternoon. It was Saturday night. I planned to cross state lines yet again when my new acquaintance picked me up at noon on Sunday. By Monday, I needed to be gone from Marquisha's house. I had just one day to figure out my next living situation. Between Saturday evening and Monday morning, I needed to begin a brand-new life.

All which had happened since I made that fateful deal with myself back in 2018; it was no longer a life which contained me. Everything; washed away to nothing with the memories of ghosts.

...

I made it. I was in a stable environment. A new life, a new location in a new time. I finally had sanctuary. The shadow of just one more tribulation loomed in the darkness on the horizon. I wasn't ready to write, but I was where I needed to be. Still unsure if my book would be my suicide note; the final test would either strengthen my resolve, or it would break me. 2022 began with thousands of miles all around the country; a continuation of four years of travel.

The next six months of 2022, in the depths of my worst addiction, began and ended in the same location. Though barely, I survived. It was then that I finally began to write. It was then that I was ready to share my experiences. Those six months were the final transcendence to my new world. I needed to include those final months, but in a different way. I had a starting point. It was finally time to begin a different type of adventure. In late 2022, I put my pen to paper, and I wrote.

www.ingramcontent.com/pod-product-compliance
Lightning Source LLC
Chambersburg PA
CBHW060821050426
42453CB00008B/537